BAROQUE SELF-INVENTION AND HISTORICAL TRUTH

for J.J.

as good a book as

his father's love

could make for him

Baroque Self-Invention and Historical Truth

Hercules at the Crossroads

Christopher Braider

Studies in European Cultural Transition

Volume Twenty Three

LONDON AND NEW YORK

First published 2004 by Ashgate Publishing

2 Park Square, Milton Park, Abingdon, Oxfordshire OX14 4RN
711 Third Avenue, New York, NY 10017

Routledge is an imprint of the Taylor & Francis Group, an informa business

First issued in paperback 2018

Copyright © Christopher Braider, 2004

All rights reserved. No part of this book may be reprinted or reproduced or utilised in any form or by any electronic, mechanical, or other means, now known or hereafter invented, including photocopying and recording, or in any information storage or retrieval system, without permission in writing from the publishers.

Notice:
Product or corporate names may be trademarks or registered trademarks, and are used only for identification and explanation without intent to infringe.

British Library Cataloguing in Publication Data
Braider, Christopher, 1950–
  Baroque Self-Invention and Historical Truth: Hercules at the Crossroads –
  (Studies in European Cultural Transition).
  1. Carracci, Annibale, 1560–1609 – Criticism and interpretation. 2. Susanna (Biblical figure) – Art. 3. Paul, the Apostle, Saint – Art. 4. Arts, Baroque. 5. Truth (Aesthetics). 6. History in art. 7. Truth. 8. Identity (Philosophical concept). 9. Hercules (Roman mythology) – Art. I. Title
  700.9'032

US Library of Congress Cataloging in Publication Data
Braider, Christopher, 1950–
  Baroque Self-Invention and Historical Truth: Hercules at the Crossroads / Christopher Braider.
      p. cm.
  Includes bibliographical references and index.
  1. Art, Baroque. 2. Art and history. I. Title.
  N6415.B3B73 2004
  709'.03'2–dc22   2004007679

ISBN 13: 978-0-7546-3881-0 (hbk)
ISBN 13: 978-1-138-37884-1 (pbk)

Contents

List of Illustrations vi
General Editors' Preface ix
Acknowledgements x

Introduction: Baroque Self-Invention and Historical Truth in Art　　1

1　The Vindication of Susanna:
　　Femininity and Truth in Baroque Science and Art　　42

2　The Fountain of Narcissus:
　　The Ontology of St Paul in Caravaggio and Rembrandt　　75

3　Hercules at the Crossroads:
　　Image and Soliloquy in Annibale Carracci　　111

4　Imaginary Selves:
　　The Trial of Identity in Descartes, Pascal and Cyrano　　144

Bibliography　　182
Index　　194

List of Illustrations

1.1	Sandro Botticelli, *The Birth of Venus*. The Uffizi, Florence. Photo: Alinari/Art Resource, NY	49
1.2	Giorgione, *Sleeping Venus*. Staatliche Kunstsammlungen, Dresden. Photo: Abteilung Foto/Repro	50
1.3	Titian, *Venus of Urbino*. The Uffizi, Florence. Photo: Scala/Art Resource, NY	50
1.4	Pieter Paul Rubens, *Perseus and Andromeda*. Staatliche Muzeen zu Berlin, Gemäldegalerie. Photo: Jörg P. Anders	52
1.5	Rembrandt van Rijn, *Susanna and the Elders* (1634). Royal Cabinet of Painting, Mauritshuis, The Hague	54
1.6	Rembrandt van Rijn, *Susanna and the Elders* (1645). Staatliche Muzeen zu Berlin, Gemäldegalerie. Photo: Jörg P. Anders	54
1.7	Jan Steen, *Oyster-Eating Girl*. Royal Cabinet of Painting, Mauritshuis, The Hague	56
1.8	Pieter Bruegel the Elder (?), *Self-Portrait with Connoisseur*. Albertina, Vienna	57
1.9	Diego Velázquez, *Rokeby Venus*. National Gallery, London. Photo: National Gallery	57
1.10	Rembrandt van Rijn, *Lucretia* (1664). Andrew W. Mellon Collection, Image © 2003 Board of Trustees, National Gallery of Art, Washington	58
1.11	Rembrandt van Rijn, *Lucretia* (1666). The Minneapolis Institute of Arts, The William Hood Dunwoody Fund	58
1.12	Jean-Baptiste-Siméon Chardin, *A Lady Taking Tea*. Hunterian Art Gallery, University of Glasgow	65
2.1	Andrea Pozzo, *Allegory of the Missionary Work of the Jesuit Order*. S. Ignazio, Rome. Photo: Alinari/Art Resource, NY	77
2.2	Caravaggio, *The Death of the Virgin*. The Louvre, Paris. Photo: Alinari/Art Resource, NY	83
2.3	Caravaggio, *Conversion of St Paul*. Cerasi Chapel, S. Maria del Popolo, Rome. Photo: Alinari/Art Resource	85
2.4	Caravaggio, *Judith and Holofernes*. Galleria Nazionale d'Arte Antica, Rome. Photo: Scala/Art Resource, NY	87
2.5	Caravaggio, *Medusa*. The Uffizi, Florence. Photo: Alinari/Art Resource, NY	88
2.6	Jan van Eyck, *Wedding Portrait of the Arnolfini*. National Gallery, London. Photo: National Gallery	93
2.7	Jan van Eyck. *Wedding Portrait of the Arnolfini*, detail with artist's self-portrait. National Gallery, London. Photo: National Gallery	93

List of Illustrations

2.8	Raphael, *The School of Athens*. Stanza della Segnatura, The Vatican Palace, Rome. Photo: Scala/Art Resource, NY	94
2.9	Raphael, *The School of Athens*, detail with artist's self-portrait. Stanza della Segnatura, The Vatican Palace, Rome. Photo: Scala/Art Resource, NY	95
2.10	Rembrandt van Rijn, *Self-Portrait with Saskia, as the Prodigal Son*. Staatliche Kunstsammlungen, Dresden. Photo: Abteilung Foto/Repro	96
2.11	Rembrandt van Rijn, *Self-Portrait as an Old Man Laughing*. Wallraf-Richartz Museum, Cologne. Photo: Rheinisches Bildarchiv Köln	97
2.12	Rembrandt van Rijn, *Self-Portrait as the Apostle Paul*. Rijksmuseum, Amsterdam	100
3.1	Annibale Carracci, *Hercules at the Crossroads*. Museo Nazionale di Capodimonte, Naples. Photo: Alinari/Art Resource, NY	116
3.2	*Judgment of Hercules*, from Jacob Locher, *Stultifera Navis* (Strasbourg, 1497). Photo: Erwin Panofsky, *Hercules am Scheidewege*, courtesy of Edition Logos, Gebr. Mann Verlag, Berlin	117
3.3	Raphael, *The Dream of Scipio*. National Gallery, London. Photo: National Gallery	118
3.4	*Judgment of Hercules*, from Christoff Murer, *XLI Emblemata miscella Nova* (Zurich, 1622). Photo: Erwin Panofsky, *Hercules am Scheidewege*, courtesy of Edition Logos, Gebr. Mann Verlag, Berlin	120
3.5	Johann Sadeler, after Friedrich Sustris, broadsheet commemorating the accession of Maximilian I of Bavaria, 1 January 1595. Photo: Erwin Panofsky, *Hercules am Scheidewege*, courtesy of Edition Logos, Gebr. Mann Verlag, Berlin	121
3.6	Johann Sadeler, after Friedrich Sustris, detail of second treatment. Photo: Erwin Panofsky, *Hercules am Scheidewege*, courtesy of Edition Logos, Gebr. Mann Verlag, Berlin	121
3.7	Niccolò Soggi, *Judgment of Hercules*, decorated coffer lid. The Ca d'oro, Venice. Photo: Erwin Panofsky, *Hercules am Scheidewege*, courtesy of Edition Logos, Gebr. Mann Verlag, Berlin	122
3.8	Girolamo di Benvenuto, *Judgment of Hercules*, decorated coffer lid, whereabouts unknown. Photo: Erwin Panofsky, *Hercules am Scheidewege*, courtesy of Edition Logos, Gebr. Mann Verlag, Berlin	122
3.9	Workshop of Pieter Paul Rubens, *Hercules at the Crossroads*. The Uffizi, Florence. Photo: Alinari/Art Resource, NY	123
3.10	Nicolas Poussin, *Judgment of Hercules*. Stourhead, The Hoare Collection (The National Trust). Photo: National Trust Photographic Library	126
3.11	Guido Reni, *The Massacre of the Innocents*. Pinacoteca Nazionale, Bologna. Photo: Alinari/Art Resource, NY	127
3.12	Gian Lorenzo Bernini, *Ecstasy of St Theresa*. S. Maria della Vittoria, Rome. Photo: Alinari/Art Resource	128

3.13 Rembrandt van Rijn, *Bathsheba at Her Bath*. The Louvre, Paris. Photo: Réunion des Musées Nationaux/Art Resource, NY   128
3.14 Georges de La Tour, *Magdalene with a Night Light*. The Louvre, Paris. Photo: Réunion des Musées Nationaux/Art Resource, NY   129
3.15 Titian, *Allegory of Prudence*. National Gallery, London. Photo: National Gallery   130

General Editors' Preface

The European dimension of research in the humanities has come into sharp focus over recent years, producing scholarship which ranges across disciplines and national boundaries. This series provides a major channel for this work and unites the fields of cultural studies and traditional scholarship. It will publish in the areas of European history and literature, art history, archaeology, language and translation studies, political, cultural and gay studies, music, psychology, sociology and philosophy. The emphasis is explicitly European and interdisciplinary, concentrating attention on the relativity of cultural perspectives, with a particular interest in issues of cultural transition.

Martin Stannard
Greg Walker
University of Leicester

Acknowledgements

Versions of several chapters have appeared elsewhere in the form of articles. Grateful thanks accordingly go to the editors of the *Yearbook of General and Comparative Literature* for permission to reprint 'The Vindication of Susanna: Femininity and Truth in Early Modern Science and Art', on which chapter 1 is based; to the editors of *Comparative Literature* for permission to reprint 'The Fountain of Narcissus: The Invention of Subjectivity and the Pauline Ontology of Art in Caravaggio and Rembrandt', on which chapter 2 is based; and to Ellen Spolsky, editor of *Iconotropisms: The Turn toward Images* (Bucknell University Press, 2003), for permission to reprint 'Hercules at the Crossroads: Image and Soliloquy in Annibale Carracci', on which chapter 3 is based. Much of this book originated in talks and conference papers, and thus in invitations to speak and in the responses this elicited. Thanks therefore to Peter Burgard, Tom Conley, Jeffrey Cox, Roland Greene, Ingeborg Hoesterey, Jeffrey Schnapp and Ellen Spolsky for prodding me into productive public speech in a variety of settings: the ACLA conference held at Indiana University in 1993; an MLA panel organized for the ACLA in 1995; the colloquium on 'Baroque Re/Visions' held at Melk Abbey and at the Internationales Forschungszentrum Kulturwissenschaften in Vienna in 1996; a conference in honour of Murray Roston hosted by Bar-Ilan University in Israel in 1998; public lectures at Princeton (1999) and Stanford (2000); and works-in-progress presentations to the Center for Humanities and the Arts at the University of Colorado, Boulder in 1999 and to the Center for Literary and Cultural Studies at Harvard in 2000. A number of colleagues have read and commented on different portions of the book. In particular Harry Berger, Jr., Jeffrey Cox, Warren Motte, Stephen Owen and Ellen Spolsky all helped me see how dark my ideas can be, how obscure their expression, and thus what they are. I am also deeply indebted to Ann Donahue, the literary studies editor at Ashgate, without whose boundless patience, tireless efforts and unfailing good humour the book would never have been at all; and to the anonymous reader to whom she entrusted the original manuscript. If, as this last remarked, the final version was not only interesting, but becomingly 'trim' and 'svelte', the honour is hers or his alone. Finally and always there is Helen—who surely knows it.

Introduction

Baroque Self-Invention and Historical Truth in Art

> In the art work, the truth of what is has set itself to work. Art is truth setting itself to work.
>
> —Martin Heidegger

' "What is Truth?" said jesting Pilate, and would not stay for an answer.' So opens Sir Francis Bacon's late essay 'Of Truth' (1625), in a volume dedicated to the then almighty royal favourite George Villiers, Duke of Buckingham, in hopes of reviving the disgraced Chancellor's career.[1] Beginning thus *in medias res*, near the close of Pilate's interrogation of the soon-to-be crucified Christ, Bacon propounds a question he believes will answer itself; the truth he invokes is meant to overcome the ironic doubt whose accents announce his topic. In the event, however, the literary performance Bacon begins *in medias res* merely deepens the question he proposes to foreclose. The essay defeats the end it sets itself; and *in* this defeat—in the process that leads the essay to sting itself with its own tail—it enacts the at once formal and historical dynamic that forms the theme of the present book.

That Bacon should cite Pilate is of course prejudicial. The example aims to discredit the author's relativist adversaries—the 'discoursing wits', the sceptics and freethinking Epicureans, Bacon takes the infamous Roman governor to epitomize. But the example further invokes a salvific irony that is meant to destroy the cynical one Pilate deploys. Against the background of the silent Christ whose impending death and resurrection vindicate the Truth to which, in the essay's locus in the Gospel of John (18.37-38), the Saviour has come to 'bear witness', the ironic jest refutes itself. Though framed as a rhetorical question to which Pilate expects no answer, the governor's derisive refusal to 'stay' betrays an uneasy sense that there *is* one. Just because Pilate '*would* not stay for an answer', peremptorily moving on before his interlocutor can reply, the cynical dismissal acknowledges the truth it denies.

It is therefore the more remarkable how little Bacon actually *says* for truth: speaking in truth's name and on its behalf, he ventures few hints as to the word's positive force and meaning—as few indeed as the Christ of his example ('for this cause came I into the world, that I should bear witness unto the truth'). To this extent, Pilate's question goes as unanswered as the governor expects. This is in part because, from the standpoint Bacon occupies, the question neither needs nor deserves an answer. For truth is 'a naked and open daylight' that, like daylight itself, both constitutes and comprises its own illumination. This is why Pilate's sneer refutes itself: the contemptuous question exposes the contemptible motives that prompt him to ask it just as, later in the story, washing his hands reveals how dirty they are. But if Bacon offers no real answer, it is also because he has none to give. If, as his metaphor suggests, truth is less what we see than the light we see by, there is no *thing* he can show for it, only the medium in which *other* things appear—the medium indeed in which *truths* appear in the feral multiplicity Bacon's unconditional singular belies. For a start, there is the sordid worldly agenda behind Pilate's jest. There are also the multifarious *lies* to which experience shows humanity to be inveterately liable, deliberate falsehoods that paradoxically speak far more eloquently for truth than Bacon's account of truth itself. Or there is the example of royal ceremonials, 'the masks and mummeries and triumphs of the world', theatrical trompes-l'œil whose factitious un-truth is indexed by the deluding 'candlelight' required to grant them a price they do not naturally possess. And beyond all of these are the truths Bacon's scientific writings expound—those to which the procedures of Baconian induction secure access through the critical discipline it enjoins, demolishing the occluding Idols it is the new science's mission to clear away.[2]

J.L. Austin makes this point in an essay ('Truth') where he too begins by citing Bacon's rehearsal of Pilate's jest, albeit in order to find in the sardonic Pilate's favour:

> 'What is truth?' said jesting Pilate, and would not stay for an answer. Pilate was in advance of his time. For 'truth' itself is an abstract noun, a camel, that is, of a logical construction, which cannot get past the eye even of a grammarian. We approach it cap and categories in hand: we ask ourselves whether Truth is a substance (the Truth, the Body of Knowledge), or a quality (something like the colour red, inhering in truths), or a relation ('correspondence'). But philosophers should take something more nearly their own size to strain at. What needs discussing rather is the use, or certain uses, of the word 'true'. *In vino*, possibly, '*veritas*', but in sober symposium '*verum*'.[3]

In evicting traditional talk about the grandiose yet comically camel-like composite *truth* in order to engage the more manageable analysis of concrete uses of the humble adjective *true*, Austin minds a lesson Wittgenstein draws.[4] Abstract nouns of the kind even abstemious Baconian empiricists find so tempting are the worst because they are the most common and thus least corrigible of idols. Because language gives a single collective name, we are led to credit the existence of a single entity that always and fundamentally answers to that name. 'Truth' insensibly becomes '*the* Truth', and this shift in turn engenders phantoms like the mysterious substance the term is held to denote, the universal quality all of its instances are expected to display or the invariant relation of correspondence that is taken to constitute the essential criterion we must satisfy in describing, expressing or delineating some portion of the general quantity the noun appears to single out.

This in turn urges the method for which Austin is famous and the theory that method proclaims: the theory of speech acts and the so-called 'linguistic' method of attending to what people are ordinarily doing when they say, not that some thing, but rather that some *statement* is true. In this perspective, truth is a variable function of the open-ended range of verbal performances in which the concept comes into play. Accordingly, what counts as true depends on the acts, contexts and enabling conventions that make the word's use intelligible. Truth—or, to speak more carefully, what is or counts as true—is then always local and conditional: a fact (and Austin would not hesitate to call it one[5]) illustrated by the case of testimony in a court of law, where what witnesses report may well be true even when it turns out to be false. For the truth they swear to tell is not what a trial of the evidence determines to be the facts of the case; it is what they know or have witnessed, or at least (since we are all naturally prone to error) sincerely believe they know or have witnessed, even if they are eventually found to be wrong.[6]

Further, the performative force Austin underscores in drawing attention to actual uses of the words true and truth informs Bacon's own analysis of Pilate's riposte. The point of Pilate's rhetorical question is less the truth or falsehood of the implied assertion that talk of truth is jejune than his cynical interest in saying so. Pilate's both unanswered and unanswerable question is not simply an indirect form of statement; it is an *act* whose force is determined by the contextual emergency to which it responds. The inconvenient demand to which the arraigned Christ bears witness—a demand that has in the end to do less with the kind of facts that preoccupy Austin and Pilate than with the morally exacting notion of the *good* a preoccupation with facts sidetracks—is not merely metaphysical; it is practical. Christ's witness requires that Pilate *do* something in a situation in which doing is fraught with perilous consequence.

This underscores a feature of the case Ann Wroe brings to light in a book devoted to the finally hopeless task of exhuming the historical person beneath the legendary personality Christian tradition has 'invented' under Pilate's name.[7] As what Bacon's contemporaries would have termed a 'politic' act adjusted to an overmastering context, Pilate's relativist jest is not just evidence of the selfish motives Bacon diagnoses; it indexes the political conjuncture Christ's arraignment, trial and death help shape. It thereby bespeaks the pressing social crisis that defines what, as an imperial functionary, the governor of Judea felt called on to do. If Pilate would not stay for an answer, it is in part because he could not. Given the official identity with which circumstance invested him and the explosive conditions of Roman rule over the fractious and resentful populace of first-century Palestine, he had no choice but to wash his hands of the matter, surrendering Christ to his clamorous local enemies. As Bacon's own unhappy experience as attorney general and chancellor might have taught him, Pilate's manœuver is the token of a truth, indeed an *historical* truth, his accuser refuses to acknowledge. Even leaving aside the careerist motives that would naturally actuate an imperial official, Pilate responds to an overdetermining *reason of State*, a consideration central to early modern efforts to rationalize an increasingly self-conscious experience of history's unforgiving necessity.

Yet this suggests how Bacon is right after all, and in a way Austin might endorse. Like Wittgenstein's related 'practices', 'language games' or 'forms of life', though local, contingent, conjunctural, the performances Austin explicates and the at once practical and conventional contexts that condition their meaning exhibit a daylight to which Bacon's essay bears witness in its very contradictions. We encounter a truth both Pilate and Bacon ironically enact at their own expense: a *dialectic* both bring to light just insofar as they fail to master what makes their proceedings visible.

The dialectic in question is that between truth and history conceived as the series of adversarial claims each directs at the other as a function of the evolving settings that give those claims dramatic salience. But it is equally the dialectic of truth and *its* history—the history of truth itself. Pilate and Bacon (like Pilate and Christ) confront each other from entirely different worlds shaped by radically different perspectives. It is important, for instance, that, however dubious his purely personal motives may be, Pilate is a pagan polytheist for whom the absolute otherworldly pretensions of Judeo-Christian monotheism are strictly incomprehensible. The example of Plato notwithstanding, the idea that there is finally only one truth whose dwelling lies wholly beyond the world of the many truths that characterize ordinary pagan belief, a truth moreover that denounces all others as sinful error and idolatrous captivity, contravenes everything that gives Pilate's experience its form, texture and coherence. And it also violates the more or less tolerant spirit of cultural coexistence on which the Roman empire depends.[8] Conversely, from the Christian standpoint Bacon champions on the occasion of this essay, Pilate's incomprehension can only seem the obdurate denial of a truth whose self-evidence springs from its spokesman's sacred identity. If Pilate fails to hear the answer Christ does not give, it can only be because he deliberately rejects it, thereby proving that he hears it just the same.[9] And yet, though incommensurable, neither perspective negates the other. On the contrary, they fuse to produce the self-defeating event both set in train. And the form of this event gives the form of the artful *essay* that, in trying to master the event by reducing one of its terms to the other, succeeds only in reproducing it as the self-defeating burden of its performance.

Whence the subject of the following book, and the theoretical ambition that inspires it. I would like to show how the conflicting claims of history and truth, of naked daylight and the contingent yet relentlessly necessary events it illuminates, find fleeting accommodation in the equivocal form of self-conscious works of art. Yet, as our introductory example demonstrates, it is in the nature of the theoretical difficulty the book addresses that it does not arise in a vacuum. The question history puts to truth and the pressures the resulting conflict exerts on individual works unfold in the dimension of history itself; the evidence for an accommodation partakes of the historical element truth endeavours to surmount. This in turn obliges us to undertake the kind of historical and critical appreciation that works of art demand as a reflex of their inescapable historicalness. If I nonetheless continue to hope, it is because there exists a body of historical works that aim to achieve just the accommodation at issue—the corpus to which Bacon's self-defeating 'Of Truth' belongs.

A longstanding problem in early modern studies is the attempt to elucidate the moral, aesthetic and intellectual unity behind the complex international phenomenon called 'the baroque'. Generations of scholars have tried to extend the term beyond art history, where it was coined, and accounts of the Counter Reformation cultures of the Catholic south, where the concept has always seemed most at home. In the 1950s, Jean Rousset advanced the still controversial thesis of the existence of a French baroque; Wylie Sypher applied the conventions of mannerist and baroque painting to English drama in the age of Shakespeare; and Mario Praz set the intricate conceits of the English Metaphysicals beside their extravagant models in Italian verse.[10] More recently, José Maravall and Anthony Cascardi have tried to ground the Spanish baroque in the deeper perspective of peninsular social ideology; Omar Calabrese and Mieke Bal have explored parallels between baroque culture and our own post-modernity; and Gilles Deleuze has interpreted the finalist defence of providence in Leibniz's *Theodicy* (1710) and *Monadology* (1714) as the philosophical expression of the otherwise inarticulate metaphysics informing the involuted 'pleats' or 'folds' that form the dominant motif of baroque ornament.[11] Above all has been the rediscovery of Walter Benjamin's failed *Habilitationsschrift* on the German baroque 'sorrowplay', *The Origin of German Tragic Drama*. To Benjamin we owe Christine Buci-Glucksmann's *La raison baroque*, linking the antinomies of baroque culture to comparable dichotomies in the poetry of Baudelaire, and her later *La folie du voir*, in which Benjamin fuses with Deleuze and Lacan in framing the basis for a diagnosis of the simultaneously flamboyant and penumbral lunacy driving the intense baroque erotics of sight. Benjamin has similarly inspired Julia Reinhard Lupton and Kenneth Reinhard's *After Œdipus*, undertaking a psychoanalysis of tragic 'mourning work' in Shakespeare. And he has even prompted exponents of Critical Theory to address pre-modern texts their ongoing quarrel with the Kantian Enlightenment encourages them to overlook.[12]

Valuable as all of these studies may be, we witness little uniformity in critical usage and, as a result, no clear consensus about what the term baroque means. Should we follow the art historian Heinrich Wölfflin in using it to designate an aesthetic *style* whose properties are logically independent of local motives,[13] or does the term more properly denote an underlying ethos or mentality of which style constitutes a mere symptom? And in analyzing the baroque as an ethos or mentality, may we see in it, as Bal and Calabrese's parallels with the post-modern or Buci-Glucksmann's with Baudelaire imply, a pervasive aesthetic tendency that transcends the immediate historical contexts in which we find it embodied; or should we focus on the socio-cultural factors defining a specific historical era? In light of questions like these, the concept looks like a protean catch-all that fails to adduce the multifaceted yet formally and historically precise phenomenon talk of *the* baroque promises. All of which explains why phases of energetic interest regularly alternate with periods of sceptical *ennui*. If we consistently fail to finger just what it is we take the baroque to be, does the term have a genuine referent? Is it not rather, as René Wellek long ago pertinaciously wondered, an *ignis fatuus* as insubstantial as the heroic trompes-l'œil and theological marsh gasses of its native home in post-Tridentine Rome?[14]

The baroque's intractability is in part a byproduct of the regional divergences alluded to a moment ago. The term's relevance to Italy, Spain or the Catholic Netherlands of Rubens, a painter whose work expressly ministers to the devotional and imperialistic tastes of Hapsburg Europe, is taken for granted. However, with the exception of professional portraitists like the dashing (and comical) Hals or the moody Rembrandt, the northern art of Calvinist Holland appears untouched. Indeed, if we accept Svetlana Alpers's assessment of the 'descriptive' temper of Dutch visual culture, Dutch art deliberately rejects the heroic illusions of Italian taste, preferring a faithful record of empirical reality observed with as much precision as the prosthetic technologies of contemporary optics could afford.[15] Later studies reinforce the anti-baroque implications of Alpers's account. Simon Schama's analysis of Dutch culture's ineffably *burgherlijk* fusion of materialism and moralism, Richard Helgerson's exposition of the political commitments implicit in Dutch painters' devotion to scenes of middleclass domesticity in open defiance of the sacramental *noblesse* defining the baroque *istoria*, Gary Schwartz's exploration of the frankly commercial interests fueling Dutch painting and Alpers's own subsequent excavation of the economic ambitions behind Rembrandt's artistic 'enterprise' all portray a climate wholly inimical to the Catholic and aristocratic values informing the paradigmatically baroque cultures of the Italian, Spanish or Flemish south.[16]

England, meanwhile, pursues an insular evolution that seems largely disconnected from continental developments—after all, the crypto-Catholic Charles I had to import Rubens to paint his father's illusionistic *Apotheosis* (1630), where angels bear the departed James I to paradise through the ceiling of the royal Banqueting House at Whitehall. Students of English literature do often expound themes we would in other contexts readily pronounce baroque. In addition to Lupton and Reinhard's analysis of Œdipal mourning work in Shakespeare, we have Stanley Fish's exposition of the 'self-consuming' habits of seventeenth-century English moralist writing. Thus, in the sermons John Donne delivered following his ordination as an Anglican priest in 1615, the devotional verses assembled in George Herbert's punningly monumental *The Temple* (1633) or Robert Burton's playfully self-dissecting *Anatomy of Melancholy* (1621), readers are seduced into adopting an interpretive outlook the work goes on to expose as morally deficient, thereby destroying the viewpoint with which the work initially identifies. Ernest Gilman's *The Curious Perspective* highlights the English fascination with what Shakespeare, Donne or the Puritan Francis Quarles, whose moral *Emblemes* first appear in 1643, regarded as the spiritual significance of painterly anamorphosis and the distorting effects of dioptric and catoptric lenses. Or again, Jonathan Dollimore expounds the radical religious sentiments shaping plays like John Webster's *The White Devil* (produced 1608; published 1612), where the political cynicism characteristic of Jacobean revenge tragedy merges with theological speculations normally associated with the more extreme Protestant sects of the Civil War era.[17] Yet such studies prove enlightening regardless of whether the material they address is baroque or not; nor in the main does the question of baroque allegiances arise at all.

Despite official commitment to the dominant ethos of its Catholic *noblesse*, absolutist France proves as hostile to the enthusiastic excesses of baroque feeling as republican Holland. Prompted by Rousset's pioneering work in the field, many scholars have asserted the existence of a distinctively French baroque. To mention some of the more memorable efforts, we have John Lyons's work on the aesthetics of disguise in French drama from 1630 to 1660 and Mitchell Greenberg's explication of the intricate 'detours' of sexual desire in baroque theatre, libertine fiction and romance. Jean-Claude Vuillemin identifies a major source of baroque effects in the at once spell-binding and critically self-conscious theatricality of dramas like Jean de Rotrou's *Les sosies* (1636), *Venceslas* (1647) and especially *Le véritable Saint Genest* (1646), where a Roman actor is converted by the role of a Christian martyr he is commissioned to perform in a play staged as an entertainment for an imperial wedding.[18] As the author reports in the preface to the revised edition, Georges Forestier's *Le théâtre dans le théâtre*, on the play-within-a-play convention in seventeenth-century French drama, turns out to say less about the baroque than he had expected. Nevertheless, the book originally meant to place Rousset's assessment of the convention's baroque character on a firmer historical footing.[19] To this we may add the byzantine complexities Louis Marin has unearthed in the Jansenist critique of classical rational discourse or in the performative allegories of the liturgical Word subtending absolutist politics and the theological aims directing period logic.[20] But where French scholars do not, like their English counterparts, simply ignore the baroque altogether, they usually apply Forestier's rule. The French baroque is mainly confined to the reign of Louis XIII (1610-43) and the period of the Frondes (1648-53), epochs enjoying a degree of political as well as artistic and intellectual licence suppressed with Louis XIV's seizure of personal power in 1661. Insofar as scholars admit that there was in fact a French baroque in the theatre of Rotrou and the younger Pierre Corneille or in libertine picaresques like Sorel's *Francion* (1623, with revisions thereafter) and Cyrano de Bergerac's *L'Autre monde* (published after his death in 1655), it is seen to have been doomed to eclipse from the start. The withering ridicule to which Boileau's *Art poétique* of 1674 exposes the elaborate conceits and punning epigrammes favoured by Saint-Amant (1594-1661) or Voiture (1598-1648) bespeaks the unconditional classicism whose inevitable triumph is taken to define the *grand siècle* as a whole.[21]

Still, the difficulties students of the early modern era encounter in coming to grips with the baroque are not only due to regional differences or to deep-seated scholarly prejudices; they also reflect the inherent slipperiness of the phenomenon itself. Part period, part sensibility, part style, the baroque is a curious (and camel-like) composite whose contours never quite coalesce in a unified pattern.

Scholars generally associate the baroque with a distinctive set of themes, tropes and rhetorical manœuvres. There is the well-documented *specularity* of baroque culture, a self-regarding temper whose most explicit expression is the era's obsession with mirrors as both a source of intriguing optical effects and an inexhaustible reservoir of analogies and examples. The mirror motif is related to the widespread taste for *mises en abyme*, elaborate framing devices (interpolated tales, pictures of pictures, plays within plays) that enable a work to incorporate its own image in the body of what it depicts. And it further coordinates with the major themes of dream and illusion, the era's compulsive interest in ghosts, twins and doubles, and the tireless manufacture of ironic reversals, strident antitheses and uncanny inversions dramatizing the deeply entrenched dualisms of baroque style—truth and falsehood, light and darkness, reason and passion, spirit and flesh.[22]

All of this bears on what Fish's analysis of English moralist literature suggests we call the self-consuming character of baroque artifacts. A recurrent feature of baroque monuments is a self-destructive impulse that produces acts of critical *anagnorisis* designed to lead readers or spectators as well as dramatic personae into an initial state of error the work then rounds on and demolishes. These self-consuming habits feed the period's addiction to anamorphic distortions of perspective designed to unmask the deluding fictions behind the realities art and thought purport to mimic. The self-destructive temper of baroque art is thereby linked to the way in which the manic desire to *see*—a desire registered not only in the proliferation of optical machines like the telescope and microscope, but also in painting, theatre and the visual extravaganzas of the nascent opera—so readily mutates into Buci-Glucksmann's *folie du voir*, binding vision and lunacy as twin faces of the same overmastering yet 'unregardable' drive. It also conditions the singular *recursiveness* of baroque culture: a trait shared by phenomena as diverse as the introspective patterns of baroque portraiture, the widespread taste for grottoes and shell motifs or (to cite Deleuze's favourite example) the complex involutions by which the doctrine of 'final causes' inverts the natural course of events to produce the ersatz providence of Leibnizian theodicy. The net effect is the bipolar volatility of baroque expression, violent mood-swings between the manic heights of heroic sublimity and the melancholy depths of madness, ruin and death to which Benjamin relates the innermost lesson of baroque allegory.

However, if such themes, tropes and devices tell us anything, it is that, while invariably pointing to the unitary principle we posit in speaking of *the* baroque, they do not unequivocally determine or contain it. It is not just that comparable phenomena may be found elsewhere; the baroque differs from analogous historico-aesthetic formations in defying ready subsumption under a single, stable doctrine or ideology. There is in its case no obvious counterpart for Renaissance humanism or the Enlightenment's commitment to universal Reason. On the contrary, the baroque is a theatre of ceaseless conflict: what in other eras represents anachronistic resistance to the theses that define the period's dominant ethos constitutes a primary engine of contemporary cultural activity.

Art historians have thus argued that what initially differentiates baroque from earlier forms of painting is the systematic naturalism it opposes to the mannered style of the later Renaissance: profoundly as baroque painters differ in other respects, they share an abiding distaste for the brooding affectations and hamstrung muscularity of Michelangelo's art. One of the many advantages of this view is that it relates changes in artistic practice to parallel transformations in the conception of material nature deployed in philosophy and science.[23] Nevertheless, as attested by the ambivalence greeting the uncompromising commitment to natural observation in Caravaggio and Rembrandt, baroque art cleaves to the Renaissance ideal of 'la belle nature', eschewing slavish adherence to things as they are for the sake of a persuasive portrayal of things as they ought to be. In Rubens, the Carraccis or Velázquez, the studied verisimilitude contemporaries found so shocking in Caravaggio and Rembrandt is harnessed to the noble fictions of monarchic absolutism or post-Tridentine faith it otherwise challenges. Similarly, in drama, the cynicism of Jacobean 'malcontents' or French 'politiques' not only coexists with the perfection of the Stuart masque and the Bourbon *ballet de cour*; it is driven by residual nostalgia for a better, more heroic world whose remoteness constitutes the pervasive theme of the pithy nuggets of relentless Tacitean realism that form one of drama's chief ornaments.

The contradictions that characterize the baroque mitigate the kind of revisionist critiques to which New Historicism subjects the Renaissance or Critical Theory the Enlightenment. But, by the same token, they complicate our efforts to pin the baroque down. Yet we can perhaps make a virtue of this necessity by modifying our expectations about what the unity we seek should look like. The baroque is less a doctrine than a *clash* of doctrines, conflicting perspectives paradoxically united by the antagonisms that yoke them in insoluble pairs. It is moreover less a style than a *jumble* of styles, each claiming centrality only to be not merely displaced, but destroyed by the next. And it is less a period than, as Mary Campbell's recent exploration of related themes suggests, a *transition* whose essentially labile character is obscured by the frozen, ritualized expression it receives in the symptomatically crepuscular cultures of Counter Reformation Rome or Hapsburg Spain.[24] What is elsewhere adduced as unwitting ideological self-betrayal forms the conscious ground of the culture we are trying to encompass.

Such is, besides, what a brief overview of the historical juncture indicates. To borrow a prescient metaphor from Montaigne's 'Des cannibales' (1580),[25] the baroque marks the moment when Europeans begin to digest the far-reaching implications of the accumulated social, intellectual, religious and geographic upheavals of the preceding age. The cosmological revolution inaugurated by Copernicus's *De revolutionibus* (1543), on the orbits of celestial bodies, shatters the reassuringly closed, anthropocentric cosmos of Aristotle and Ptolemy to unveil the infinite intersideral spaces whose 'eternal silence' will later so frighten Pascal.[26] The related progress of scientific naturalism intensifies the materialism derived from Lucretian Epicureanism, laying the basis for a systematically reductive picture of natural processes that reshapes the conception of moral as well as physical nature.[27] The Protestant Reformation begun with Luther's refusal to recant his heretical doctrines in 1519 divides the Christian world along at once denominational and territorial lines hardened by the militant reaction galvanized at the Council of Trent (1545-63); and in the violent debates surrounding the theology of justification and scriptural hermeneutics, the era refashions faith itself as a field of corrosively sectarian perspectives and interests. The advance of humanist scholarship revives the values of pagan antiquity, setting secular Stoic and rhetorical models of self and civic association against the fractured Christian picture of human destinies and community. Worse still, in the textual criticism whose notoriously poisoned fruit is Erasmus' *Novum instrumentum* (1516), correcting the authorized Latin translation of the New Testament by comparing it with the original Greek, humanism exposes the linguistic and cultural contingency of the Word of God enshrined in holy writ.[28] In Machiavelli's *Il Principe* (1532), Guicciardini's *Storia d'Italia* (1561) and the recovered writings of the Roman historian Tacitus, we observe the rise of a critical historicism promoting a starkly relativized (if not yet relativistic) image of political conduct grounded in the black arts of dissimulation, prudential calculation and the cynical pursuit of *raison d'Etat*.[29] We witness the shift of economic and therefore political power (the tightening link is itself significant) from the dynastic Catholic south to the mercantile banking centres of the increasingly industrial Protestant north.[30] Above all, as a kind of emblem in which Renaissance writers tried to capture all of the metamorphoses the times endure, stands the discovery of America. The encounter with a 'new world' hitherto wholly concealed from Europe not only convulses the face of the planet, but, in the ensuing extermination of the continent's pre-Columbian peoples, explodes 'old world' delusions about Europe's moral privilege.[31]

The seventeenth century is in the main the inheritor of these things; it would thus be a mistake to claim that it makes changes that in many respects antedate the Renaissance itself.[32] It is nonetheless only now that the moral and ontological consequences sink in. Though modeled on the 'natural magic' of sixteenth-century technology, the experimental mastery of the axioms of physical law that Bacon's *New Organon* (1620) calls for goes far beyond mere local improvements. Bacon aims to transfigure the human condition as a whole; and for all he adopts the eschatological tones of the prophet Daniel or John of Patmos to describe it, the radical reform he proposes represents the worldly triumph of self-determined human intelligence and will. Indeed, the exclusion of divine agency forms the very basis of Baconian 'natural history': what grants human reason its transformative power over nature is a reduction to natural law and to the observable phenomena that express it without which reason as such cannot properly function.[33] On the eve of the baroque, Giordano Bruno's *De l'infinito universo et mundi* (1584) tries to draw the cosmological implications of Copernicus's 'solar hypothesis' by frankly asserting the universe's infinite scale and the countless worlds it must logically harbour. But it takes the *Sidereus nuncio* of 1610, reporting Galileo's work with the telescope, and in particular the discovery of Jupiter's moons and the starry composition of the Milky Way, to give infinite space the properly physical definition Bruno's speculations lack. At one level, this opens the way for radical thought experiments like Kepler's *Somnium* (1634), Godwin's *The Man in the Moon* (1638) or Cyrano's alarmingly freethinking *Etats et empires de la Lune et du Soleil* (1655), endowing the alternate worlds inhabiting the numberless immensity of Bruno's space with increasingly thick historical and sociological as well as physical detail. But Galileo's discoveries also promote the reductive physical monism systematically codified in Newton's *Principia* (1687). Despite the residually magical and theocentric commitments motivating his ongoing alchemical and chronological interests, it is Newton who conclusively demonstrates that all things, as *things*, as physical products of equally physical principles, fall under a single set of mathematical laws that are nature's alone.[34]

The critical energies set loose in astronomy and physics also shape period anthropology, the evolving picture of human as well as physical nature. As Campbell shows, a central dynamic in early modern accounts of the New World is the shift from the discourse of 'wonder' animating Thevet's *Singularitez de la France antarctique* (1558) or *Cosmographie universelle* (1575) to the discourse of sober science embodied in the emerging discipline of ethnography of which Lafitau's *Mœurs des Sauvages amériquaines* (1724) becomes the model. If only as a means of managing Europe's vast colonial dominions, observers strive for an 'anaesthetic' objectivity whose rhetorical expression is a studied elimination of first-person pronouns and a systematic preference for the passive voice of impersonal natural process.[35] However, the objective precision achieved in the description of colonized peoples is paid for by a corresponding reduction of the human as such. Descartes is in more whiggish moods as liable as Bacon to grant human intellect a demiurgic potency. His sense of methodic consequence nonetheless leads him to apply the principles of mechanics to the human psyche, spawning the nightmare vision of godlike Man as the soulless automaton that stalks the pages of the Second Meditation (1641).[36] Reinforced by Hobbes's *Leviathan* (1651), Richelieu's posthumous *Mémoires* (1650) and *Testament politique* (1688)[37] give institutional respectability to the amoral political realism traditionally vilified in Machiavelli. Moreover, in subversive texts like the Digger Winstanley's *Law of Freedom* (1652), a spiritual protest the more telling for espousing the viewpoint of history 'from below', the century anticipates later socialist critiques of the emergent capitalist order by denouncing the role of property as the 'original sin' of political community.[38]

All of which lays the moral as well as intellectual basis for consummating the historical reading of scripture still merely latent in Erasmus. The Oratorian priest Richard Simon's *Histoire critique du Vieux Testament* (1678) is a guilelessly pious work devoted to disinterring the Word of God from the accretions produced by Christian ignorance of Hebrew. But rightly perceiving the threat to Catholic orthodoxy Simon's philology poses, Simon's superior Bossuet expelled him from the Oratory in an effort to silence him. The doctrinal questions Simon raises without meaning to form the central burden of Spinoza's *Tractatus theologico-politicus* (1670), a deliberately historical critique expounding the creaturely interests determining the Torah's composition in ancient Palestine. The critical viewpoint Spinoza and Simon adopt toward the Old Testament is then generalized by the Huguenot exile Pierre Bayle's *Dictionnaire historique et critique* (1697) to the entire history of Western philosophical as well as religious belief.[39]

When Montaigne writes, a full century has passed since the discovery of America, overturning Western self-conceit by disclosing whole civilizations unassimilated by the natural order as seen from Europe. But the full force of the challenge registers only *after* Montaigne, in the systematic moral relativisms inspired by Hobbes's misanthropic anatomy of the material bases of social might, Spinoza's political critique of the great historical religions or the sarcastic behaviourism framing Pascalian apologetics. The sceptical Montaigne confesses his inability to tell the difference between the self-reproducing truth of nature and the self-displacing revolutions of fallen human custom. Yet a reassuringly personified nature remains an essential postulate, a sort of cosmological constant enabling him to gauge the otherwise unimaginable dislocations to which he counterposes her. So it is up to Pascal, in the sardonic fragment (126/159) on the presumed 'unnaturalness' of youths eager to dispose of inconvenient fathers, to give doubt its characteristically modern voice by administering the chiastic twist through which custom as 'second nature' turns into nature as mere 'second custom'.

This brings us to the argument at the heart of the following book. What distinguishes the baroque, forging the unity we sense behind the conflicting themes and tendencies endemic to the age, is the experience of unsettling *secondness* Pascal articulates with Montaigne in view. And the underlying thrust of Pascalian secondness is *history* and the coercive process of dialectical mediation history sets in train. In denouncing Montaigne's faith in nature as an artifact of the denaturing customs the Renaissance sceptic calls in doubt, Pascal undermines the paradoxical assurance Montaigne derives from custom's overthrow. But he also *temporalizes* that assurance. Insofar as Montaigne's thought is true, it occurs in the enduring present of timeless verities. But to the extent that it is false, it embodies a state of error Pascal consigns to the past. What the sceptic took for nature was already mystified custom the moment Montaigne adduced it as custom's redeeming opposite. The authority of Pascal's critique thus springs from its belatedness: because he writes in every sense *after* Montaigne, Pascal is in a position to see what Montaigne cannot, developing ironic second thoughts his predecessor occasions at his own expense. But, by the same token, in voicing the second thoughts to which Montaigne falls subject, Pascal reveals the temporal machinery that ensnares the critical present he himself inhabits. The goal behind Pascal's critique of Montaigne is finally apologetic: where the sceptic sacrifices custom for the sake of abiding nature, the Jansenist sacrifices even nature in defence of his hidden God, radicalizing scepticism at scepticism's expense. Yet the upshot of Pascal's critique, foreshadowed by the very chiasmus that brings the conversion about, is the Godlessness conversion aims to preempt. The inscription of Pascal's second thoughts unfolds in the recursive dimension of what Bal, borrowing from Patricia Parker, would call the 'preposterous' incorporation of its own critical posterity—pointing toward the still further thoughts his second thoughts engender in their turn, and from there toward the defeat of apology itself.[40]

The Pascalian sense of secondness encodes an insight that is both radical and pervasive. Baroque artists, poets and thinkers are fitfully yet acutely aware of the historical contingency of the choices, conventions and motives embodied in their works. But they are also aware of how the effort to disentangle themselves from historical contingency seconds history's tyrannical grip. The experience of chiastic belatedness illuminates the logic of dialectical mediation for which Pascal's chiasmus serves as a paradigm. More precisely, it highlights the uncanny *supervenience* Pascal's chiasmus enacts: the blind yet ineluctably self-accusing difference between the moral or aesthetic task a work sets out to perform and the result by which it is dialectically overtaken to an effect it cannot predict. What gives the exponents of baroque culture their urgency and point is the degree to which they not only acknowledge, but practise the dialectical ground of their own literary, artistic and intellectual performances.

As this suggests, a first feature of such experiences is the fact that they are unintended. The poets, painters and philosophers they visit perceive them as a version of what, in a fragment on the nature of thought (542/459) designed to defeat its pretensions, Pascal ambiguously calls 'chance'. Accordingly, the work not only unearths an otherwise hidden truth about itself; it is transformed, taking an orientation as unlooked for as the discovery that precipitates it. This is one reason for calling such moments dialectical. The act of unprogrammed self-discovery that brings the work face to face with its own contingent nature *makes a difference*, creating as it were a new work that usurps the place of the one originally meant. But this points to another sense in which such moments are dialectical. For in the act of self-discovery, and in the difference the discovery makes, the work suddenly becomes what it learns it was from the start: something fully if at first unconsciously historical. It is not just that, among the other features of its own character and ground made known to it, it meets the historical condition inscribed in the socio-cultural occasion of its composition. The work makes history in the movement by which the encounter first displaces and then changes it. What most indelibly marks the poetic, artistic and philosophical monuments of the baroque, defining them as *baroque*, the unmistakable products of the period, sensibility and style to which we give that name, is the way they both register and work through the historical dialectic that governs them.

In proposing this view, I do not mean to say that the protagonists of the baroque era either would or could have formulated their experience in the historical terms suggested here. The dialectical theory of their self-consciously historical practice demands a conceptual vocabulary unavailable until the development of a thoroughgoing *philosophy* of history by the German Romantics, and in particular Hegel and Marx.[41] Indeed, the lack of the philosophical idiom required to explicate and formalize the baroque's historical insights explains why the experiment that baroque painters and writers find themselves performing turns out to be so short-lived. The era remains, after all, precariously suspended between two periods endowed with complementary notions of 'nature' that inevitably limit (where they do not preclude) an historical sense of the sort the baroque exhibits.[42] Because it is conceptually empty, reduced to an ironic *pointe* he cannot develop beyond mere tautological restatement, Pascal's chiastic rejoinder to Montaigne's profession of faith fails to prevent the revived confidence in natural categories that characterizes the century to come.

Thus, at the height of the Enlightenment, Hume's remorselessly reductive application of the 'experimental method' to moral and aesthetic as well as physical science gives scepticism a renewed life paradoxically nourished by disciplined adherence to observable fact. To this extent, the *Treatise of Human Nature* (1739-40) articulates the genuinely critical potential underlying the effort to disentangle the principles of reason and aesthetic imagination that Campbell chronicles. In the idol-smashing tradition of Baconian natural history, the point is to eliminate what Thomas Browne's *Pseudodoxia epidemica* (1672) calls the muddled 'amphibologies' of baroque science. Like Browne's sardonic survey of the epidemic fallacies that bedevil the search for knowledge, Humean scepticism clears the way for the properly modern model of science the method of experiment announces.[43] But as his book's very title reminds us, the perspective Hume embraces is no less 'natural', and therefore *ahistorical*, for the reductive picture of human knowledge, taste and conduct on which it is based.

Hume shares the baroque sense of human nature as the plaything of passion, prejudice, chance association and blind appetite: his analysis of the unsavoury sources of religion in the superstitions induced by ignorance and fear reproduces the one Spinoza proposes in ascribing the Hebrew Bible to the cynical policy needed to forge a Jewish state.[44] This yields the comic spectacle of deluded human self-importance that surfaces as early as the Hogarthian portrait of the 'present imperfect condition of the sciences' in the *Treatise*'s introduction:

> [E]ven the rabble without doors may judge from the noise and clamour, which they hear, that all goes not well within. There is nothing which is not the subject of debate, and in which men of learning are not of contrary opinions. The most trivial question escapes not our controversy, and in the most momentous we are not able to give any certain decision. Disputes are multiplied, as if every thing was uncertain; and these disputes are managed with the greatest warmth, as if every thing was certain. Amidst all this bustle 'tis not reason, which carries the prize, but eloquence; and no man needs ever despair of gaining proselytes to the most extravagant hypothesis, who has art enough to represent it in any favourable colours. The victory is not gained by the men at arms, who manage the pike and sword; but by the trumpeters, drummers, and musicians of the army.[45]

Yet *as* a comic spectacle, a comedy of manners close cousin to the 'comic epic poem in prose' Fielding defines in the contemporary form of the novel, Hume's picture of human nature presents consoling 'regularities'. Like the novel, Humean philosophy draws a proto-ethnographic map of human presumption and error, a diverting inventory of intellectual follies and character types whose very inveteracy enables human enquiry to police its own distorting foibles.[46]

The *Treatise*'s breezy good-humour carries all the way to the late *Dialogues Concerning Natural Religion*, drafted in the 1750s, but not published until 1779, after Hume's death. The coupled importance and obscurity of the issues Hume's speakers join, produce not the manic oscillations between enthusiastic heat and anguished doubt characteristic of baroque engagements with such themes, but rather the tempered tones of private conversation conducted in the comfortable surroundings of a well-appointed library. What the baroque would seize on as a matter for tortured tragedy becomes a social amenity that 'unites the two greatest and purest pleasures of human life, study and society'.[47] The baroque, then, proves both ephemeral and unique, a transient crisis whose anxious incapacity to formalize the insights on which it feeds induces the condescending incomprehension to which the Enlightenment treats it. But it is exactly here that we perceive what makes the period exemplary. Just because its protagonists cannot reduce their experience to formal concepts, the baroque is compelled to enact the historical process that traverses the monuments it leaves. And it is to this enactment, and to the critical self-consciousness with which enactment invests the ineffably singular works that form its medium and occasion, that we owe the dialectical light baroque culture sheds on the nature of historical experience and on the agonistic truth of the monuments charged with expressing it.

The following book develops the broad argument outlined here through a series of readings keyed to signal episodes in seventeenth-century cultural history. Chapter 1 shows how, not only despite, but in large measure as a direct reflex of what Mieke Bal terms the 'semiotics of rape' implicit in the Cartesian ideal of 'mastery' and 'possession' informing early modern science and art,[48] baroque representation asserts the finally indigestible alienness of both physical nature and the female form that artists and scientists deploy as nature's symbol. The allegories of rape Bal documents thus become emblems of the paradoxical inviolacy that Rembrandt makes the central focus of his exemplary treatment of the rape tale inscribed in the apocryphal History of Susanna. Chapter 2 unpacks the aesthetic and ontological entailments of this inviolate alienness as played out in the relation between self-portraiture and the Pauline view of carnal nature at work in Caravaggio and, again, Rembrandt. To the extent that, in Caravaggio and Rembrandt, the self-portrait becomes an icon of the irredeemably carnal character of the art to which it affixes an authorial face, it identifies painting as the preeminent exponent of the metaphysics of immanence on which the baroque era turns. Immanence, and more specifically the aesthetic *principle* of immanence whose self-conscious application lends baroque artistic production the character of a coherent system embracing literary as well as visual art, is the subject of chapter 3. A review of the history of representations of the Stoic legend of Hercules at the Crossroads that gives this book its subtitle will enable us to link the ontological burden of baroque painting as Caravaggio and Rembrandt expound it to the radical (as Wölfflin would call it, 'painterly') temporality of baroque drama. The result is a comparative analysis of the art of dramatic monologue and the soliloquistic habits of baroque visual art embodied in Annibale Carracci's epoch-making treatment of the tale. Finally, in chapter 4, the book returns to baroque philosophy, exploring how the text of Cartesian metaphysics, traditionally construed as the archetypal adversary of dialectical reason, engenders its own deconstruction. One locus for this deconstruction is the critical revision to which Cyrano and Pascal subject Descartes's work. Another is the series of dreams recorded in the 'Olympica', a repressed text dating from Descartes's youth whose uncanny return in the main body of his mature writings generates all of the major symbolic figures that mark the salvific road of methodic doubt.

As this suggests, we will cover a wide variety of media and forms: paintings and plays, scientific treatises and apologetic writings, moralist maxims and philosophical essays, the repressed dream text of Descartes's 'Olympica' and, in the case of Cyrano's 'Sur l'ombre que faisoient des arbres dans l'eau', a pyrotechnical *exercise de style* in the guise of a satiric letter to an anonymous friend. The variety of media is in turn cashed out in the variety of individual works, each of which is defined in the first instance by the local, historically licensed end it has in view. In Caravaggio's Cerasi *Conversion of St Paul*, for instance, as also (though very differently) in Rembrandt's *Self-Portrait as the Apostle Paul*, we meet votive images illustrating the lesson of Christian faith, hope and charity spelled out in 1 Corinthians 13.12-13. By contrast, in Carracci's *Hercules* we find the representation of a legendary or historical exemplum initially calculated to celebrate the current political order of post-Tridentine Rome. Meanwhile, for all the radical acuity that makes it a primary reference for the Marxist Louis Althusser, the social semiologist Louis Marin or the social constructivist Pierre Bourdieu, Pascal's *Pensées* is first and last a theodicy defending Catholic belief in its most intransigent (if heterodox) form.[49]

This points at one level to each work's inescapable dependence on the wider cultural and historical context all of them share and on the pervading aims, norms, self-understandings and needs that shape this context. The combination of interdisciplinarity and attention to the mediating settings in which individual works appear evokes the whole of which each work and the socio-cultural episode it refracts are conditional expressions. But, at another level, because the argument focuses on the exemplary occasions of which these works and episodes are at once vestiges and vehicles, the book illustrates the logic of mediating historical enactment and the role this plays in determining the period's historical testimony. The baroque thus has a wider pedagogic value bearing on theory and the dialectical method theory recommends.

To see more clearly how, we will turn to a telltale source of the recent revival of interest in the baroque in Benjamin's book on the German *Trauerspiel*. However, to understand the *Origin*'s testimony, we must first consider the issues raised by two later works of which it is the forerunner: the ill-starred monograph on 'The Paris of the Second Empire in Baudelaire' and the *Passagen-Werk* or 'arcades project' from which the Baudelaire essay was culled. For what drew Benjamin to the baroque was precisely the set of simultaneously historical and theoretical problems for which his later writings provide a conceptual apparatus.

The Baudelaire monograph and arcades project employ the 'mosaic' technique of historical montage. Like the *flâneur* of Baudelaire's *Spleen de Paris*, wandering the boulevards and back alleys of the modern city in pursuit of the curious and rare, Benjamin patrols libraries, antiquarian bookshops and the hulks of abandoned arcades in search of the *disiecta membra* of the forgotten past. By this means, he not only retrieves but, as he also liked to hint, messianically 'redeems'[50] a wide variety of intriguing totemic objects: commercial fliers, tintypes, engraved illustrations or the stray scraps of superannuated knowledge and discarded insight contained in his beloved collection of quotations. These items are then stitched together to form discrete constellations whose artful juxtaposition conjures up fleeting images of the bygone lifeworld of which they are the relicts. It is crucial, however, that the application of what the 'Theses on the Philosophy of History' calls the 'constructive principle' behind these juxtapositions is an essentially forensic enterprise: the construction follows the process of historical destruction that has given the assembled vestiges the form Benjamin preserves.[51] The lost world that the mosaic conjures up reproduces the state of *ruin* that both motivates and conditions historical research. But it is also crucial that, as his affection for the ruins motif suggests, Benjamin makes no attempt to weave the fragments he rescues into an explicit explanatory narrative. He presents them, rather, as 'monads', discontinuous and therefore seemingly random 'crystallizations' of historical remnants whose critical exegesis lies dormant in the material itself and in the principles of selection Benjamin's constructions hint at but never expound (pp. 262-263).

It is in the cryptic nature of the historical project made known to him in the Baudelaire monograph that it should provoke the notorious impatience voiced in Theodor Adorno's letter of 10 November 1938, explaining its rejection by the Institute for Social Research, to which Benjamin had submitted it for publication. Though Adorno found the material suggestive, he deplored the lack of he kind of encompassing theoretical frame needed to give the monograph's content the 'concretion' and intelligibility dialectical historiography demands. Benjamin's mosaic fragments struck him indeed as hopelessly 'abstract' precisely because they were cut off from the mediating socio-historical matrix that conditions what they are, how they came to be and what they signify. Shrewdly linking the text's theoretical underdevelopment to his correspondent's crypto-Kabbalistic interests, Adorno writes:

> The theological motif of calling things by their names tends to turn into a wide-eyed presentation of mere facts. If one wished to put it very drastically, one could say that your study is located at the crossroads of magic and positivism. That spot is bewitched. Only theory could break the spell—your own resolute, salutarily speculative theory.[52]

Though Adorno does not expressly say so, Benjamin's monads were not only unintelligible, but came across as an antiquarian counterpart of the commodity fetishes of contemporary mass culture. Like the popular movies to which Benjamin was also powerfully drawn, they are idols whose phantasmagoric hold on the imagination is determined just by their alienated abstraction from the social economy that, in manufacturing and marketing them, assigns their true agency and meaning. Not, of course, that Adorno responds here as the sort of 'vulgar' Marxist both he and Benjamin despised—a one-way determinist for whom the superstructure of historical culture is the mere mystified reflex of an all-powerful socio-economic base.[53] But though his view was tempered by a neo-Hegelian sense of the role conscious agency plays in determining its own historical conditions, he held fast to a Marxist stress on the social whole that Benjamin's fetishized fragments sacrifice. Whence, however, Benjamin's rejoinder, no less pointed for the mysteriously gnomic form in which he eventually came to express it. If the monads are theoretically undigested, it is because they are fundamentally *indigestible*, resisting subsumption in the kind of perspicuous theoretical scheme Adorno wants. And what makes them so is the destructive operation of the socio-historical whole whose ruins they reproduce.

Such is at least what I take to be the thrust of the formal responses to Adorno's criticisms contained in the characteristically fragmentary essay the Institute did agree to publish, 'On Some Motifs in Baudelaire', and in the still more fragmentary 'Theses on the Philosophy of History'. The 'Theses' make seemingly extravagant claims in defence of Benjamin's eccentric procedures. The monads not only prove consonant with the method Adorno recommends; they embody the fundamental principles that distinguish a properly 'materialistic historiography' from the retrograde 'historicism' Benjamin derisively associates with Ranke (p. 255). For Benjamin, the Rankean ideal of a seamlessly 'universal' history promotes a mechanically 'additive' conception of the historical past. In the absence of the kind of 'theoretical armature' Benjamin now purports to supply, it 'musters data to fill the homogeneous, empty time' that the finally impossible goal of securing an integral reconstruction of the past 'as it really was' [*wie es eigentlich gewesen*] requires.[54] By contrast, the 'historical materialist' breaks history down into discrete moments of crystallized symbolic tension and focus, producing none other than the monads Benjamin sets out to construct (pp. 262-263).

This theoretical adjustment has formal consequences. In pursuing an integral restoration of the past as it really was, Rankean historicism creates the illusion of a seamless 'transition' from the past itself to 'the "eternal" image' in which it is now preserved as an object of disinterested historical contemplation. Benjamin counters by asserting that such timeless disinterest is not only implausible, but immoral. Materialist historiography expressly inhabits the embattled present of historical writing as such; and in this present, 'time stands still and has come to a stop' under the pressure of the critical interest the historian takes in the past. Benjamin characterizes this interest in typically idiosyncratic terms as the simultaneously 'revolutionary' and 'Messianic' desire to *rescue* the past, a goal that can only be achieved by demolishing the at once deluded and oppressive continuities of conventional historiography (pp. 262-263).[55] But Benjamin's method also reflects a deeper motive for the sort of prophetic iconoclasm he preaches.

What inspires the historical materialist to 'blast a specific era out of the homogeneous course of history' by 'blasting a specific life out of the era or a specific work out of the lifework' (p. 263) is the desire less for dispassionate knowledge *of* the past than an empathic 'experience *with* it' (p. 262; my emphasis). And what we experience with the past is the condition we share with it: the condition of *being historical* and the dimension of inexorable change, decay, alienation and loss such being entails (p. 255).

To be sure, however materialistic its inspiration may purport to be, the deepest sources for Benjamin's method are poetic rather than historiographical.[56] The phenomenon of 'involuntary memory' Proust derives from Bergson is one such source; and Goethe's *Farbenlehre*, from which Benjamin borrows the epigraph for the *Origin*, is another.[57] But the nearest (in part, no doubt, because the most 'splenetic' and disenchanted) model is the one on which the arcades project so heavily drew: Baudelaire's *correspondances*, enigmatic episodes of heightened moral and sensory perception crystallized in the discontinuous mode of prose poems. As the 'Motifs' essay tries to explain in terms Adorno will countenance, what attracts Benjamin to Baudelaire is the lucidity with which the poet freezes the sensation of historical becoming in moments of vivid yet fleeting poetic experience that no mere theory can accommodate. The scent of a woman's hair, the glare of gaslight in the new cafés, the oceanic vistas of urban rooftops, the measureless vastness of Parisian boulevards all seem to *betoken* something. But what they betoken escapes us because the element that calls them into being is the relentlessly modern experience of resistless historical change the poems try to overcome. Baudelaire's symbolic correspondences originate in the very process of social dislocation that destroys the moral framework needed to make them speak.[58]

In both Baudelaire and Benjamin, but also, we recall, in Pascal before them, this insight produces the tautological form of the alienated monadic present: fugitive atoms of experience that, in the absence of an articulate moral frame, can only repeat themselves, circularly restating the broken terms of their inscrutable equations. But it likewise yields a constitutive temporal paradox: the present the correspondences tautologically rehearse is composed of fragments of the *past* to which history relegates it. As Benjamin acutely notes, the vivid 'data' of Baudelairean prose poetry, the mute facts endlessly recycled in the here and now of poetic encounter, are already as such 'data of remembrance' wrested from a flood of social change that carries all before it. This is how Baudelaire's correspondences express the consciousness of their historical destiny. Yet it remains of the essence of the destiny thus exhibited that we can never perceive it directly. As Althusser puts it, adapting an insight borrowed from Spinoza, history is an 'absent cause' apprehensible only in its *effects*, causal telltales available only once the contingent relations of force that produced them have moved on.[59] History is then, by definition, what is past beyond recall and cannot therefore be rescued from the wreck to which its own onrush consigns it. Accordingly, Benjamin goes on to specify that Baudelaire's data of remembrance are 'not historical data, but data of prehistory' (p. 182). This formula refers of course, in one of its aspects, to the longing with which Benjamin and Baudelaire both turn back toward an edenic past of which philistine modernity is the Moloch-like destroyer. In speaking of 'prehistory', Benjamin thereby denotes one of the aims he and his chosen poet characteristically pursue, that of resurrecting the childlike paradise from which modern alienation satanically expels us. But the notion also has a deeper charge. To experience history at all is to do so *in medias res*, in the 'prehistoric' mode of anxious anticipation. It is thus in the nature of the historical condition we experience with the past that it assume the 'arrested' form of the monads Benjamin models on the *Spleen de Paris*. What is to be recovered from the past in the mode of historiographical experience is the prehistoric registration of the irresistible destruction on the point of overtaking a lost historical present.

In explaining the grounds of Benjamin's mosaic method, the 'Theses' and 'Motifs' further explain how the method is justified by the materialistic historiography in whose light it seems an enigmatic fetish. Benjamin turns the lack of a mediating thesis that Adorno laments into a theoretical virtue: the method's monadic inscrutability measures its historical veracity. But this in turn pinpoints the challenge the method poses to the perspective Adorno champions. If history is what Marxism alleges, what happens 'behind our backs' even as we try to shape it, and indeed just because we try to shape it from the standpoint of interested agents caught up in its alienating course, then it remains fundamentally inaccessible in the form Adorno requires. Students of Benjamin will recognize the insight behind the famous passage in the 'Theses' on the expressionist Paul Klee's *Angelus Novus* (pp. 257-258). Klee's image of an angel looking back on a landscape of ruins as storm winds carry it into an ominous future provides an emblem of the sense of historical being Benjamin identifies in Baudelaire. At one level, the *Angelus* embodies the historical nostalgia recalled a moment ago—the poignant regret informing the 'Storyteller' essay or the later discussion of the 'loss of aura' art undergoes in the 'age of mechanical reproduction'.[60] But the icon of historical reality Benjamin perceives in Klee's painting is not merely nostalgic; it mirrors the critical idea embedded in the parable of the chess machine with which the 'Theses' open:

> The story is told of an automaton constructed in such a way that it could play a winning game of chess, answering each move of an opponent with a countermove. A puppet in Turkish attire and with a hookah in its mouth sat before a chessboard placed on a large table. A system of mirrors created the illusion that this table was transparent from all sides. Actually, a little hunchback who was an expert chess player sat inside and guided the puppet's hand by means of strings. One can imagine a philosophical counterpart to this device. The puppet called 'historical materialism' is to win all the time. It can easily be a match for anyone if it enlists the services of theology, which today, as we know, is wizened and has to keep out of sight. (p. 253)

The parable's Marxist automaton is meant to prove not only that it wins, but that it wins *because it is an automaton*. Victory is assured by the apparent elimination of the human player, the living subject of historical experience. Victory is thus presented as a mindless reflex of the deterministic necessity that historical materialism appoints. But if the automaton wins, the real reason is that it cheats: victory is achieved through the all-too-human agency of the ignoble hunchback concealed inside. The parable calls the hunchback 'theology'. To this extent, it echoes the classic denunciation of Marxist scientism, a denunciation to which Critical Theory also subscribes. If Marxism passes for the infallible science of history its exponents are tempted to claim materialism makes it, it is because it masks the metaphysics sustaining the transhistorical posture that the supporting notion of science presumes. Still, at the tip of Benjamin's pen, theology is by no means an unequivocally pejorative term; one of its functions here is indeed to announce the messianic Angel soon to come. If theology nonetheless remains a 'wizened' figure obliged to hide its shameful misshapenness, it is because, browbeaten by a materialist outlook that historical experience shows to be unanswerable, we fail to keep the faith materialism itself unconsciously enjoins.

To keep this faith demands acknowledging what remains an irrevocable consequence of the materialism history teaches: the exclusion of the metaphysical outside on whose promise faith depends. To be faithful, then, requires that we envision redemption in the perspective of radical immanence Spinoza's absent cause prescribes—from *within* the historical world whose demonic headlong flight eradicates all hope of salvation. But this is just where Benjamin's prehistoric method of monadic correspondences comes in—and why, though looking backward even as the storm winds carry it forward in time, the messianic Angel prophesies a redemption mysteriously at hand. Held in the prism of the historical fate that shortly overtakes it, the historical moment turns the spectacle of its destruction into the kind of *witness* that historical experience otherwise compels us to foresake.

All of this illuminates Benjamin's early interest in the baroque, and in particular its late efflorescence in the German baroque of Gryphian 'graveyard thoughts', the already outmoded taste for emblem books and above all the German 'sorrow play'. What Benjamin contrives to find in the baroque is an historical culture—but also an historical *moment*, both period and phase, epoch and episode—that contains the prehistoric intuition of its own historical destruction as an inner productive impulse. This coalescence of perspectives informs Benjamin's important distinction between the German *Trauerspiel* and Greek tragedy. The classical Greek picture of sacrificial human grandeur in the face of the inescapable ironies of suffering, error and death is as it were parodied by baroque protagonists whose besetting sin is less heroic hubris than dithering indecision. What undoes the royal Heinrich of Filidor's *Ernelinde* (c. 1660) or the odious Herod of Hallmann's version of the Mariamne story (1670) is a Hamlet-like failure to act, creating a vacuum tragic fate occupies at their expense (pp. 60-68). The same coalescence of viewpoints justifies the weight Benjamin lays on the theme of melancholy and the perverse pleasure baroque poets take in it, actively savouring the acedic *ennui* discovered at the heart of mortal experience (pp. 138-158). This in turn prompts the famous interpretation of baroque allegories as constituting, 'in the realm of thoughts, what ruins are in the realm of things': a fusion of symbolic monuments and the sceptical demolition to which time exposes them whereby the baroque incorporates decline, decay, corruption and death in the constructive principle that pretends to vanquish them (p. 178). Whence, finally, Benjamin's conception of German *Trauer* as a mode of mourning work conducted *in advance* of the mortal end toward which it compulsively turns—a dress rehearsal for the dismembering loss that awaits us all. Like the *fort-da* game of Freud's *Beyond the Pleasure Principle*, a collection of late graveyard thoughts designed to redeem the aging psychoanalyst's growing presentiment of failure and death by transforming his fears into the suicidal 'wish' that forms the book's chief theoretical innovation, the period, sensibility and style we call baroque encompass the ruin history makes of them.[61]

Benjamin's view is abetted by the vestigial form in which the era's productions survive. As for the past in general, what we know of the baroque is what *remains* of it. The baroque just *is* the fossil record of historical documentation unearthed in discarded emblem books, designs for long-vanished triumphal entries, *Festbuch* illustrations of defunct court entertainments and rituals, the inventories of dismantled *Wunderkammer* collections of now meaningless curiosities or the lost learning buried in forgotten archives.[62] This general truth has special point in the German case given the phenomenon's provincial character as an outdated excrescence on the neglected outer fringes of metropolitan Europe. Composed in a German that is hard to read, and adopting forms that show little of the finesse its French, Spanish or Italian counterparts display, German baroque literature was largely obsolete even in its own day, constituting a corpus only Benjamin-like antiquarians could love. This antiquarian obsolescence emerges, moreover, as a deliberate feature of one of German drama's most prestigious exemplars, the tragedy of *Sophonisbe* (produced 1669; published 1680) by the 'German Seneca' Lohenstein.[63]

The play's historical heroine is the daughter of the dead Hasdrubal and niece of the beleaguered Hannibal, heroic defenders of the once great city of Carthage, soon to be vanquished by the Roman armies of Scipio Africanus. Eager to avenge her father's defeat and death, Sophonisbe overcomes the understandable reluctance of her weak-willed husband Syphax, king of Numidia, to wage war on the victorious Romans. When Syphax is defeated and imprisoned, Sophonisbe consents to a bigamous second marriage to the infatuated Masinissa, an ally of Rome whose passion for the heroine leads him to espouse her cause. In a fanatical effort to revive the powers of Carthage's tutelary gods, Masinissa's bigamous queen prepares at one point the ritual sacrifice of one of her own sons—a fate her willing child is spared at the last moment when Roman captives are found, who die in his stead. Nevertheless, unnerved when Scipio's troops arrive on the scene, Masinissa reneges on his conjugal promise, whereupon Sophonisbe poisons herself in an ultimate act of defiance. If she cannot defeat her enemies, she will at least escape the disgrace of being led in chains in Scipio's triumphant train.

The tragedy rehearses a violent tale of passion and intrigue all the more sensational for the lurid elements on which Lohenstein dwells: Sophonisbe's unscrupulous manipulation of the feeble men in her thrall; a bigamous marriage other versions avoid by having Syphax killed before his wife's union with his besotted rival; the intricately staged ritual in which Sophonisbe first prepares to immolate her son Hierba and then sacrifices the Roman captives in his place; and scenes of cross-dressing in which the heroine clads herself in male armor to defend her husband's besieged city, dons the same costume again as a disguise in order to rescue Syphax from prison and arrays her son Vermina in a woman's garments as a mandated part of the sacrificial ritual performed at the altar of Baal.[64] It is moreover hard to imagine anything either more self-explanatory or better suited to Lohenstein's chosen genre: the *Haupt-* or *Staatsaktionendrama*, a kind of *grand guignol* spectacle modeled (in one of the odder episodes of early modern literary influence) on Jacobean revenge tragedies mounted in their original tongue by itinerant troops of London players displaced by the closure of English theatres in 1642.[65]

Still, Lohenstein finds it impossible to leave the story alone, allowing it to work its magic on its own. On the contrary, he adds an enormous apparatus of learned footnotes documenting the items of local historical colour the play parades, glossing his scholarly sources and pointing each incident's moral. He also interrupts the central action itself by introducing allegorical interludes that supply a running commentary in the intervals between the play's five acts. Thus act 1's exposition of the doomed queen's furious defiance at the approach of Scipio's army is followed by a psychomachic masque in which the heroine's disembodied Soul looks on while her personified Passions (Discord, Love, Rage, Hate, Joy, Desire, Dread, Envy and Fright) lyrically wrestle for supremacy. And act 4, which features a 104-line solioquy in which, torn between passion for Sophonisbe and politic awe in the face of Rome's invincible might, Masinissa decides to abandon his wife to her fate, gives way to a portrayal of the legend of Hercules at the Crossroads. The symbolic reenactment of the Greek demigod's choice of heroic Virtue (*Tugend*) over carnal Pleasure (*Wollust*) in turn evolves into a hymn of praise to the Genius, Spirit or Ghost (*Geist*) of the emperor Leopold, a living reincarnation of Hercules' glorious example offered as a pattern for the noble patron to whom the poet dedicates the play. Lohenstein's *Trauerspiel* is thus doubled by its own proleptic archaeology, an erudite substitute for an active knowledge that the author fears will prove deficient. Even in its own time, the play anticipates an eclipse against which Lohenstein arms it with donnish punctiliousness.[66]

It is true and important that, despite all the evidence in its favour, we cannot take Benjamin's picture of baroque culture uncritically. Placed in their immediate historical context, the allegories in which he perceives the petrified remnants of a lost lifeworld are imbued with an irrepressible vitality to which he is stubbornly blind. Even in the proleptically archaeological form Lohenstein gives it, *Sophonisbe* retains a vigorous sense of *theatre*. If only in the mode of reception Harry Berger calls the 'imaginary audition' that its status as drama demands on the reader's part,[67] the play invokes the resuscitating energies of scenic performance: the animate heat of bodies and voices; the deployment of painted scenery, candlelight and the music to which Lohenstein's interludic figures dance their masquing measures; above all, a responsive public capable of discerning the action's moral bearing. As Lohenstein's allegorical interludes suggest, contemporary spectators needed instruction; but much of this instruction takes place, precisely, in the form of dramatic interludes projected against the background of established conventions that make perfect theatrical sense of them. In *Verliebtes Gespenst/Die geliebte Dornrose* (1661), a comic 'Mischspiel' by the 'German Sophocles' Gryphius, two different plays alternate act by act until fusing in a common finale: one a polite comedy, set in a pleasure garden, whose hero pretends to be poisoned by sweets his beloved laces with a love potion meant for another man and then woos her in the form of his own infatuated ghost; the other a knockabout farce in which cloddish swains compete for the hand of the winsome Thornrose. Meanwhile, in Bidermann's *Cenodoxus* (1602), where the hosts of heaven and hell do battle for the eponymous protagonist's soul, scenes of human interaction are interspersed with spirit encounters invisible to the play's human agents. Even leaving aside prestigious if eccentric experiments like these, Lohenstein's procedures find ready precedents in Jesuit 'school' drama and the emergent opera, where commentary in the form of choric dances is common.[68]

What is more, Lohenstein trades on a conception of history quite different from the one by which Benjamin sees him as overtaken. To cite an idea whose consequences we will explore in chapter 3, the notion that history contains moral lessons of the sort Lohenstein points is a period commonplace. To contemporary readers of the ancient historians Lohenstein draws on, Plutarch, Livy, Polybius or Tacitus, history is first and last a repository of practical examples designed to enable those who use them to map a successful passage through the maze of present emergencies.[69] Lohenstein's public would thus have taken it for granted that the dark forces driving *Sophonisbe*'s characters have a saving moral valence. And they would also have taken it for granted that the divided human loyalties the play portrays have transcendental referents in the Christian faith to which the poet implicitly appeals and in the social order that Christian belief underwrites in the person of the fourth interlude's ghostly emperor.

Yet impoverished as it may be, Benjamin's reading of the baroque points to something essential. Though more 'painterly' and dynamic than Benjamin's saturnine picture allows, the sense of impending eclipse that Lohenstein's interludes and learned footnotes evince is both real and central. Beyond underscoring the obsessional fixation on decay, decline, corruption and death to which the dark matter of his fable testifies, Lohenstein registers both the chiastic secondness to which Pascal bears witness and the dialectic that Pascalian secondness unleashes.

Of this too the double structure of Lohenstein's *Trauerspiel* offers proof. A major function of *Sophonisbe*'s interludes is to stage a kind of secular theophany. They constitute a ritualized mode of dramatic action designed to manifest the cosmic order more directly but, for that very reason, more obscurely embedded in the main body of the tragic plot. Invoking the metaphysical certainties underpinning the conventions and commonplaces on which the interludes depend, the aim is to achieve a moral transparency the play itself cannot. This produces the almost disinterested pertinacity with which, in the psychomachia appended to act 1, the Soul of Sophonisbe points the lesson of the allegorical dance of Passions her words round off:

> Ja! alle die beherbergt meine Brust /
> Seit mein verletzter Geist für Rach' und Eyfer glühet.
> Die Liebe schöpft an meinen Kindern Lust /
> Wenn sie die Mordlust sich in ihnen wittern siehet.
> Ich hasse Rom / und fürchte seine Macht.
> Mich tröstet Syphaxs Flucht / ich neide's Feindes Glücke.
> Mich schreckt die schon zweymal verlohrne Schlacht.
> Nimm / Rache / dir den Preiß. Doch Blitz zerbrich die Stricke![70]

> [Yes! My breast harbours all of these
> Since my wounded spirit began to burn with rage and redhot passion.
> Love labours to secure my children's happiness
> When she sees bloodlust begin to stir in them.
> I hate Rome, and fear her might.
> Syphax's flight brings me solace, I envy my enemy's good fortune.
> The already twice-lost battle frightens me.
> Rage, take thou the prize. May lightning snap these binding snares!]

Set beside the more sophisticated methods of a playwright like the French Corneille, Lohenstein's device is endearingly clumsy and literal. In a comparable scene from *Cinna* (1642), Corneille conveys the sense of demonic possession Sophonisbe shares with his play's Emilie, torn between an overpowering thirst for revenge and fear on behalf of the lover from whom she demands the murder of the emperor at whose hands her father died. But where Lohenstein resorts to personification allegory in order to portray Sophonisbe's inner conflict, Corneille presents a soliloquy composed of artful apostrophes addressed to the raging passions by which Emilie is beset:

> Impatients désirs d'une illustre vengeance
> Dont la mort de mon père a formé la naissance,
> Enfants impétueux de mon ressentiment,
> Que ma douleur séduite embrasse aveuglément,
> Vous prenez sur mon âme un trop puissant empire:
> Durant quelques moments souffrez que je respire,
> Et que je considère, en l'état où je suis,
> Et ce que je hasarde, et ce que je poursuis.[71]

> [Impatient desires of illustrious revenge
> To which my father's death has given birth,

> Impetuous children of my resentment
> That my misguided pain blindly embraces,
> You exert too potent an empire over my soul:
> Suffer for a few moments that I may breathe
> And contemplate, in the state to which I am led,
> Both what I risk, and what I pursue.]

Still, artless as it may be, Lohenstein's psychomachia achieves the same general effect, simultaneously presenting and judging the fearful moral dismemberment unbridled emotion inflicts.

Yet at the same time as the psychomachia clarifies the moral issues joined and the moral judgment we are meant to apply to the heroine's demonic blindness, the device's very literalness underscores the unbridgeable gulf between the clarity it secures and the lifeworld on which it comments. The radical divorce between moral experience and the moral lessons it contains is after all what makes the device seem necessary, thereby undermining the pious certainties the play wants to endorse. What is more, blind, dismembered, villainously possessed as the interludes appear to make her, Sophonisbe is also *magnificent*; the moralistic horror her crimes inspire is overbalanced by the identificatory relish they invite. In this she resembles not only Corneille's regicidal Emilie, but the still more unrelievedly monstrous heroine of the French poet's earlier *Médée* (1634): appalling as the Colchean witch's decision to punish her faithless husband by murdering her own children may be, the action's very extravagance commands respect. Lohenstein's African queen further recalls the Satan of Milton's *Paradise Lost* (1667), the full measure of whose wicked influence is the admiration his willful defiance of divine authority extorts.[72] Sophonisbe is a figure of proud resistance and self-determined right all the more seductive for her hyperbolic transgressiveness.

Sneaking admiration for the play's Luciferic heroine explains the widespread interest in the historical anecdote—the complex resonance that, in France notably, led not only Corneille (1663), but his sometime rival Mairet (1634) to devote tragedies to the theme.[73] For despite the criminal lengths to which resentment drives her, Sophonisbe is predestined to suffer lamentable defeat: it is indeed her defeat and the defiant suicide with which she resists it to the end that define her exemplary appeal. In depicting the fall of the last of Hasdrubal's line, the fable also forecasts the definitive (and bloody) triumph of imperial Rome: a city in which early moderns saw a model both of the growing empires the emergent states of modern Europe were in the process of creating and of the absolutist monarchies to which the goal of empire was regularly hitched. In this sense, by an effect of contrast with its eponymous heroine's hyperbolic crimes, Lohenstein's play becomes an encomium of the stern heroic virtues whose exercise historically ordains Scipio's victory over the defeated ethos his adversary defends. Scipio represents the second, positive leg of the legend of Hercules the fourth interlude stages, a role confirmed by his status as the recipient of the hieroglyphic dream recorded in Cicero's *De republica* (6.9.29) that forms part of the legend's topical intertext. But to the precise extent that the play invites us to sympathize with the monstrous Carthaginian, Scipio becomes the focus of an ineffaceable ambivalence in whose light his cold-blooded virtues appear as baleful as his enemy's excesses.

Noble as history paints him, Scipio is a moral automaton whose triumph ironically deepens our appreciation of Sophonisbe's vanquished humanity. Like the chess machine in Benjamin's parable, he wins just because he disowns the disordered attributes of human subjectivity—a point underscored late in the play (act 4, verses 203-344) when he scolds the feckless Masinissa for letting womanish love unhinge his manly reason. The result is that the human feeling the play evokes lies with his backward-looking adversary. Sophonisbe embodies the sense of historical loss that is the price of Roman victory. In the process, she crystallizes what, in an English context, Christopher Hill calls the 'experience of defeat' endemic to the seventeenth century. As Hill documents, defeat is universal in England, sooner or later visiting all parties to the social, political and religious conflicts of the age—Jacobites and Cromwellians, Diggers and Independents, Fifth Monarchists and Catholic recusants, Quakers and cavaliers. Against this background, it is entirely appropriate that the key figure in Hill's survey should be Milton, author not only of the attempt to 'justify the ways of God to men' in *Paradise Lost*, but of *Samson Agonistes* (1671), where blind self-sacrifice redeems still blinder self-betrayal. But the English example typifies a condition observed throughout seventeenth-century Europe. Violently as they may differ in everything else, reformers and counter reformers, naturalists and apologists, ancients and moderns, royalists and republicans, *nobles de robe* and *nobles d'épée* all taste the bitterness of impotence and failure. Like the Roman Lucretia whose exemplary suicide so resembles her own, Sophonisbe epitomizes a work of mourning that pervades the era as a whole.[74]

All of this accounts for what drew Benjamin to the baroque; it is hard indeed to imagine a period or a body of works better suited to the would-be Kabbalist's saturnine temperament. But it also suggests that the baroque appealed to him not merely as an appropriate object for his style of reading; it served, further, as a model for the mosaic method Adorno disliked. In ambiguously espousing its heroine's at once doomed and demonic vitality in the face of her enemy's automatized virtue, *Sophonisbe* seeks refuge from the impossible choices that the pressure of historical events compels human agents to make. In answer to the virtuous example the fourth interlude proposes as a paradigm identified with the reigning emperor Leopold, the play temporizes in order to remind us of the cost Scipio's virtues exact. The baroque's artful equivocations mirror Benjamin's own refusal to submit to the Scipionic rigour Critical Theory requires, a refusal that colours even those texts in which he does his best to kiss the rod. Like the baroque itself, Benjamin keeps faith with the dialectic to which historical materialism shows all cultural acts to be bound. But, as in the baroque, the measure of his fidelity is its *aesthetic* character. If, from the dialectical standpoint as Benjamin conceives it, the baroque faithfully records the historical emergencies that produced it, it is because, like the data of Baudelaire's *Spleen de Paris*, it remains stubbornly prehistoric: the monuments of baroque culture are artful monads designed to arrest the process of historical change on the point of consuming them. In this sense, Lohenstein's anarchic heroine incarnates the aesthetic itself envisaged in the fundamental vulnerability that defines its historical truth. Even, if not especially, at its most lucid and critical, in the theoretical writings of Spinoza or Pascal as well as in the categorically aesthetic form of Caravaggiesque painting or the dramas of Lohenstein and Shakespeare, what guarantees the veracity of the baroque response to historical necessity is its calculated assumption of the equivocal mode of art.

This is in part a reflex of the lack of determining concepts noted earlier. Period painters, poets and philosophers are obliged to figure what, in the absence of later notions of history, the unconscious, social construction or the performative grounds of human natures and identities, it cannot articulate in expressly categorical form. By this means, baroque representation answers, in the mode of historical accident, to the second of Kant's four 'moments' of aesthetic judgments. As in Kant, the beautiful here evinces a contingent 'liking' (*Wohlgefallen*) that, for want of a categorical term, is simultaneously subjective and universal. It springs from a fortuitous conjunction whose appeal to a missing concept sets the beholder's faculties in a state of free and therefore pleasing yet interminable play.[75] But the resort to the aesthetic is also a reflex of the faith Lohenstein's Sophonisbe keeps and of the backward-looking resistance her faith's inevitable defeat inspires even as we acknowledge the justice of Scipio's triumph.

This remarkably foreshadows the role the aesthetic performs in Kant. It throws a bridge across the insuperable gulf between the illusionless world of fact and a world of moral choices made all the more urgent by turbulent desires over which moral reason has no control. The monadic aestheticism of baroque monuments induces the brute contingencies of historical experience to speak on morality's behalf.[76] The preeminent philosophical expression of the dilemma baroque aesthetics engages is perhaps Spinoza's posthumous *Ethics* (1677). The *Ethics* decrees the Scipionic triumph of immanence—of nature construed as reductive matter. Whence the initial force of Spinoza's declaration that God and Nature are in fact one and the same thing, viewed under complementary aspects. Where God is not merely a figment of human imagination, an irrational reflex of the ignorance and fear natural to our species, he is the name we give natural law conceived as the irresistible determinism to which Nature subjects all things. Yet the ultimate effect of Spinoza's declaration is the chiastic reversal by which, in fusing God and Nature, he transforms both terms. In sacrificing the idea of God to that of Nature, in sacrificing transcendence to the immanence that negates it, Spinoza secures the belated victory of transcendence as such. More precisely, God becomes the prophetic achievement of the human mind insofar as mind acknowledges its absolute enthrallment to natural determinism. But the crucial point is that this redemptive paradox is accomplished in the *form* of Spinoza's text rather than its argument. It is indeed enacted far more than it is argued, a product of inventive play with the figure of chiasmus and the artful reversals of perspective chiasmus promotes.

To seek the truth of the baroque thus demands that we seek its truth *as art*. This speaks to the continuity linking Benjamin's book on the German baroque to his later defence of the aesthetic, an arena to which Critical Theory generally turns with iconoclastic intent. In Adorno, art either exposes the false consciousness of a subjacent ideology or, as in his notoriously elitist embrace of avant-gardist music, it negates the mass-produced commodities of deluded popular taste. But the conjunction of truth and art in the baroque also underscores the relevance of my epigraph from Heidegger, striking the keynote for what is to follow: 'In the art work, the truth of what is has set itself to work. Art is truth setting itself to work.'[77]

That the work of art should become the theatre of truth is a paradox for the baroque itself. On the one hand, art is a triumph of self-determined human 'genius' and 'invention', terms whose relation to the semantic field of art is attested by their coalescence in the 'engines' of 'engineering'—the French *génie*. This is what Bacon has in mind in extolling the 'vexations' by which the art of empirical experiment forces personified Nature to reveal the hidden laws that govern her underlying 'operations'.[78] It is then to inventive art that we look to escape mere natural givenness, transcending the misleading evidence of natural sight in order to penetrate nature's secrets and transform our natural condition. But, on the other hand, as the ambiguous resonance of Bacon's 'vexations' reminds us, art is also an epitome of error, violence and fraud. Though a near synonym of 'genius', 'art' is the antonym of 'truth' and 'nature' alike, a trick or ruse, a fount of coercive illusion that, like the deceitful 'engines' and 'inventions' of politic ministers, conceals and deforms the native face of things. Art is to this extent a focus of ambivalence quite as insoluble as that surrounding both Sophonisbe's vices and her Roman conqueror's orthopedic virtues.

Yet the deceitful illusions with which the baroque associates art underscore its ambiguous salience. A major, therapeutic function of baroque art is to spotlight the elusive difference between truth and falsehood in order to restore the reader or beholder's power to distinguish reality from illusion. The point of a play like Calderón's *La vida es sueño* (1635), a goal curiously yet characteristically shared with the philosophical analysis of dream in Descartes's First Meditation, is not merely to alert us to the disturbing proximity of dream and wakefulness; it is to arm us against mistaking deluded carnal appearance for the deliverances of God-given reason.[79] To achieve this end, art deploys the very deceptions it sets out to explode. If *La vida* convinces us of the ease with which dream passes for real, it is because the play itself induces us to credit its own dreamlike illusions. And what is true of Calderón's play is equally so of Descartes's meditation, which shakes our faith in a distinction we take for granted by exposing the shallow grounds on which it stands. Art frames an image of truth precisely by exhibiting its power to cast a spell over fallen human consciousness: the very impossibility of entrusting truth to art in view of art's truth as illusion confirms our vulnerability to error. In the mirrorlike inversions by which the self-consuming form of a self-denouncing work of art unmasks its own deceitfulness, art fingers a truth *only* art could disclose.

This insight refines the topic and method of the present book—what is enacted by the specific works and issues it addresses and how these in turn bear on the dialectic of 'self-invention' encoded in its title. The book examines a series of critical aesthetic encounters in which, on the occasion of pursuing some higher, more orthodox goal, a variety of artists, poets and thinkers working in a variety of media meet the historical ground and the related historical contingency of their own artistic, intellectual or literary performances. The term 'invention' thus resounds in a double register. At one level, it possesses the primary sense derived from rhetoric, preserved in our contemporary 'inventory'. To this extent, it points to a finding or discovery: it denotes what the work is forced to acknowledge about itself, faced with the errors, interests, anxieties and illusions endemic to its defining historical moment. And the preeminent form of this acknowledgement is what Hill calls the 'experience of defeat'. Despite the hubristic project of 'mastery' and 'possession' they share with Cartesian science, the paintings of Rembrandt register their failure to penetrate nature's secrets; and in Pascal's *Pensées*, theodicy argues for faith in a 'hidden' God beyond the reach of argument as such. But 'invention' also has the sense current usage foregrounds: that of a creation, fiction or fabrication, some new thing not there before, the dialectical product of the contingencies from which it arises. Insofar as the baroque work meets something other than it planned for, it mediates and thus changes the historical conditions in which it began. Defeat thereby engenders a series of paradigms with which European culture reckons to this day. The fathomless inwardness of Rembrandt portraits, the sceptical recursiveness of baroque soliloquy, the self-directed duplicities of Pascalian irony set standards by which Western aesthetic practice continues to be measured.

As a fundamentally aesthetic phenomenon, baroque self-invention inhabits the objects it creates and the performances these objects encode. Yet, by the same token, it also informs the dual consciousness that arises as its instrument, its register and its precipitate. This is, finally, why I speak of *self*-invention, designating not merely the works of art the baroque produces, but the states of mind of which those works are both a correlate and a condition. And this mindfulness in turn explains the media within whose spatio-temporal coordinates baroque consciousness is inveterately entangled: self-portrait and excursus, soliloquy and moralist maxim, theological fragment and dream.

What characterizes all of these forms is their contingent secondness. They arise as parasitic asides on the margin of the larger enterprise that calls them into being and yet fails to digest them precisely because they mark the enterprise's limits. This is in fact the source of the prehistoric salience to which the following book owes a Benjamin-like discontinuousness: we cannot finally subsume the readings presented here in a single overarching story. In the language of Jacques Lacan, the self-inventive enactments explored here constitute the unpredictable yet, in retrospect, both infallible and unanswerable incursions of the Real. In one of its aspects, the Real is whatever, in experience, 'resists symbolization absolutely'.[80] It is the indigestibly Other, at once coercive and recalcitrant, to which Fredric Jameson gives the misleadingly tragic name of uppercase Necessity itself.[81] (History hurts; but as Lacan understood better than most, it also makes us laugh.) Yet if the Real resists the symbolisms in which we envelop it in order to blunt its force, imposing itself on us as what we can neither acknowledge nor wholly repress, it is because, at the subterranean level of dream, compulsion rituals and *actes manqués*, we already know what the unconscious has to say, namely, what it perpetually labours to conceal. In Lacan, this determines the exhausting repetitions of the *imaginary*, simultaneously masking and pinpointing the truths our defences underwrite.[82] But it further determines the form of the present book. The circular compulsiveness with which the logic of repression fuels the machine of self-discovery generates the baroque inventions I have taken as my theme. The monadic method of fleeting symptomatic glimpses mirrors the phenomenon it aims to comprehend.

Notes

1 Sir Francis Bacon, 'Of Truth', *The Essays, or Counsels Civil and Moral*, ed. Brian Vickers (Oxford: Oxford University Press, 1999), pp. 3-5.
2 See Bacon's discussion of the 'Idols of the Mind', *The New Organon and Related Writings*, ed. Fulton H. Anderson (Indianapolis, IN: Bobbs-Merrill, 1960), bk. 1, aphorisms 36-68.
3 J.L. Austin, 'Truth', in *Philosophical Papers*, 2nd ed., ed. J.O. Urmson and G.J. Warnock (Oxford: Oxford University Press, 1970), p. 117.
4 Wittgenstein traces the fallacy to the 'picture of the essence of language' in Augustine's *Confessions* (1.8), where the saint recounts learning to speak. The fallacy 'is this: the individual words in language name objects—sentences are combinations of such names.—In this picture of language we find the root of the following idea: Every word has a meaning. This meaning is correlated with the word. It is the object for which the word stands.' *Philosophical Investigations*, 2nd ed., German text with parallel trans. by G.E.M Anscombe (New York: Macmillan, 1958), p. 2. See too Austin, 'The Meaning of a Word', *Philosophical Papers*, pp. 55-75.
5 See Austin, 'Unfair to Facts', *Philosophical Papers*, pp. 154-174, where emphasizing use and the variable contexts and conventions that condition both use and canons of 'meaning' and 'truth' does not vitiate a commitment to facts as arbiters of the truth of statements—so long as such statements are about alleged *facts* rather than something else.
6 See Austin's analysis of the class of performative utterances (verdicts, findings, rulings, etc.) he calls 'verdictives' in *How to Do Things with Words*, 2nd ed. J.O. Urmson and Marina Sbisà (Cambridge, MA: Harvard University Press, 1975), pp. 153-155.
7 Ann Wroe, *Pilate: The Biography of an Invented Man* (London: Jonathan Cape, 1999).
8 The conflict between the worlds of pagan and Judaeo-Christian experience is the theme of Robin Lane Fox's extraordinary *Pagans and Christians* (New York: Knopf, 1987).
9 Compare this with Milton's attitude as set forth in Stanley E. Fish, *How Milton Works* (Cambridge, MA: Harvard University Press, 2001), chap. 3, 'Problem Sol-

ving in *Comus*', where all of the apparent paradoxes and contradictions critics traditionally find in Milton's masque vanish the moment we understand that (a) the rival perspectives respectively championed by Comus and the Lady are strictly and absolutely incommensurable, and (b) there is just as absolutely no question about where Milton stands, such that everything Comus says, no matter how plausible or seductive, is wrong by definition.

10 Jean Rousset, *La Littérature de l'âge baroque en France: Circe et le paon* (Paris: J. Corti, 1953), Wylie Sypher, *Four Stages of Renaissance Style: Transformations in Art and Literature, 1400-1700* (Garden City, NY: Doubleday, 1955), and Mario Praz, *The Flaming Heart: Essays on Crashaw, Machiavelli, and Other Studies in the Relations between Italian and English Literature from Chaucer to T.S. Eliot* (Garden City, NY: Doubleday, 1958). Rousset has returned to these questions in a swan song, *Dernier regard sur le baroque* (Paris: J. Corti, 1998).

11 José Maravall, *The Culture of the Baroque: Analysis of a Historical Structure*, trans. Terry Cochran (Minneapolis, MN: University of Minnesota Press, 1986), Anthony J. Cascardi, *Ideologies of History in the Spanish Golden Age* (University Park, PA: Pennsylvania State University Press, 1997), Mieke Bal, *Quoting Caravaggio: Contemporary Art, Preposterous History* (Chicago: University of Chicago Press, 1999), Omar Calabrese, *Neo-Baroque: A Sign of the Times*, trans. Charles Lambert (Princeton, NJ: Princeton University Press, 1992), and Gilles Deleuze, *Le pli: Leibniz et le baroque* (Paris: Minuit, 1988).

12 Walter Benjamin, *The Origin of German Tragic Drama*, trans. John Osborne (London: New Left Books, 1978), Christine Buci-Glucksmann, *La raison baroque: de Baudelaire à Benjamin* (Paris: Galilée, 1984) and *La folie du voir: de l'esthétique baroque* (Paris: Galilée, 1986), and Julia Reinhard Lupton and Kenneth Reinhard, *After Œdipus: Shakespeare in Psychoanalysis* (Ithaca, NY: Cornell University Press, 1993). Mitchell Greenberg's *Canonical States, Canonical Stages: Œdipus, Othering, and Seventeenth-Century Drama* (Minneapolis, MN: University of Minnesota Press, 1994) projects the theme of recursive Œdipal mourning work on the broader European scene. Critical Theory chiefly focuses on Benjamin's *Ursprung* independent of German baroque drama as such. However, in a talk at the University of Colorado, Boulder, in Fall 1999, Samuel Weber evinced an incipient interest in the drama at least to the extent of checking Benjamin's claims against some of the texts.

13 Heinrich Wölfflin, *Principles of Art History*, trans. M.D. Hottinger (London: G. Bell and Sons, 1932; repr. New York: Dover, 1950).

14 René Wellek, 'The Concept of the Baroque in Literary Scholarship', in *Concepts of Criticism*, ed. Stephen G. Nichols (New Haven, CT: Yale University Press, 1963), pp. 69-114. Wellek closes by suggesting that the term promises a future 'synthesis' that might yield a refined sense of literature as a 'fine art', but he does not seem hopeful.

15 Svetlana Alpers, *The Art of Describing: Dutch Art in the Seventeenth Century* (Chicago: University of Chicago Press, 1983).

16 Simon Schama, *The Embarrassment of Riches: An Interpretation of Dutch Culture in the Golden Age* (New York: Knopf, 1987); Richard Helgerson, *Adulterous Alliances: Home, State, and History in Early Modern European Drama and Painting* (Chicago: University of Chicago Press, 2000), chap. 4, 'Soldiers and Enigmatic Girls'; Gary Schwartz, *Rembrandt, His Life, His Paintings* (New York: Viking, 1985); Svetlana Alpers, *Rembrandt's Enterprise: The Studio and the Market* (Chicago: University of Chicago Press, 1988).

17 Stanley E. Fish, *Self-Consuming Artifacts: The Experience of Seventeenth-Century Literature* (Berkeley, CA: University of California Press, 1972), Ernest B. Gilman, *The Curious Perspective: Verbal and Pictorial Wit in Seventeenth-Century Literature* (New Haven, CT: Yale University Press, 1978), and Jonathan Dollimore, *Radical Tragedy: Religion, Ideology, and Power in the Drama of Shakespeare and His Contemporaries*, 2nd ed. (Durham, NC: Duke University Press, 1993).

18 John D. Lyons, *A Theatre of Disguise: Studies in French Baroque Drama* (Columbia, SC: French Literature Publications, 1978), Mitchell Greenberg, *Detours of Desire: Readings in the French Baroque* (Columbus, OH: Ohio University Press, 1984), Jean-Claude Vuillemin, *Baroquisme et théâtralité: le théâtre de Jean Rotrou* (Paris: Papers on French Seventeenth-Century Literature, 1994).

19 Georges Forestier, *Le Théâtre dans le théâtre sur la scène française du XVIIe siècle*, 2nd ed. (Geneva: Droz, 1996), pp. viii-x.

20 Louis Marin, *La Critique du discours: sur la 'Logique de Port-Royal' et les 'Pensées' de Pascal* (Paris: Minuit, 1975), *Le portrait du roi* (Paris: Minuit, 1981), and 'La parole mangée ou le corps divin saisi par les signes', in *La parole mangée et autres essais théologico-politiques* (Paris: Klincksieck, 1986), pp. 11-35.

21 The notion that seventeenth-France was inherently inimical to the baroque is largely an artifact of the standard model of French literary history. We will explore this in chap. 4.

22 On baroque specularity, see Rousset, *La Littérature de l'âge baroque en France*, Pierre Charpentrat, *Le mirage baroque* (Paris: Minuit, 1967), Greenberg, *Detours of Desire*, Anthony J. Cascardi, *The Limits of Illusion: A Critical Study of Calderón* (Cambridge: Cambridge University Press, 1984), and Maravall, *The Culture of the Baroque*. On the vogue of anamorphic imagery, see Gilman's *The Curious Perspective* and Jurgis Baltrusaitis, *Anamorphoses ou perspectives curieuses* (Paris: O. Perrin, 1955), *Anamorphoses ou magie artificielle* (Paris: O. Perrin, 1969), and *Anamorphoses ou Thaumaturgus opticus* (Paris: Flammarion, 1984).

23 For characteristic statements of this classic view, see Giulio Carlo Argan, *The Baroque Age* (1964; 1st paper ed. Geneva: Skira; New York: Rizzoli, 1989) and John Rupert Martin, *Baroque* (New York: Harper and Row, 1977).

24 Mary Baine Campbell, *Wonder & Science: Imagining Worlds in Early Modern Europe* (Ithaca, NY: Cornell University Press, 1999).

25 Michel de Montaigne, 'Des cannibales', *Essais* 1: 31 (Paris: Garnier-Flammarion, 1969), p. 251: 'J'ay peur que nous avons les yeux plus grands que le ventre, et plus de curiosité que nous n'avons de capacité.' 'Des cannibales' dates from the first edition of books 1 and 2 of the *Essais* in 1580. Though the essay was subject to revision right up to Montaigne's death in 1592, the first edition already sports the formula quoted here.

26 Blaise Pascal, *Pensées*, ed. Louis Lafuma (Paris: Seuil, 1962), fragment 201. See also the edition by Philippe Sellier (Paris: Classiques Garnier, 1991), which assigns the same fragment the number 233. As an unfinished work descending through two different manuscript copies composed by the author's entourage shortly after his death, the order and, in minor respects, even the text of the *Pensées* pose intractable problems. Given the impossibility of referring to *the* text of the work we call the *Pensées*, I cite both editions, noted henceforth parenthetically by the corresponding fragment numbers in each one. All translations from French are my own.

27 On the impact of Lucretius' version of Epicurean materialism, see Ernst Cassirer, *The Individual and the Cosmos in Renaissance Philosophy*, trans. Mario Domandi (New York: Barnes and Noble, 1963), emphasizing *De rerum natura*'s contribution

to the Renaissance assertion of freedom of thought, and Michel Serres, *La Naissance de la physique dans le texte de Lucrèce* (Paris: Minuit, 1977), stressing how Epicurus' theory of the chance 'swerve' (Latin *declinatio*, Greek *clinamen*) that created the physical universe authorizes the anti-metaphysical picture of nature required for a genuinely critical science. However, in *The Legitimacy of the Modern Age*, trans. Robert M. Wallace (Cambridge, MA: MIT Press, 1983), Hans Blumenberg stresses the *anti*-scientific potential of Lucretian Epicureanism. The Epicurean 'exhibition of the world's form as contingent' promotes humanity's power over physical nature and the self-assertive 'curiosity' underlying European modernity (p. 156). But the revelation of the world's contingency is also linked to the mystic moment in Ockhamite nominalism (pp. 152-153), supplying a proof of God on the grounds of his remoteness from an utterly fallen, chance-driven world. Blumenberg further reminds us that the Epicurean myth of distant, uncaring gods serves a therapeutic function, schooling us in healing *ataraxia* by demonstrating nature's fundamental inanity and the corresponding emptiness of human desire (pp. 264-267). The Cassirer/Serres interpretation is taken up (and problematized) in Jacques Lezra, *Unspeakable Subjects: The Genealogy of the Event in Early Modern Europe* (Stanford, CA: Stanford University Press, 1997), where the very forces of chance that legitimize the intellectual autonomy on which the modern subject depends call the subject in question.

28 See Robert Coogan, *Erasmus, Lee and the Correction of the Vulgate: The Shaking of the Foundations* (Geneva: Droz, 1992), and David Daniell, *William Tyndale: A Biography* (New Haven, CT: Yale University Press, 1994). But see the next note for Anthony Grafton, whose work on the historical content of humanist scholarship suggests that Erasmus's contribution was somewhat less epoch-making than focus on scriptural philology suggests.

29 On the Renaissance reception of Tacitus, see Anthony Grafton, *Commerce with the Classics: Ancient Books and Renaissance Readers* (Ann Arbor, MI: University of Michigan Press, 1997), pp. 204-208. The recovered Tacitus and Suetonius, together with the 'modern' Machiavelli and Guicciardini, do for early moderns what new historicism does today—whence the renewed interest in these writers in Victoria Kahn, *Rhetoric, Prudence, and Skepticism in the Renaissance* (Ithaca, NY: Cornell University Press, 1985), Albert Russell Ascoli and Victoria Kahn (eds), *Machiavelli and the Discourse of Literature* (Ithaca, NY: Cornell University Press, 1993), John D. Lyons, *Exemplum: The Rhetoric of Example in Early Modern France and Italy* (Princeton, NJ: Princeton University Press, 1989), and Timothy Hampton, *Writing from History: The Rhetoric of Exemplarity in Renaissance Literature* (Ithaca, NY: Cornell University Press, 1990). See too Perez Zagorin, *Ways of Lying: Dissimulation, Persecution, and Conformity in Early Modern Europe* (Cambridge, MA: Harvard University Press, 1990), where dissimulation and Machiavellian prudence are put in context with the intersections of political and religious thought.

30 See Fernand Braudel, *Civilisation matérielle, Economie et Capitalisme, XVe-XVIIIe siècle* (Paris: Armand Colin, 1979), vol. III, *Le Temps du Monde*, chaps. 1-4, where the spatio-temporal logic of 'economy-worlds' yields analysis of the mechanisms conditioning the successive economic heydays of Venice, Genoa, Antwerp, Amsterdam and London. While the shift from South to North has confessional markers, Braudel seconds H.R. Trevor-Roper's critique of Max Weber's *The Protestant Ethic and the Spirit of Capitalism*, trans. Talcott Parsons (New York: Scribner, 1930), in *The Crisis of the Seventeenth Century: Religion, the Reformation and Social Change* (New York: Harper and Row, 1968), chap. 1. For both writers, the 'Protestant ethic'

may express and even further, but does not *cause* capitalist ideology since the essentials antedate the Reformation by three centuries.

31 See, e.g., in addition to the already-cited 'Des cannibales', Montaigne's 'Des coches' (*Essais* 3: 6) and 'De l'expérience' (3: 13). The discovery of America also generates one of the many arguments for doubt in the *Apologie de Raimond Sebond*: 'c'eust esté Pyrrhoniser, il y a mille ans, que de mettre en doute la science de la Cosmographie, et les opinions qui en estoient receuës d'un chacun; c'estoit heresie d'avouer des Antipodes; voilà de nostre siecle une grandeur infinie de terre ferme, non pas une isle ou une contrée particuliere, mais une partie esgale à peu près en grandeur à celle que nous cognoissons, qui vient d'estre decouverte.' (2: 12, p. 237). For a classic commentary on these issues, see Richard H. Popkin, *The History of Scepticism from Erasmus to Spinoza*, rev. ed. (Berkeley, CA: University of California Press, 1979), and, from a literary viewpoint, Hampton's *Writing from History*. In addition to her recent *Wonder & Science*, see Mary Baine Campbell, *The Witness and the Other World: European Travel Writing, 400-1600* (Ithaca, NY: Cornell University Press, 1988), Stephen Greenblatt, *Marvelous Possessions: The Wonder of the New World* (Chicago: University of Chicago Press, 1991), Anthony Grafton, with April Shelford and Nancy Siraisi, *New Worlds, Ancient Texts: The Power of Tradition and the Shock of Discovery* (Cambridge, MA: Harvard University Press, 1992), and Roland Greene, *Unrequited Conquests: Love and Empire in the Colonial Americas* (Chicago: University of Chicago Press, 1998). Despite a misguided attempt to assign Petrarchism a leading role in the literary assimilation of the Americas, Greene has interesting things to say about the 'Columbian First Person' (chap. 1) and the representation of Brazil (chap. 2).

32 Medievalists urge this point with some heat. See David Aers, 'A Whisper in the Ear of Early Modernists; or, Reflections on Literary Critics Writing the "History of the Subject"', in David Aers (ed.), *Culture and History, 1350-1600: Essays on English Communities, Identities, and Writing* (Detroit, MI: Wayne State University Press, 1992), pp. 177-202. Bernard Guenée, *Histoire et culture historique dans l'Occident médiéval* (Paris: Aubier Montaigne, 1980), makes a similar case, as does Steven Justice, *Writing and Rebellion: England in 1381* (Berkeley, CA: University of California Press, 1994), analyzing popular understanding of the social function of writing.

33 Alongside Descartes, Bacon is one of the heroes of Blumenberg's account of modern meliorist self-determination and the 'overcoming' of the 'Gnostic' depreciation of the natural world and self-determining humanity alike. But see the very different valuation of self-determinative reason and will in Charles Taylor, *Sources of the Self: The Making of Modern Identity* (Cambridge, MA: Harvard University Press, 1989), where Bacon and Descartes contribute both to an overemphasis of human agency as the basis of an authentic 'ontology' of human identity and to the consequent 'disengagement' of human reason from a world of which it is a living part.

34 The best general account is still Thomas S. Kuhn, *The Copernican Revolution: Planetary Astronomy in the Development of Western Thought* (Cambridge, MA: Harvard University Press, 1957). See too Campbell's excellent analysis of the role that the science fiction of Bruno, Godwin, Kepler, Cyrano and Fontenelle play in the absorption of the new astronomy, *Wonder & Science*, chap. 4, 'On the Infinite Universe and the Innumerable Worlds', and chap. 5, 'A World in the Moon: Celestial Fictions of Francis Godwin and Cyrano de Bergerac'. On Newton's residual commitment to magic and the traditional Christian picture of the universe, see Michael White, *Isaac Newton: The Last Sorcerer* (Reading, MA: Addison-Wesley, 1997). On the nonetheless monistic naturalism implicit in Newtonian science, see Carl Friedrich von

Weizsäcker, *The Unity of Nature*, trans. Francis J. Zucker (New York: Farrar Straus Giroux, 1980), esp. pt. 2, 'The Unity of Physics'.

35 As her title indicates, Campbell analyzes the transition from literary and 'natural philosophical' accounts of 'other worlds', where the 'sensational' pleasures of imaginative wonder predominate, to the soberly 'anaesthetic' modes of discourse constitutive of modern physical and ethnographic science. Campbell's primary focus is the rise of modern ethnography as a social science of the type Lafitau embodies in contrast to the 'narcissistic' literary inhabitation she finds in Thevet. But her analysis of the emergence of ethnography is accompanied by exploration of comparable developments in physical science, and in particular astronomy, where the antic speculations of Bruno give way to the mathematized mechanics of Newton.

36 René Descartes, *Méditations métaphysiques*, in *Œuvres philosophiques*, ed. Ferdinand Alquié (Paris: Garnier, 1988-92), vol. 2, pp. 426-427. Here again Campbell has interesting things to say, albeit only in passing. See *Wonder & Science*, pp. 104-105.

37 Though traditionally attributed to the cardinal's own hand, both the *Mémoires* and the *Testament politique* are pseudonymous works composed by members of Richelieu's secretarial entourage. For a vivid picture of the operation of Richelieu's secretariat, see Christian Jouhaud, *La Main de Richelieu, ou le pouvoir cardinal* (Paris: Gallimard, 1990), pp. 85-122.

38 On Winstanley's life and work, see Christopher Hill, *The World Turned Upside Down: Radical Ideas during the English Revolution* (London: Maurice Temple Smith, 1972), chap. 7.

39 On Spinoza, see Leo Strauss, *Spinoza's Critique of Religion*, trans. E.M. Sinclair (New York: Schocken, 1965), and 'How to Study Spinoza's *Theologico-Political Treatise*', in *Persecution and the Art of Writing* (Glencoe: The Free Press, 1952), pp. 142-201. On Richard Simon, see Henri Margival, *Essai sur Richard Simon et la critique biblique au 17e siècle* (1900; repr. Geneva: Slatkine, 1970). On Bayle, see Ruth Whelan, *The Anatomy of Superstition: A Study of the Historical Theory and Practice of Pierre Bayle* (Oxford: Voltaire Foundation, 1989), and Thomas M. Lennon, *Reading Bayle* (Toronto: University of Toronto Press, 1999).

40 For Bal's initial formulation, see *Quoting Caravaggio*, pp. 6-7. For her source, see Patricia Parker, 'Preposterous Events', *Shakespeare Quarterly* 43.2 (1992), pp.186-213.

41 For two sharply contrasting accounts of the crucial German Romantic contribution to the philosophy of history, one traditional, the other heavily influenced by Franco-German discourse analysis and cultural criticism, see R.G. Collingwood, *The Idea of History* (Oxford: Oxford University Press, 1946), pp. 104-126, and Hayden White, *Metahistory: The Historical Imagination in Nineteenth-Century Europe* (Baltimore, MD: The Johns Hopkins University Press, 1973).

42 The contrast between 'history' and 'nature' is a major theme in Collingwood's *Idea of History*, as in his discussion of the limits of Greek historical thought (pp. 20-21). However, insofar as, for Collingwood, what makes the essential difference between history and nature is 'man', a being possessed of a nature ('human nature') of its own, he reproduces the ahistoricism he wants to avoid. If we owe Michel Foucault's *L'Histoire de la folie à l'âge classique* (Paris: Plon, 1961; repr. Paris: Gallimard, 1972) or *Les mots et les choses: une archéologie des sciences humaines* (Paris: Gallimard, 1966) anything, it is insistence on the need to denaturalize what history itself (as, e.g., the history of ideologies) constantly urges us to imagine in natural terms. See Richard J. Evans, *In Defense of History* (New York: Norton, 1999), who occasionally succumbs to temptation in defending history against its own historicism.

43 For a preliminary account of his 'experimental method', see David Hume, *A Treatise of Human Nature*, ed. Ernest C. Mossner (Harmondsworth: Penguin, 1969), pp. 44-46. On the 'amphibologies' disciplined 'experiment' eliminates, see Campbell, *Wonder & Science*, pp. 85-96. The term 'amphibologies' originates in Browne's *Pseudodoxia Epidemica*, a critique of popular fallacies and superstitions that nonetheless remains attached to the overdetermined symbolic duplicities it tries to police. Here again Campbell's book (pp. 71-85) is instructive.

44 For Hume's account of the origins of religion, see his tellingly-entitled *Natural History of Religion*, ed. H.E. Root (Stanford, CA: Stanford University Press, 1957), sections 2 and 3, and 'Of Superstition and Enthusiasm', in *Essays Moral, Political, and Literary*, rev. ed. Eugene F. Miller (Indianapolis, IN: Liberty Classics, 1987), pp. 73-79. For Spinoza's, see the preface to *Theological-Political Treatise*, trans. R.H.M. Elwes (1883; repr. New York: Dover, 1951), pp. 3-11. Both writers make a point of distinguishing 'true' religion from mere 'superstition'. The terms nonetheless prove synonymous in the perspective of the all-too-human 'originals' their 'natural history' reveals.

45 Hume, *Treatise*, pp. 41-42.

46 For Fielding's formula, see *Joseph Andrews*, ed. A.R. Humphreys (London: Everyman, 1973), p. i. A central thread of Campbell's analysis of the transition from 'wonder' to 'science' is how, once science and fiction part company in the later seventeenth century, a space opens for a form of 'world-making' that adjusts the two in the realm of imaginative (aesthetic) pleasure. This space is occupied by the novel, one of whose cultural conditions is to transfer to Europe itself the ethnographic viewpoint honed in Europe's dealings with colonized peoples. See *Wonder & Science*, chap. 8, 'Anthropometamorphosis: Manners, Customs, Fashions, and Monsters'.

47 David Hume, *Dialogues Concerning Natural Religion*, ed. Martin Bell (Harmondsworth: Penguin, 1990), p. 38.

48 Mieke Bal, *Reading Rembrandt: Beyond the Word-Image Opposition* (Cambridge: Cambridge University Press, 1991), p. 60.

49 Pascal's critical authority is a major theme in Marin's *Critique du discours*. Despite a disappointing tendency to cite rather than analyze his model, Bourdieu's Pascalian credentials are openly displayed in *Méditations pascaliennes* (Paris: Seuil, 1997).

50 The theme of messianic 'redemption' pervades all of Benjamin's writings, but one of its most moving (and topical) expressions is 'Unpacking My Library: A Talk about Book Collecting', which characterizes book collectors as 'interpreters of fate' whose rescue of the volumes that enter their collections achieves nothing less than their 'rebirth'. See Walter Benjamin, *Illuminations*, ed. Hannah Arendt, trans. Harry Zohn (New York: Schocken, 1968), pp. 59-67. See too 'Theses on the Philosophy of History', ibid., p. 254.

51 Benjamin, 'Theses on the Philosophy of History', *Illuminations*, p. 262. Compare the famous statement about the historical meaning of private book collecting in 'Unpacking My Library': 'But, as Hegel put it, only when it is dark does the owl of Minerva begin its flight. Only in extinction is the collector comprehended.' (p. 67) Subsequent references to the essays assembled in *Illuminations* appear in parentheses in the text.

52 I cite the translation by Harry Zohn in Ronald Taylor (ed.), *Aesthetics and Politics* (London: New Left Books, 1977), pp. 129-130.

53 But see Giorgio Agamben, 'The Prince and the Frog: The Question of Method in Adorno and Benjamin', in *Infancy and History: Essays on the Destruction of Ex-*

perience, trans. Liz Heron (London: Verso, 1993), pp. 107-124. Agamben argues that, though claiming to distance his hostility from vulgar Marxist reductionism, Adorno's almost willful incomprehension lapses into just that. For a more sympathetic view, see Martin Jay, *The Dialectical Imagination: A History of the Frankfurt School and the Institute for Social Research, 1923-1950* (Berkeley, CA: University of California Press, 1972; repr. 1996), pp. 206-208.

54   This is the standard translation of Ranke's phrase; but Evans (*In Defense of History*, p. 14) argues that a better version would read 'as it *essentially* was'. I am not convinced that Evans's softer version is quite right or makes the difference he thinks, but share the view that Ranke is a victim of caricature.

55   For a recent commentary on this aspect of Benjamin's project, see Michael André Bernstein, *Five Portraits: Modernity and the Imagination in Twentieth-Century German Writing* (Evanston, IL: Northwestern University Press, 2000), pp. 84-85.

56   The theme already appears in Hannah Arendt's introduction to *Illuminations* and Peter Demetz's introduction to the companion volume, *Reflections: Essays, Aphorisms, Autobiographical Writings*, ed. Hannah Arendt, trans. Edmund Jephcott (New York: Schocken, 1978).

57   For Proust, see Benjamin, 'The Image of Proust', *Illuminations*, pp. 201-16, and 'On Some Motifs in Baudelaire', ibid., pp. 180-185. For the epigraph from Goethe's *Farbenlehre*, see *The Origin of German Tragic Drama*, p. 27. (Subsequent references to the *Origin* appear in parentheses in the text.) The full title of Goethe's speculations on colour, *Materialien zur Geschichte der Farbenlehre*, promising an undigested collection *toward* a history that is never adduced, could not be more congenial to a sensibility like Benjamin's.

58   For the complete essay, see *Illuminations*, pp. 155-200. For another published outtake, see 'Paris, Capital of the Nineteenth Century', in *Reflections*, pp. 146-162. The encompassing source is *The Arcades Project*, trans. Howard Eiland and Kevin McLaughlin (Cambridge, MA: Harvard University Press, 1999). The Eiland/McLaughlin volume also contains a new translation of the 'Paris' essay (pp. 3-13), which dates from 1935, and a translation of the fuller (and more theoretical) prospectus of the same name, written in French in 1939 (pp. 14-26).

59   Louis Althusser and Etienne Balibar, *Reading Capital*, trans. Ben Brewster (New York: Pantheon, 1970), p. 189. See Fredric Jameson's commentary on Althusser's theory of 'effective' causality in *The Political Unconscious: Narrative as a Socially Symbolic Act* (Ithaca, NY: Cornell University Press, 1981), pp. 23-38.

60   See 'The Storyteller: Reflections on the Works of Nikolai Leskov', in *Illuminations*, pp. 83-110, and 'The Work of Art in the Age of Mechanical Reproduction', ibid., pp. 217-252.

61   The reading of Freud's *Beyond the Pleasure Principle* hinted at here is inspired by Jacques Derrida, 'Coming Into One's Own', trans. James Hulbert, in Geoffrey H. Hartman (ed.), *Psychoanalysis and the Question of the Text* (Baltimore, MD: Johns Hopkins University Press, 1978), pp. 114-148. As Derrida notes, *Beyond the Pleasure Principle* is a textbook case of the kind of unconscious overdetermination Freud made a name for himself by exposing. As revealed, notably, by Freud's intervention in the *fort-da* game he observes his grandson Ernst playing, the book's focus on the 'reality principle' and the related 'death wish' or 'death drive' attempts to solve the strictly autobiographical dilemma posed by the ailing Freud's awareness of his own mortality. The question is, will the science of psychoanalysis survive its progenitor? More pointedly, is it even a *science*, a method and doctrine grounded in reality rather than (as its own theory of desire would propose) in its author's unconscious

wishes? This in turn suggests what is at issue not only in the aim (the desire) to ground psychoanalysis in something 'beyond' the 'pleasure principle' on which the epochal *Interpretation of Dreams* is based, but in Freud's characterization of the 'death drive' as an urge to recover the 'mineral' condition in which organic life originates. In willing his own death, Freud wills that he be *turned to stone*, the medium of the sort of monumental afterlife he wishes for the science he hopes to bequeath to future generations.

62 Compare this picture of the baroque with a passage in Joseph de Maistre's *Les Soirées de Saint-Pétersbourg* that Benjamin cites in the context of Baudelaire's *correspondances* in the J Convolute of the *Arcades Project*: 'One can form a perfectly adequate idea of the universe by considering it under the aspect of a vast museum of natural history exposed to the shock of an earthquake. The door to the collection rooms is open and broken; there are no more windows. Whole drawers have fallen out, while others hang by their hinges, ready to drop. Some shells have rolled out into the hall of minerals, and a hummingbird's nest is resting on the head of a crocodile. What madman, though, could have any doubt of the original intention, or believe that the edifice was built to look this way? [...] The order is as visible as the disorder; and the eye that ranges over this mightly temple of nature reestablishes without difficulty all that a fatal agency has shattered, warped, soiled, and displaced. And there is more: look closely and you can recognize already the effects of a restoring hand. Some beams have been shored up, some paths cut through the rubble; and, in the general confusion, a multitude of *analogues* have already taken their place once again and come into contact.' (p. 377) It is hard to imagine a more beautifully apt picture not only of Baudelaire's poetic enterprise, but of the picture of the German baroque Benjamin's *Origin* conveys. For a commentary, see Christopher Prendergast, *The Triangle of Representation* (New York: Columbia University Press, 2000), chap. 7, 'Representation or Embodiment? Walter Benjamin and the Politics of *Correspondances*'.

63 Daniel Casper von Lohenstein, *Sophonisbe*, ed. Rolf Tarot (Stuttgart: Reclam, 1970). The editor reports Lohenstein's contemporary sobriquet, the 'German Seneca', in the afterword (p. 233). I use the same source below for Gryphius's identification as the 'German Sophocles'.

64 For a fuller discussion of cross-dressing in *Sophonisbe*, see Jane O. Newman, *The Intervention of Philology: Gender, Learning, and Power in Lohenstein's Roman Plays* (Chapel Hill, NC: University of North Carolina Studies in the Germanic Languages and Literatures, 2000), pp. 47-58.

65 Phyllis Hartnoll, *The Theatre: A Concise History*, rev. ed. (London: Thames and Hudson, 1985), pp. 132-135.

66 For a general analysis of the uses to which Lohenstein put his considerable scholarship and of the ideological consequences for the intelligence both of the ancient past and of the often conflictual role Lohenstein assigns the past in understanding the present, see Newman, *The Intervention of Philology*.

67 Harry Berger, Jr., *Imaginary Audition: Shakespeare on Page and Stage* (Berkeley, CA: University of California Press, 1989).

68 Andreas Gryphius, *Verliebtes Gespenst/Die geliebte Dornrose*, ed. Eberhard Mannack (Stuttgart: Reclam, 1985), and Jacob Bidermann, *Cenodoxus*, ed. D.G. Dyer with parallel trans. by D.G. Dyer and Cecily Longrigg (Austin, TX: University of Texas Press, 1974). For an overview of Jesuit school drama in the German-speaking world, of which Bidermann's *Cenodoxus* is a masterpiece, see Jean-Marie Valentin, *Theatrum catholicum: les Jésuites et la scène en Allemagne au XVIe et au XVIIe

siècles (Nancy: Presses universitaires de Nancy, 1990). See too Marc Fumaroli, *Héros et orateurs: Rhétorique et dramaturgie cornéliennes* (Geneva: Droz, 1990), section 2, 'Corneille et la Société de Jésus'. Fumaroli provides a stimulating discussion of the Jesuit use of chorus and dance and its relation to the nascent opera (pp. 159-166).

69 All four historians (Plutarch, Livy, Polybius, Tacitus) appear in the 17-page bibliography the editor of the Reclam edition has extracted from *Sophonisbe*'s 110 pages of notes.

70 Lohenstein, *Sophonisbe*, p. 40. I have replaced the original's diacritical superscript *e*'s with modern umlauts. The translation is my own.

71 Pierre Corneille, *Cinna*, in *Œuvres complètes*, ed. Georges Couton (Paris: Gallimard, 1980-87), vol. 1, 1.1.1-8.

72 The seductiveness of Milton's Satan is central to Stanley E. Fish, *Surprised by Sin: The Reader in Paradise Lost* (Berkeley, CA: University of California Press, 1967). In a rehearsal for *Self-Consuming Artifacts*, Fish analyzes how Milton's theodicical epic manipulates readers' responses, arguing that Blake's famous claim that Milton was of the Devil's party without knowing it misses Milton's point: i.e., that, as a result of the primal Fall, *we are ourselves* of the Devil's party and must be *made* to know it.

73 For an edition of Mairet's version, see Georges Couton (ed.), *Théâtre du XVIIe siècle* (Paris: Gallimard, 1975-92), vol. 1, pp. 669-729. For Corneille's, see *Œuvres complètes*, vol. 3, pp. 379-446.

74 See Christopher Hill, *The Experience of Defeat: Milton and Some Contemporaries* (New York: Viking Penguin, 1984). For related developments in France, see Paul Bénichou, *Morales du grand siècle* (Paris: Gallimard, 1948), which chronicles the role the defeat of the Frondes plays in shaping the classical culture of the later seventeenth century; Lucien Goldmann, *Le Dieu caché: étude sur la vision tragique dans les Pensées de Pascal et dans le théâtre de Racine* (Paris: Gallimard, 1959), which adduces the 'tragic vision' in Pascal and Racine to their social affiliation as Jansenists, a sect largely recruited from the ranks of the judicial and administrative ranks of the *parlements* displaced by the system of royal commissions introduced under the Bourbon monarchy; Marc Fumaroli, *Le Poète et le Roi: Jean de La Fontaine en son siècle* (Paris: Fallois, 1997), which views La Fontaine as the ironical champion of an aristocratic freedom of thought suppressed by the triumphant court culture of Louis XIV; and Joan DeJean, *Ancients against Moderns: Culture Wars and the Making of a Fin de Siècle* (Chicago: University of Chicago Press, 1997), which focuses on the anti-modern losers in the 'culture wars' with which the *grand siècle* closes. Maravall's *Culture of the Baroque* and Cascardi's *Ideologies of History* make a similar case for Spain, with this difference: that a major function of Spanish court and Church ideology was to disguise the Hapsburg defeat to which it mightily contributed.

75 See Immanuel Kant, *Critique of Judgment*, ed. and trans. Werner S. Pluhar (Indianapolis: Hackett, 1987), pp. 53-64.

76 This is what literally happens, albeit in the amphibological name of 'Mother Nature', in the famous footnote on the inscription above the Temple of Isis in section 49 of the Third Critique.

77 Martin Heidegger, 'The Origin of the Work of Art', in *Poetry, Language, Thought*, trans. Albert Hofstadter (New York: Harper and Row, 1971), p. 39.

78 See Campbell's stimulating discussion in *Wonder & Science*, chap. 3, 'The Nature of Things and the Vexations of Art'.

79 See Descartes, *Œuvres philosophiques*, vol. 2, p. 406.
80 Jacques Lacan, *Les écrits techniques de Freud, Le séminaire de Jacques Lacan*, bk. 1, ed. Jacques-Alain Miller (Paris: Seuil, 1975), p. 80.
81 See Jameson, *The Political Unconscious*, pp. 101-102, including the memorable formula according to which 'History is therefore the experience of Necessity'. It should go without saying that Lacan's uppercase Real is just as misleading as Jameson's uppercase Necessity.
82 See, e.g., in addition to the source cited in note 79, Jacques Lacan, *Les quatre concepts fondamentaux de la psychanalyse, Le séminaire de Jacques Lacan*, bk. 11, ed. Jacques-Alain Miller (Paris: Seuil, 1973; 'Points' paper ed.), pp. 25-75, for a memorable discussion of the complexly imbricated themes of the unconscious, the real, chance, dream and ego defence inspired by a reading of the famous dream of the burning son in Freud's *Traumdeutung*.

Chapter 1

The Vindication of Susanna: Femininity and Truth in Baroque Science and Art

As we saw in the introduction, the term baroque exhibits a camel-like complexity. Not only does it indiscriminately identify a period, a sensibility and a style that, though related, remain different things; it also embraces the wide variety of conflicting themes, forms and conventions with which period, sensibility and style are traditionally associated. In painting, for instance, the naturalist commitment to the human body's native colours, contours and attitudes is regularly hitched to idealizing fictions whose moral, political and devotional valence leaves unedified nature behind. Similarly, the taste for the breathtaking illusions of the art of trompe-l'œil goes hand in hand with the aggressive iconoclasm of the *vanitas* motif, exposing the euphoric delights of aesthetic experience to the *memento mori*'s melancholy reminder of sinfulness and death. Yet as contradictory as its concrete expressions may be, the baroque as a whole encodes a number of deep-seated constants; and chief among these is a tireless fascination with visual representation and the heightened acts of vision that representation mimics and promotes. The baroque marks indeed at once the apogee and crisis of early modern visual culture, simultaneously magnifying and deprecating human sight and the modes of depiction calculated to model and enhance it.[1]

As Christine Buci-Glucksmann reports, the period's insatiable appetite for novel visual experiences and for artful materials designed to satisfy it amounts to a kind of mania.[2] Even in the Protestant north, where iconomachic suspicion of idolatrous likenesses is a pious commonplace, we witness the production and consumption of pictures on an unprecedented, quasi-industrial scale. Artists, travelers, antiquarians, scientists and the publishers and dealers who merchandise their work generate an encyclopedic record of things seen and things imagined. The output is indigestibly multifarious and vast, flooding the new market in visual matter with paintings, drawings and prints depicting scenes and objects drawn from every field of human interest, every sphere of human activity and every corner of the globe.[3] We find portraits, genre vignettes and still lives; landscapes and maps; pictures of notable buildings and diagrammes outlining the workings of complex machines; engravings of ancient coins and medals and of the ruins of ancient monuments; illustrations of human and animal anatomies and of the theatres in which physicians dissected them; emblems, allegories and 'histories' drawn from the Bible, classical mythology and epic poetry; representations of the sieges, battles, coronations, dynastic marriages and public executions that marked the highpoints of contemporary political events; and woodcuts illustrating the exotic flora, fauna and artifacts discovered in Europe's growing colonies, jumbled together with images depicting the still more exotic physiognomies, mores and modes of dress by which Europe's new colonial subjects were systematically classified.

The baroque craving for visual matter is invariably accompanied by anxieties about the reliability of the testimony such materials offer and their dubious moral influence on consumers. This is partly a function of sheer novelty. As Mary Campbell argues, the promiscuous taste for sensational wonders deepens an unsettling acquaintance with the 'monstrous' and strange that challenges the supposedly 'natural' arrangements of life in the metropolis. Exposed to models imported from distant cultures, homegrown canons of beauty, morality and social order look increasingly makeshift and impermanent. Whence one of Campbell's richest case studies, the Puritan physician John Bulwer's *Anthropometamorphosis*. First published in 1650, with angry enlargements in 1653 and 1654, Bulwer's book-length diatribe is the more telling in that the author's animus toward contemporary fashions inspired by the outlandish costumes and cosmetic practices cultivated by colonized 'savages' leads him to apply the corrosive insights of cultural anthropology to his own society. The tattoos, pierced noses, moulded skulls, distended lips and ornamented 'privy parts' in which Bulwer sees disgusting and degrading disfigurations of the human body's natural form become a template for the abominable mutations of metropolitan taste.[4]

The appetite to which the proliferation of images ministers is itself far from blameless. As Augustine of Hippo (*Confessions* 10.34) had long ago pointed out in acknowledging his own sinful susceptibility in this regard, the faculty of sight not only exposes us to temptations, but is a seat of prurient interest in its own right. From this viewpoint, the vogue for graphic depictions of the depraved customs exhibited in Europe's colonies, where unbridled lust, cannibalism and unspeakable tortures are imagined to be the norm, is entirely of a piece with a highbrow taste for subjects drawn from ancient myth, whose concupiscent gods are just as lawless (and just as naked) as any African or American. But even at its most innocent, the growing curiosity to which the ever more widespread dissemination of images ministers constitutes a *diversion* in Pascal's austerely disapproving sense.[5] Instead of encouraging the exclusive focus on the at once 'final' and 'invisible' things that pertain to the cure of our eternal souls, pictures feed a desire for trivial escape into the world of carnal sensation. Where images are not directly criminal, they inveterately distract us from the true business of human life, namely, the pursuit of personal salavation in the world to come.

Yet if only because the period's intense visual interests both survive and, as in *vanitas* and *memento mori* emblems, actively thrive on the uneasy second thoughts they occasion, the moral concerns representation causes merely confirm the phenomenon's dominance. A logical place to start the present study is accordingly where the baroque does: in the decisive role pictures play in the concerted arts of vision on which early Western modernity depends.

Many things determine the critical position pictures occupy as a form and an ideal. Dating from Giotto's great cycles of the Lives of Christ, his Virgin Mother and his earthly counterpart, St Francis of Assisi, visual narrative serves as a crucial means of popularizing the complex system of Christian belief. By engaging beholders in the face-to-face immediacy of direct visualization, images lend their special rhetorical weight to impressing the articles of the faith on believing hearts and minds. The holy stories that scripture records, the exemplary lives of the saints collected in the Golden Legend and even arcane points of doctrine concerning the holy Trinity, the antecedents of the virgin birth or the number, nature and function of the divine sacraments are granted a form the largely illiterate mass of the faithful can grasp and remember. In granting these things dramatic visual presence, pictures also propagate a fundamental change in late-medieval and Renaissance piety. In reenacting scenes from the Saviour's life, images literalize the Franciscan programme of 'imitating' Christ. Artists accomplish in the medium of paint what St Francis does in the Christlike pattern of his works and sayings; and both demonstrate the same commitment to the twin mysteries of the incarnate Word and Christ's real presence in the Eucharist. In the visceral present of direct visual encounter and the acts of private meditation for which images provide a frame and a spur, art renews the work of intercession Christ's humanation performed by representing sacred truth in a form adjusted to the carnal conditions of human experience.[6]

We witness a similar turn in secular verse. Breaking with the preeminently oral conventions of song informing the medieval *chanson de geste* and ballad, Renaissance poets redefine epic and lyric poetry as modes of imagery. Poets respond in this to the profound shift in taste and outlook theorized in the humanist doctrine of the Sister Arts distilled in a pair of slogans that dominate European aesthetics from the Renaissance to the Romantics: Simonides of Chios' 'witty' chiastic conflation, *poesia tacens, pictura loquens* ('painting is mute poetry, poetry a talking picture'), and the celebrated Horatian dictum, *ut pictura poesis* ('as in painting, so in poetry'). Whatever other goals it may pursue, poetry's presiding ambition is a visual one. In refining the techniques of rhetorical *enargeia*, creating vivid word pictures intended to rival painting itself, verse mimics the clarity and concreteness poets enviously identify with pictorial art.[7]

Finally, in the context of the problems I mean to explore more specifically in this chapter, notions of picturing become a major formative influence at the heart of Western philosophy and science. And nowhere is this influence more signally at work than in the baroque.[8] Pictorial models of knowledge and thought begin to move to the formative centre of Western natural philosophy as early as the fourteenth century. For the *via moderna* of Ockhamite nominalism, the concept or 'universal' is 'only a kind of picture' (*non est nisi fictio quaedam*), a mental image constructed with a view to sorting the anarchic particulars of ordinary experience;[9] and the mathematician and naturalist Nicole Oresme plots graphs enabling him to image ratios and proportional relations or to map otherwise impalpable temporal phenomena like the parabolic trajectory of an arrow.[10] Still, it is with the inception of modernity proper in the seventeenth century that the philosophic picture comes fully into its own. Pictorial norms contribute to what Svetlana Alpers calls the 'descriptive' moment of Baconian induction. This visual emphasis is reflected not only in the enormous interest in prosthetic aids to sight in the form of microscopes and telescopes, but in the desire, most eloquently expressed by Robert Hooke's *Micrographia* (1665), that the secrets of nature such instruments disclose be preserved in images. The 'sincere Hand' of art thereby supplements the 'faithful Eye' of direct observation by fixing its findings in the both stable and readily reproducible form of pictures.[11] The commitment to pictures also dictates a guiding axiom in Johannes Kepler's correction of the optical science of his time, *Ad Vitellionem paralipomena* [*Supplement to Vitellius*] (1604). Where Alberti's *De pictura* of 1435 adheres to what would seem the natural order by constructing linear perspective on the model of empirical sight, Kepler's *ut pictura, ita visio* sets optics on a rational footing by assigning vision a geometry derived from pictorial forms.[12]

But the philosophic picture receives perhaps its most influential expression in the person of Descartes. In a passage in the *Discours de la méthode* (1637) to which we will return in greater detail in a later chapter, Descartes summarizes his first major scientific work, the unpublished *Le Monde*, which sets out a complete system of the physical universe and the natural laws governing its genesis and operations. However, Descartes's synopsis opens by describing not the system the earlier work contained, but rather the pictorial structure he gave its exposition. Faced with the task of conveying a notion of physical nature as a volumetric whole, Descartes adopts a mode of perspective foreshortening akin to the one employed by painters obliged, like him, to recover an image of three-dimensional truth in a two-dimensional medium. In painting, the reduction to two dimensions stems from the planar form of the panel or canvas on which the artist works. In philosophy, it is an artifact of the equally flattening medium of language and the temporal ordering language demands:

> [J]ust as painters, being unable to represent equally all of the faces of a solid body on a flat canvas, choose one of the most important and, turning it alone toward the light source, leave the others in shadow, causing them to appear only so far as one can see them while looking at the first, so I, fearing I could not put in my discourse everything I had in thought, undertook to expose fully only what I understood of light; then, on the the occasion of light, to add something of the sun and the fixed stars, because it almost entirely proceeds from them; of the heavens, because they transmit it; of planets, comets and the earth, because they reflect it; and in particular of all the bodies that lie on the earth, because they are either coloured, transparent or luminous; and finally of man, because he is its spectator.[13]

Yet the pictorial structure the treatise attributes to physical science is not confined to its exposition. As witnessed by the place of 'man' at the close of the passage, as the 'spectator' whose ocular presence conditions the very possibility of scientific description and understanding, Cartesian method rationalizes a process of intellection systematically represented in visual terms as an at once light-borne and light-bearing act of vision. With the rise of the doctrine of 'ideas' as forming the basic units of perception and thought, the mind itself becomes a visual machine. Pictured now as a 'mirror', now as a 'camera obscura', the mind is a mechanical device designed to stock the human brain with more or less clear and distinct portraits or simulacra reproducing the phenomena it meets in the natural world.[14] The picture in general, and painting in particular, thus emerge as a dominant paradigm for the whole system of modes of representation constitutive of early modern philosophy, religion and science as well as literary or aesthetic culture. To understand the baroque—and to understand the modernity of which the baroque is the preeminent bearer and expression—means understanding early modern representation; and this in turn means grasping the critical contribution the pictorial imagination makes to shaping not only representation's essential forms, aims and canons, but the world that arises as its object, theatre and creation.

A fertile approach to these problems, capturing not just the structure, but the underlying affect of early modern visual culture, concerns the place of gender in the dominant pictorial régime of baroque Europe. The growing body of work on the European imagination's gendered character sheds a powerful light on representation's disciplinary ambitions. Emphasizing the essential unity behind apparent differences in medium and form, and especially how, whatever the medium, women so often emerge as passive objects of visual analysis and consumption, the image of women set forth in painting, poetry, philosophy or science confirms the *systemic* character of baroque pictorial practices. Indeed, the feminist critique reveals just the kind of generalized visual 'discourse' that Foucaldian theory posits as the correlate of the hegemonic *episteme* by which early modern culture constitutes a single, self-organized and self-reproducing whole.

But the portrayal of women also brings the régime's characteristic *violence* into sharper focus. In painting, a telling symptom of this violence, notably explored by Mieke Bal, is the link between painterly portrayals of the female body and the Cartesian rhetoric of 'mastery' and 'possession' informing the investigation of nature in modern science.[15] Ever since the Renaissance, the ocular objectivity of early modern pictorial practices in the broadest sense, encompassing literature and philosophy as well as visual or plastic art, has now patently, now latently fed on what Bal calls a 'semiotics of rape'. Drawing on the cultural studies of Laura Mulvey, Teresa De Lauretis and Kaja Silverman, seconded by Evelyn Fox Keller's classic feminist revaluation of the history of science, Bal assigns the Western canon a visual rhetoric of domination, reification and penetration that extends to the whole of visible creation. Recent work on the genre of 'anatomy lessons' and the related fascination with the dissection of human bodies encourages a more general application of Bal's thesis.[16] But the violence at issue is most clearly and systematically observed in the portrayal of women.[17]

In the *Magna instauratio* (1620), Bacon distinguishes the method of 'true induction' from the logic-chopping wordgames of Aristotelian schoolmen. The new philosophy's superiority stems, however, not simply from its fidelity to natural observation, but from its power to 'command' the world of created things; and what grants this power is the fact that the knowledge it acquires is 'extracted' not merely out of the depths of the mind, but out of the very bowels of nature'. Science is thus a Caesarian delivery of the fruits produced by the 'marriage' of virile intellect and fecund female nature consummated in the experimental laboratory conceived as the 'bridal chamber' in which 'mind' and 'universe' meet as one.[18] Nor is the latent violence of Bacon's imagery limited to the process of Caesarian 'extraction' by which nature is delivered of the infant knowledge mind sires on her. Using the relevant legal term of art, Bacon likens the procedures of experiment to 'vexations', forms of judicial torture to which reticent witnesses are exposed during police inquiries. Baconian natural science also examines nature 'free and at large', as observed in the unfettered flow of ordinary experience. Nevertheless, its primary object is 'nature under constraint and vexed; that is to say, when by art and the hand of man she is forced out of her natural state, and squeezed and moulded'. Like a suspect in a criminal proceeding, nature conceals the secrets interrogators desire to wrest from her. If then Bacon chiefly relies on the violent interventions of experiment rather than on the relaxed procedures of ordinary observation, it is because 'the nature of things betrays itself more readily under the vexations of art than in its natural freedom'.[19]

Descartes's sexual metaphors are less overt: committed to the frighteningly hubristic and, as we will see in chapter 4, strikingly Œdipal task of reinventing both science and his own historic identity as its epochal progenitor, he tends to repress them. When they do surface, it is only indirectly, as, notably, in the symbolically charged setting for the narrative of the great Illumination of 10 November 1619—the heated room, the maternal *poêle*, where, shut up on his own in the amniotic fluid of undistracted thought, the philosopher undergoes the conversion from which he emerges quite literally 'reborn', *rené* as 'Descartes', the self-determined father of modern science.[20] However, unavowable as Descartes's sexual imagery may remain, the ambition sustaining the picture of his universal method and of everything it will enable him to achieve is the same as Bacon's. And just as Baconian is the interventionist imagery Descartes employs in the famous picture of the 'long chains of reasons' modeled on the demonstrations of geometry whose power and reach entitle him to 'imagine' that

> everything capable of falling within the compass of human knowledge follows after the same fashion, and that, provided only one abstain from receiving anything for true that is not, and maintain throughout the order required to deduce them one from another, there can be nothing so remote that one cannot finally reach it, nor anything so hidden that it cannot be discovered.[21]

Comparable testimony is offered by the doctrine of 'qualities', a theory closely related to Bacon's idea of science not just as empirical description, but as an analytic 'interpretation' recovering, behind and beneath empirical appearances, the underlying 'axioms' or causal laws that produce them.[22] A strategic moment in the development of modern scientific method is the distinction between 'primary' and 'secondary' qualities and the explicit formulation of the principle of ontological reduction this distinction encodes. Primary qualities (solidity, extension, form or figure, motion and number) are deemed real in and of themselves as we perceive them in experience. By contrast, secondary qualities like temperature, colour, smell or taste are seen as being wholly subjective in origin, and the properties they present are accordingly quite unreal in the form in which we initially detect them. They are mere epiphenomena, derivative 'images', 'tokens', 'footsteps', 'vestiges' or 'signs' produced in our senses by primary forces too rapid, powerful or minute to register directly.[23] This is what both licenses and requires the reductive Baconian method of interpretation, reading back from the illusions of sensory appearance by writing them down to causes that, in explaining, also explode them. It is important to observe, however, what defines primary qualities as a class. In the first place is the fact, later adduced by Kant, that they condition the possibility of cognizable objects per se, as properties any such object must possess to exist for us at all.[24] Yet primary qualities further share a double reference denied their epiphenomenal counterparts. While secondary qualities engage only one sense (smell, taste, touch or, in the case of colour, sight), the primary appeal to two working in concert, sight and touch, fusing the hand that lays bare with the eye that sees. Primary qualities thus exhibit and confirm, in the form of the object of rational experience, the attributes presupposed by the underlying architecture of knowledge itself: the powerful amalgam of vision and prehension grasped in the German for 'concept', *Begriff*.

The main business of science is to rifle the physical universe in search of the deep causal structures that determine it. And just as a feminized nature surrenders her secrets to the invasively prehensile gaze of a Bacon or Descartes, so does its aesthetic counterpart in the synecdochic nude of Renaissance art. One obvious symbol is the personification of Truth. In Cesare Ripa's *Iconologia*, the great handbook of allegorical types first published in 1593, Truth is a naked female whose nudity is understood to indicate 'that truth is a natural state and, like a nude person, exists without need for any artificial embellishment'.[25] To be sure, the figure is 'modestly covered with a bit of drapery': like the *Venus Pudica* with whom Rona Goffen reminds us she is commonly linked,[26] Truth withholds herself from basely lascivious attention. Even in portrayals of the energetic theme of 'Truth revealed by Time', where a male personification strips Truth of her protective drapery, an air of respectful solemnity inhibits an openly carnal response. Nevertheless, coupled with the absolute requirement of physical beauty, the venereal suggestion of the figure's nakedness is inescapable.

What applies to nature even in the abstract character of naked truth does so all the more obviously when we address her naked truth as nature. Take Botticelli's *Birth of Venus* (c. 1485; fig. 1.1). The painting embodies a classicizing and humanizing ideal of form cherished for its own sake, a formalism expressed by the goddess's sculptural coolness. But the *Birth of Venus* also opens an Albertian window on a natural world of physical beauty candidly enjoyed and, as enacted by the strong if as yet still somewhat clumsy spatial recession in the

Fig. 1.1 Sandro Botticelli, *The Birth of Venus*. The Uffizi, Florence

background, actively explored as such. Moreover, portrayed here issuing directly from that world, rising full-grown from the womb of the sea as a personification of the fruitful natural landscape she simultaneously graces and epitomizes, the goddess assumes the form of an object of visual exploration and enjoyment identical to that bestowed on the world itself. Venus incarnates an erotic potential tantalizingly underscored by the prettily ineffectual gesture of concealing a naked sex and breasts all the more palpable for the attempt.

Or consider Giorgione's *Sleeping Venus* of circa 1510 (fig. 1.2). The painting's construction underscores its own voyeuristic character by hinting that our approach to the goddess is faintly illicit, occasioned by her unconsciousness of our furtive presence. Giorgione's Venus thereby amplifies the forces observed in Botticelli. She may not yet be what Kenneth Clark calls the *Venus Naturalis* of High Renaissance art, a knowing and inviting figure of the type Titian models on her in the *Venus of Urbino* of 1538 (fig. 1.3).[27] Yet for all her 'Gothic virginity', she emerges as the correlate of an act of carnal possession proleptically rehearsed not only in the characteristic Venetian colourism that lends the flesh the warmth and texture of an eminently tactile substance, but in our relation to the framing landscape whose composition mirrors the supple horizontal contours of her reclining form. Through the metonymy of compositional association, the landscape derives a certain divinity from the goddess. In the process, it both

Fig. 1.2 Giorgione, *Sleeping Venus*. Staatliche Kunstsammlungen, Dresden

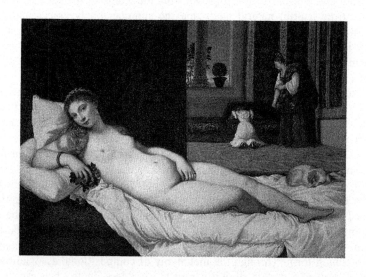

Fig. 1.3 Titian, *Venus of Urbino*. The Uffizi, Florence

certifies and promotes painting's status as *imitatio naturae*. But the goddess in turn falls under the beholder's optico-tactile grasp after a fashion inscribed in the way the receding horizon, the winding road leading up to the town in the right middleground and, above all, the folds and undulations of the landscape reproduce those of Venus' own body to invite our implicitly erotic exploration.

Nor is the erotic enjoyment implied here as benign as the foregoing examples might suggest. Even leaving aside the fact that the overwhelming majority of the images that have reached us were composed by and for men, there is a wafer-thin boundary between Titian's *Venus of Urbino* and his *Rape of Europa* (c. 1559-62) or a painting like Rubens' *Perseus and Andromeda* (late 1630s), a baroque image modeled on a Titian original. Rubens' picture relates (more accurately, draws its pretext from) the story of Andromeda's rescue from the devouring sea monster, and to this extent portrays less a rape than its frustration. The artist nonetheless clearly takes advantage of the situation to enable the tacitly male beholder vicariously to indulge the sadistic pleasures that the supporting legend denies the monster (fig. 1.4). Manacled to the rock in a classic pornographic pose assuring maximum exposure, manual as well as ocular, Andromeda is represented as a thrillingly sentient target of invasive male objectification and desire.[28]

Once we confess the seamless regularity with which portrayals of women in the European canon pass over into portrayals of rape, we begin to see how far the canon is itself a kind of rape, the symbolic equivalent of the violence it depicts. As Bal and, in a wider perspective encompassing not just early modern culture, but the entire history of Western art, Griselda Pollock insist, one consequence of this insight is to politicize our sense of the cultural past.[29] The exploration of representations of sexual violence frankly acknowledged as such, stripped of the alibi by which the tradition converts them into harmless aesthetic fictions, compels us to admit how pervasive rape is not only as a fiction, but as a fact—a fact moreover that not only explains, but is perpetuated by the fictions whose sheer number betokens its pervasiveness. Precisely in the light it sheds on how fact and fiction evoke and confirm each other, the exploration of canonical rape indicts the fundamental collusion between the gender régime that encourages and the aesthetic régime that depicts the violence to which women remain subject both in fact and as fiction. That and how the canon figures rape is thus not merely a symptom; it is a constituent of the reality it marks. Endowed with causal as well as conditional force, it proves at once a source and vehicle of the violence it represents.

And yet there is a danger here. We have learned to discern the underlying identity the canon masks as aesthetic difference—to see, for instance, how metaphors of rape are versions of the deed they invoke in fictional terms. But in identifying the representation *of* rape as evidence of representation's function *as* rape, we are insensibly led to perpetrate the kind of violence we allege. The great virtue of discovering the identity linking rape to its portrayal lies in our enlarged sensitivity to the distinction between the portrayal and the experience it depicts—between how rape is represented and what rape means to the women

52 *Baroque Self-Invention and Historical Truth*

Fig. 1.4 Pieter Paul Rubens, *Perseus and Andromeda*.
Staatliche Muzeen zu Berlin, Gemäldegalerie

who are its victims. But this is just the sort of distinction of position, understanding and perspective we risk losing sight of. Once we have refigured the representation of rape so as to see how readily it serves as rape, how do we tell the difference where we find a difference to tell?

The problem of telling this difference suggests that, self-evident (and damning) as the acknowledgement of the tradition's violence may seem, the question is more complex than the prosecution of such iniquities encourages us to think. Gendered violence conditions both science and art, and by examining the intricate links between scientific procedures and painterly practices, we sensitize ourselves to its underlying patterns and effects. But the relation between visual representation and its objects is by no means as unilateral as may appear. In the book cited a moment ago, Bal confesses how Rembrandt often evinces sympathy for his female subjects.[30] Nor is this sympathy simply conveyed by the studied rejection of Italian conventions of feminine beauty made out in his loving respect for what was conventionally devalued as 'common' or 'ugly', things the Italianate French critic and connoisseur Roger de Piles wrote off as tasteless surrender to 'the poverty of ordinary nature' in contrast to the idealizing 'grandeur' expected of the 'perfect' painter.[31] Rembrandt's sympathy is more deeply expressed by a tendency to represent women as *resisting* the quasi-pornographic exposure that constitutes the Western norm.

Whence the *Susannas* of 1634 and 1645 (figs. 1.5 and 1.6). The paintings invoke the Apocryphal tale of two elders who, lusting after the ravishing Susanna, conspire to assail her virtue while she bathes alone, naked, in the garden of her house during her husband's absence. She cries out for help at their approach. Yet when her servants arrive on the scene, the elders claim to have surprised her with a lover; and because they are elders while she is a mere woman, the people believe them, condemning her to death for adultery. The story already addresses the theme of 'appearances', of representation—indeed, of what contemporary cultural criticism calls 'construction'. On the strength of their authoritative account of what they saw in the garden, the elders determine how the people see Susanna. She effectively becomes what their version of events makes of her, the image or likeness, the *eidolon* of an adulteress—and the polyvalent Greek term *eidolon*, with its connotations of idolatry as well as resemblance, is relevant here, bearing as it does on a story written in Greek recording a tale current among the supremely rational Jews of Alexandria.

But it is at this point that the great unmasker of idols and likenesses, the young iconoclast Daniel, steps forward from the popular mass. The History of Susanna is indeed the story of how the prophet-to-be, nemesis of the idols of Babylon and decrypter of dreams and of the famous Writing on the Wall, first singled himself out for notice. Daniel alone remains undeceived by the idolatrous likeness; nor does respect for the elders enjoin his silence, forcing him to deny the evidence of his own intelligence. Permitted to interrogate the elders, he draws each one aside in turn and asks where Susanna stood when discovered in her lover's embrace; and when one says under a mastic tree while the other says

Fig. 1.5 Rembrandt van Rijn, *Susanna at the Elders* (1634).
Royal Cabinet of Painting. Mauritshuis, The Hague

Fig. 1.6 Rembrandt van Rijn, *Susanna and the Elders* (1645).
Staatliche Muzeen zu, Berlin, Gemäldegalerie

under an evergreen oak, the fraud is exposed and Susanna vindicated while the elders themselves are put to death.

Rembrandt's depiction of his heroine is the more remarkable given the character of the tale. Shown naked, and to this extent a standard object of concupiscent male attention, Susanna is at one level an ocular possession wholly in the beholder's power. Yet faithful to the text in which the pictures find their occasion, this nakedness is thoroughly problematic. We see something the story tells us we ought not to, Susanna's naked beauty, concealed in the enclosed garden of her husband's house. But unlike Rubens' *Perseus and Andromeda*, where the portrayal of a frustrated rape transposes into its fetishized aesthetic consummation, Rembrandt's Susanna shelters her nakedness not only from the invading elders, but from *us*. Though she cannot hide everything, the protective clutching of her clothes and the way her body closes in self-defence prevent us from seeing her breasts and sex. And that we too are so prevented is asserted by the emphatic direction of her surprisingly self-collected gaze. For it is unmistakably at us that she looks. We too are indelibly present, and it is from us as much as the elders that she conceals what we too desire to and, in other art, would in fact see: the sexual organs she contrives with Rembrandt's help to hide.

I want to suggest that, unwonted as all of this seems, anti-canonical as Rembrandt's practice proves in this as in so much else, it is perhaps not quite as unique as we suppose. The norm itself merits further thought: the proto-feminism made out in Rembrandt is more widespread and representative than we might at first credit. Painting, after all, is not just a way of seeing and portraying; it is an object of inspection formed for an eye as proprietary and concupiscent as the one trained on the beautiful women it depicts. Nor is the painting of a beautiful woman just (though it is also) a demonstration of art's power to master and possess beautiful nature; it doubles as the personified embodiment of painterly beauty itself. The Venus of a Titian or Giorgione images artistic as well as feminine beauty: painting is prized as the finished form in which beauty is captured or, better, actively realized and created as well as the instrument by which mere reproduction is achieved. This is why, in the iconophobic art of the Zwinglian or Calvinist North, a Cranach will present a Venus who, like the equally iconophobic Duessa of the Protestant Spenser's *Faerie Queene*, at once conceals and discloses the baited hook of sin and death behind the vision of carnal beauty and delight that meets us at first sight. And it is also why, more subtly and forgivingly if in the end no less emphatically, Jan Steen's alluring yet soberingly prostituted *Oyster-Eating Girl* (c. 1658-60; fig. 1.7) yields a problematic pleasure that calls both visual art and its beholder to book. The unmistakable direction and fathomless ironic clarity of the girl's gaze extorts the admission that it is to us that she offers the tempting aphrodisiac oyster, emblem of the sex whose hire is even now transacted in the room at the back.

Implicit then in the representation of feminine beauty is a fundamental solidarity between female form and the art that, in and by portraying it, offers itself up for visual consumption of precisely the sort it practises. Nor is the act of looking to which art is subjected any less questionable than that addressed to women. The elders in Rembrandt's second *Susanna* double for the connoisseur looking over the artist's shoulder in the satiric self-portrait attributed to the elder Pieter Bruegel in the Albertina in Vienna (c. 1565; fig. 1.8).[32] Even in a painting

Fig. 1.7 Jan Steen, *Oyster-Eating Girl*. Royal Cabinet of Painting, Mauritshuis, The Hague

as potentially pornographic as Velázquez's *Rokeby Venus* of c. 1648 (fig. 1.9), luxuriously serving up the mistress of the notorious débauché who commissioned it,[33] we encounter a certain ambivalence. A hallmark of this image is the way it subverts the exposure of the woman's body by revealing a Venus who turns her back, setting a limit simultaneously surmounted and underscored by a mirror showing the self-absorbed remoteness of the face she turns away.

What is true of Venus is also true of figures like Lucretia, to whom Rembrandt devotes two paintings, the first in 1664, the second in 1666 (figs. 1.10 and 1.11). As Bal argues when analyzing these paintings in her broader account of the 'semiotics of rape', the pronounced preoccupation with the Rape of Lucretia from classical antiquity to the baroque affords a fruitful focus for the feminist revision of Western cultural history.[34] The reason is the thematization of rape itself. Early modern interest in the tale provides an opportunity to talk both about a phenomenon that is still painfully with us and about how our patriarchal culture appropriates and distorts an experience that is centrally feminine while

The Vindication of Susanna 57

Fig. 1.8 Pieter Bruegel the Elder (?), *Self-Portrait with Connoisseur*. Albertina, Vienna

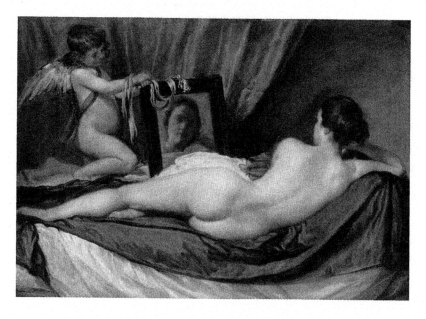

Fig. 1.9 Diego Velázquez, *Rokeby Venus*. National Gallery, London

Fig. 1.10 Rembrandt van Rijn, *Lucretia*. National Gallery of Art, Washington

Fig. 1.11 Rembrandt van Rijn, *Lucretia*. Minneapolis Institute of Arts, Minneapolis

perpetuating the myths and power relations responsible for it. In this double register, Bal denounces how poets and artists 'literally need to touch the woman's body—to partake in its rape'.[35] Through what she calls the 'semiotic use of the raped body', Livy, Ovid and Shakespeare as well as Rembrandt exploit Lucretia for their own ends. Often these are political, citing her rape as an example of generalized monarchic tyranny and a call to resistance. But they are often more narrowly aesthetic, as in Rembrandt, 'the *sculpteur manqué*, the toucher' par excellence. Thus, according to Bal, in the second *Lucretia*, Rembrandt associates the bloodstain that serves as a sign both of the rape and of the suicidal wound the heroine has just administered with the 'thick paint' that represents them. The blood becomes a metonymy for his characteristic impasto effects, an element of facture that constitutes a signature of the kind of paintings we think of as 'Rembrandts'. To this extent, the painter 'uses [Lucretia's] death to attract attention to his skill, the craft which he is at this very moment promoting into an art'.[36]

Everything Bal claims about Rembrandt's appropriation of Lucretia could as easily be said of his representations of Christ, the Jews of the Old Testament or the Jewish quarter of Amsterdam, the self-important burghers of *The Night Watch* (1642) or even the dogs and horses he paints throughout his career. It is hard, in other words, taking a broader view of Rembrandt's work, to detect the sort of difference in the way he appropriates female as opposed to other bodies required to license the special inferences Bal draws.[37] Yet even granting the point, as important as acknowledging the way Rembrandt's portrayal of Lucretia duplicates the rape it depicts is recognizing how far his art *identifies* with her martyred body.

It is worth asking, for instance, why Rembrandt (or Livy, Ovid and Shakespeare for that matter) should wish to take over just this figure from this tale. One motive, related to the specifically political message the tale repeatedly bears, is the sense in which all non-noble political subjects tended, in early modern Europe, to represent their relation to power as rape. The Rape of Lucretia is thus one of many tales of violation made to serve the critical political purpose of denouncing tyranny on behalf of the 'commons' from whose ranks all painters and the great majority of poets were recruited. Confining ourselves to Rembrandt's own century, theatre in particular abounds in examples of rapes serving to channel political protest. Lope de Vega's *Fuenteovejuna* (1619) and Calderón's *El alcalde de Zalamea* (published in 1651) use rape as a symbol of general social crisis—the symptom of a pathology that forms the very basis of unreformed political association. Lope's play is all the more revealing in that, in addition to the violation of the heroine Laurencia, who incidentally eschews suicide in order to lead the popular revolt her rape precipitates, we also have the torture of the hedonistic Mengo. The political violence Lope documents observes no distinction of sex. Similarly, in Alexandre Hardy's *Scédase*, published in 1624, the rape and murder of the daughters of a worthy peasant by Spartan nobles occasion a hearing in which the father is denied a trial of his daughters' killers. The obdurate Spartan authorities thereby drive home the lesson that the lower orders of society can expect no justice at the hands of the ruling élite. Nor is it indifferent that—though resulting, like the Rape of Lucretia, in a suicide—the father takes his own life in his daughters' place. Without wishing to minimize the degree to which tales of rape can (and do) act out the violence they portray, these counterexamples suggest that there is no reason for assuming that they *must* serve this purpose. They may also provide a means of representing a suffering painters and poets conceive themselves as sharing with their victims.[38]

What is at least possible in the case of representations of rape in general seems probable in that of Lucretia. For the core of the tale is less the rape itself than the suicide by which the victim transforms it into a political symbol—the gesture by which she refigures her rape as self-determined meaning. And it is in fact here far more than in Bal's association of Lucretia's blood with Rembrandt's paint or of her violated body with his tactile impasto that we see why this particular story recommended itself.[39] What Rembrandt represents is not just the victim, but the victim on the verge of death: in the *Lucretia* of 1664, the moment when the heroine prepares to plunge the dagger into her breast; in that of 1666, the moment immediately following the deed, when death overtakes her. In both cases, we are given a poignant image of interiority. Rembrandt's Lucretias embody not only suffering and injustice, but what it is to *experience* these things, to be an individual subject—a point reinforced by their utter isolation in a three-quarters view from which every extraneous detail is systematically eliminated. If, from the standpoint of artistic practice, these paintings may be said to represent Rembrandt's art as such, it is not merely in their characteristic colour tones and impasto. It is also in the signature inwardness of the heroine's gaze: an inwardness that distinguishes virtually all of Rembrandt's paintings, and especially his portraits, male as well as female, of himself as well as others. Embodying their consciousness of the death they embrace in answer to the uniquely intimate violence they have endured, the Lucretias become the embodiments of the peculiar intimacy that is consciousness itself, an essential theme of all of Rembrandt's paintings. Rembrandt chooses Lucretia as a means of affirming and portraying his art less because her victimhood predisposes her for a victim's part than because it motivates a unique expressiveness, the soulful in-turning melancholy we identify as 'Rembrandt'.

Against this background, let us return to the pictures we began with, the two versions of Susanna.[40] As the foregoing suggests, one weakness in Bal's interpretation of these pictures—a weakness representative of a more general precipitancy at work both in feminist or cultural studies and in new historicism or the 'new' art history as well—is that, engrossed in unmasking the hegemonic male desires to which Susanna is subjected, it overlooks the ways in which images of rape may identify with their victims. The gesture by which Rembrandt's Susannas resist the invasive attentions of the elders enacts a similar resistance on painting's part. We have, for instance, to reckon here with the cultural context in which these images were made. It is Rembrandt's fate (as also, from another angle, his good fortune) to work in a reformed Netherlands where, for all the unprecedented interest in and consumption of pictures of every sort chronicled by Alpers and Schama, images remain subject to deep and abiding mistrust.[41] To paint, for him, is to be caught up in what Schama styles the ambivalent cycle of 'feasting and fasting' whereby pictures are simultaneously desired and reviled. Art works are openly coveted, and eagerly created, in answer to a widespread public appetite. Yet there hangs over them a guilty sense both of the carnal vices with which they are confederate and of the active, literally destructive hostility they at once inspire and, as our examples from Rembrandt and Steen hint, even endorse.[42]

But a deeper weakness, related to the first, is blindness to the bearing the identification of art and the all too visible female nude has on the *Susannas*' true subject, the invisible hero Daniel: the prophet and judge in whose eyes alone Susanna and painting are alike truly seen. Daniel is the key to the ultimate burden of Rembrandt's visual texts. As noted earlier, at the same time as Rembrandt's Susannas turn away from the lustful and mendacious elders, they look to the position we ourselves occupy as beholders in a space outside of yet continuous with that of the image. At one level, these gazes challenge us, asserting (among other things) how painting, and thus even the female beauty painting at once captures and identifies with, has the power to look back. This challenge reminds us, however, not only of the erotically suspect status of our own looking, but of what Maurice Merleau-Ponty describes as the essentially reciprocal and chiastic structure of vision itself. As an expression of the 'intentional' form of our relation to the visible, each object, however eyeless and inanimate, returns our gaze as a reflex of that conscious presence to things by which we grant them visibility.[43] Yet beyond challenging our implicit engagement as beholders, the gazes that Rembrandt's *Susannas* return our own appeal to a mode of vision for which, as the hero of the story Rembrandt tells, Daniel offers the example. They invoke a way of looking we ourselves enact precisely insofar as we are conscious of the place Daniel occupies as the last in the series of beholders in whose sight Susanna is made to appear.

What is exemplary in Daniel is a property he shares both with the iconoclastic art of Rembrandt and with the idol-smashing thrust of early modern science: the capacity to look beyond the ostensibly self-evident (and theoretically self-ratifying) constructions we impose on the world.[44] When, toward the end of the first of the two books of aphorisms composing the *New Organon* (1620), Bacon sets out to depict natural philosophy's millenarian power to revolutionize the human condition, it is to the Book of Daniel that he turns. This biblical text recommends itself in the first instance for prophylactic reasons, as one in which Christian exegetes were accustomed to see a typological 'shadow' of their own Apocalypse:

> Nor should the prophecy of Daniel be forgotten touching the last ages of the world: 'Many shall go to and fro, and knowledge shall be increased'; clearly intimating that the thorough passage of the world (which now by so many distant voyages seems to be accomplished, or in course of accomplishment), and the advancement of the sciences, are destined by fate, that is, by Divine Providence, to meet in the same age.[45]

Daniel is to this extent a reassuring scriptural type for the literally eschatological promise Bacon claims for the new science, and thus too for himself as its progenitor. Yet what singles Daniel out for this role is less the godlike power of prophecy the Bible assigns him than the iconomachic gift of independent judgment that enables him to explode the idolatrous illusions that enthrall his contemporaries.

The Daniel Bacon invokes is the hero of another story Rembrandt paints: the regicidal tale of *Belshazzar's Feast* (c. 1635-39) in which the apparently omnipotent worldly despot is undone by the proverbial Writing on the Wall (Dan. 5) that only Daniel knows how to read.[46] Bacon's Daniel is also the interpreter of Nebuchadnezzar's Dream (Dan. 2). In this character, he penetrates the prognostic message of the 'little stone' that razes the dream's complex 'image' of gold, silver, bronze and iron to the dust by destroying the 'feet of clay' on which it stands, thereby exposing the illusory majesty with which the Babylonian tyrant is idolatrously invested. Or again, the allusion points to the Daniel of the Apocrypha's history of Bel and the Dragon to which Bacon's successor Locke seems to owe the 'footsteps' metaphor he uses to portray the forensic methods by which science infers underlying natures and causes from outward signs that bear no resemblance to the natural forces they express.[47] Confronted with apparently irrefutable evidence of Bel's divine nature, Daniel unmasks the fraud of the pagan priests by scattering ashes on the floor of the temple housing the idol of their false god. The incriminating footprints the priests leave in the ashes at night reveal how the food the idol appears miraculously to eat has in fact been consumed by the priests themselves. At one level, the story affirms the monotheistic basis of Judaeo-Christian belief: there is only one true god; all others are empty fakes. But this pious reading admits another that is less so. The story's theological point depends on the sceptical, and in this sense entirely rational, contrivance that Daniel devises in order to drive it home. In this light, the exposure of the false god of the pagans becomes an allegory of Baconian experiment. More specifically, it images the principle of reduction by whose means empirical science refers the misleading appearances of ordinary experience to the hidden substances and laws of which they are mere tokens. To discover the truth, we must seek its origin in an order of things quite other than the one that meets untutored sight.

All of these stories underscore the need to which Daniel ministers and the intellectual gift that sets him apart: the perhaps unteachable power to transcend the forms in which things first appear in order to perceive and thus represent them in something approaching their native truth. The Daniel of Rembrandt's *Susannas* sees through the overdetermined projections of his own fears and desires, as also through the heroine's inability to show herself in a light that will not misrepresent her, to something like the woman (the truth) herself. Truth is a likeness whose discovery demands our readiness to accept that it remains in the end *only* a likeness—the image of something that, however asymptotically close representation may come, ultimately withholds itself. Susanna's truth is not simply her innocence of the crime of which she stands accused; it is her refusal to grant the knowledge the elders crave, the treasure forever concealed in the secret garden where her naked form is displayed.

Nor are Rembrandt's paintings alone in being vindicated in this way; we see how science requires further thought as well. At the close of the preface to the *New Organon*, Bacon appeals, Susanna-like, to a reader possessing the same powers as the Daniel to whom Rembrandt's Susannas look:

> It is but reasonable, however (especially in so great a restoration of learning and knowledge), that I should claim of men one favour in return, which is this: if anyone would form an opinion or judgment either out of his own observation, or out of the crowd of authorities, or out of the forms of demonstration (which have now acquired a sanction like that of judicial laws), concerning these speculations of mine, let him not hope that he can do it in passage or by the by; but let him examine the thing thoroughly; let him make some little trial for himself of the way which I describe and lay out; let him familiarize his thoughts with that subtlety of nature to which experience bears witness; let him correct by seasonable patience and due delay the depraved and deep-rooted habits of his mind; and when all this is done and he has begun to be his own master, let him (if he will) use his own judgment.[48]

For all the authority natural science derives from the system of disciplined experiment and the principle of reduction on which experiment is based, it proves as subject to misconstruction as the world it seeks to rescue from the idolatries it supplants. Its power to lay bare the true nature of things is in the end only visible to those who share its outlook and are therefore parties to the dispute in which it is engaged. In the absence of the at once autonomous and disinterested judge Bacon invokes, science is thus no more capable of defending its veracity than Susanna is her innocence. On the contrary, it must, like Susanna, await the advent of a mind freed of the 'depraved and deep-rooted habits' that determine how contemporaries take it. What Bacon looks for is the candid intercessor whom, in Shakespeare's *Merchant of Venice* (c. 1595), Shylock hails in the disguised person of Portia: 'A Daniel come in judgment! yea, a Daniel!'[49] But as Shylock's fate reminds us, even Daniel is only '*a* Daniel', a creation of our need that presents as such a potential for fraud and mistake.

Yet more striking still is how the ambitions of Baconian science are eventually qualified even on their own terms. In the *New Organon*'s second book, concerned less with the general idea of science than with its actual practice, Bacon tempers the rhetoric of mastery and possession featured in manifestos like the *Magna instauratio* or the preface to the *New Organon* by confessing that natural philosophy can never in fact capture nature itself at all. As Bacon puts it here, the knowledge of nature qua nature, independent of the interests, needs and perceptions of the human subject of such knowledge, demands addressing it 'with reference to the universe' rather than limiting (and idolatrous) reference 'to man'.[50] But this means that, just insofar as knowledge is a self-determined achievement of human intellect, it remains a prisoner of its own conditions of possibility, cut off from the very thing it seeks. For all his pride and certainty, Bacon marks the inception of the critical turn by which the philosophy of science becomes a dependency of the philosophy of mind. The first systematic exposition of this turn is Locke's *Essay Concerning Human Understanding* of 1690; and its immediate result is a new programme of knowledge focused on limited, practical goals that expressly foreswear both Bacon's apocalyptic promises and the totalitarian ambitions that Descartes's *Le Monde* lays out:

> When we know our own strength, we shall the better know what to undertake with hopes of success; and when we have well surveyed the *powers* of our own minds, and made some estimate what we may expect from them, we shall not be inclined either to sit still, and not set our thoughts on work at all, in despair of knowing anything; nor on the other side, question everything, and disclaim all knowledge, because some things are not to be understood. It is of great use to the sailor to know the length of his line, though he cannot with it fathom all the depths of the ocean. It is well he knows that it is long enough to reach the bottom, at such places as are necessary to direct his voyage, and caution him against running upon shoals that may ruin him. Our business here is not to know all things, but those which concern our conduct. If we can find out those measures, whereby a rational creature, put in that state in which man is in this world, may and ought to govern his opinions, and actions depending thereon, we need not to be troubled that some other things escape our knowledge.[51]

What begins as aphoristic *Diktat* turns into a complex chiastic *dialogue* that transforms both of the terms it joins.

Similarly, perhaps the most decisive feature of modern Western painting, emblematic in this of representation at large, is the degree to which it engages less what we see than what we cannot: less the gaudy operatic exposures of Italian art than an elusive interior forever evading visual grasp.[52] Michael Fried shows how modern art as such begins in an exemplary problematic surrounding the relation to the beholder in the painting of eighteenth-century France. Painting's fundamental purpose is of course to be seen, and to this extent the presence of a beholder constitutes an ontological condition of visual art, essential to its very nature and existence. And indeed, from the great religious narratives of the later Middle Ages, and more especially the heroic perspective constructions of the Italian Renaissance, to the Academic art of the nineteenth century, most paintings are deliberately and consciously grounded in this fact. The awareness of being seen informs every feature of composition, expression and pose, yielding what Fried's chief contemporary witness, Denis Diderot, derisively calls 'theatrical' art.[53] In direct and explicit contrast to such art, however, is a mode of painting that counters and even denies the beholder's presence: a denial expressed in images that not only withhold all overt acknowledgement of being seen, but maintain the fiction that there is no beholder at all. For pictures of this sort Fried coins the term 'absorptive', testifying to the way in which they contrive to subsist (or at any rate appear to subsist) entirely in, by and for themselves alone, independent of any onlooker.

To take an example from an eighteenth-century painter Fried cites as an important exponent of absorptive art, Chardin's *A Lady Taking Tea* (1735; fig. 1.12) presents us with the characteristically understated treatment of an equally understated theme: the representation of a lady taking tea. However, beyond the decidedly ordinary, insignificant and to this extent already antitheatrical character of the action, the crucial thing is the *concentration* the subject involves and how this in turn determines our relation to it. Engrossed in the absorbing if

Fig. 1.12 Jean-Baptiste-Siméon Chardin, *A Lady Taking Tea*.
Hunterian Art Gallery, University of Glasgow

mundane task of preparing a cup of tea, though wholly visible to us, wholly in our presence as a reflex of our presence to her, the lady is wholly oblivious to us—to the point where, so long as she remains absorbed in the task in hand (which, in the time of the picture, is forever), we do not exist at all. But this also means that she *eludes* us in the very form by which she seems to be given. What we see is in fact the curious absence entailed by her absorbed attention to her task, a recentring of the universe which, by excluding us, extracts itself from our field of vision, becoming the indelible trace of its own disappearance.

Yet the truly extraordinary thing is not simply the lady's (and so the painting's) self-absorption and how this in turn engenders the formal autonomy in which Fried sees the ontological basis of a specifically modern art. It is the link between painterly absorption and the ontology of modernity itself expressed in natural philosophy.[54] As Michael Baxandall argues, the true subject of this painting is less the lady than a certain drama of vision, the history of a beholding. Chardin creates subtly disjunctive zones of distinctness of colour and focus, volume and depth, so as to rehearse the act of viewing in the representation's form:

> Chardin is one of the great eighteenth-century narrative painters: he can and often does make a story out of the contents of a shopping bag. He narrates by representing not substance—not figures fighting or embracing or gesticulating—but a story of perceptual experience masquerading as a moment or two of sensation: sometimes he jokes about this fiction with momentary substances like spinning tops or frozen steam from a tea-cup. There is a degree of symmetry between the experience he represents and our experience of his picture but the symmetry is not complete. What we have in *A Lady Taking Tea* is an enacted record of attention which we ourselves, directed by distinctness and other things, summarily reenact, and that narrative of attention is heavily loaded: it has foci, privileged points of fixation, failures, characteristic modes of relaxation, awareness of contrasts, and curiosity about what it does not succeed in knowing.[55]

What we see is not a lady seated at a table, preparing a cup of tea, but what is involved in *seeing* such a lady. In particular, the painting features gentle deviations between what at one level we know we see and what at another we actually do see. The lady's right hand, for example, is more distinct than her face; and the teapot manages to belie, in the visual 'sensation' out of which we construct our 'perception', the three-dimensionality the painting at once alleges and contradicts. The result is that the picture plays out a specifically Lockean tension between the inherent 'substance' of a thing and the 'ideas' by which we come to know it. The image gives us the sensations out of which we build up our perception of the 'complex substance' we look at, 'a lady taking tea'. But it also tactfully refrains from giving the substance itself, enacting the Lockean notion that we never in fact know or experience substance directly at all, but only mediately, in the forms in which it registers as the hidden source of our ideas about it. And it is to this, finally, that we owe the picture's absorptiveness; for it is essential to the understanding of beholding the image enacts that the object it represents, the lady herself, escape. Even as a representation of the complex idea of the lady's complex substance, by depicting the lady as engrossed in stirring her tea, the picture presents her as absorbed in herself and to that extent as withdrawn from the beholder in whose perceptual field she appears.[56]

Rembrandt's *Susannas*, like Chardin's *Lady*, identify with a striking blindness of the sort Bal is fascinated by. For Bal, swept up in the drama of ocular hubris for which the Bacon of the manifestos or the Descartes of *Le Monde* are models, blindness is a wound inflicted to punish the arrogant desires vision carries out. Its preeminent icons would accordingly be paintings like *The Blinding of Samson* (1636), where the emphatically male embodiment of the heroic agency with which Bal's Rembrandt identifies his art suffers a symbolic castration that reduces him to feminized passivity.[57] By contrast, the blindness at issue here constitutes less a punitive negation than a *condition* of representation, the admission of a limit that enables both art and science to expound the dialogical ground of their relation to the world. In Bacon's terms, the key to true as opposed to merely apparent induction, to authentic rather than deluded because idolatrously self-referential apprehension, is the acknowledgement that representation instigates a movement toward its natural, feminine other that will never either master or possess what it aims to grasp. The third aphorism in book one of the *New Organon* opens in the accents of proprietary right: 'Human knowledge and human power meet in one; for where the cause is not known the effect cannot be produced.' Nevertheless, the power knowledge bestows depends on a prior surrender in which it cedes the authority it hopes to regain in return: 'Nature to be commanded must be obeyed; and that which in contemplation is as the cause is in operation as the rule.'[58]

In conclusion, the gendered imbalance at work in baroque representation, and the violence it simultaneously expresses and encourages, are obvious and undeniable. And yet even as representation ceaselessly reproduces, it also undermines the régime to which it subjects both women and the whole world of 'other' realities for which, in this culture, women are the synecdoche by locating the place or space from which the other radically arises. What this other may be in itself it can neither say nor show. But perhaps the essential point is just the difficulty of saying or showing as such. The Naked Lady that images both nature and truth is an *idea* in Kant's strict sense, a principle that guides us precisely because it can never be realized in the realm of representable experience.[59] To this extent, she is an emblem of everything that eludes us as a condition of everything that falls within our reach.

In a famous note to the chapter on 'the powers of the mind which constitute genius' near the close of the deduction of pure aesthetic judgments in the Third Critique, Kant suggests that

[p]erhaps nothing more sublime has ever been said, or a thought ever been expressed more sublimely, than in that inscription above the temple of *Isis* (Mother Nature): 'I am all that is, that was, and that will be, and no mortal has lifted my veil.'[60]

It is of course essential to the act that Kant performs here that a personified nature appears, and can in fact only appear, in the context of *aesthetics*. More precisely, it is crucial that Isis speaks at that point where, in bringing the closed world of positive science purged of all metaphysical admixture into direct contact with the teleological longings that spring from moral interest, the text adduces the radical disjunction at the heart of the Kantian experience of the sublime—an experience whose moral testimony the aesthetic is meant to legitimize. Isis is indeed expressly cited as the spokeswoman for the unrepresentable, and yet for that very reason irreducible, excess to which the hermetic closure of the world accessible to empirical science bears witness in the face of the moral interest that actuates specifically human consciousness. To this extent, the phenomenological bridge that the aesthetic sets out to throw between the realms of fact and value, of being and bearing, paradoxically reinstates the gulf it sets out to cross, and not least because Kant's eloquent Isis amounts as such to a ventriloquistic fiction: it is in the end only *as if* nature spoke, leaving us finally where we were at the start. Yet what authenticates Isis' speech just the same is exactly what animates the feminized objects of baroque science and art, transforming them into the antithetical protagonists of their own alienated reification. By virtue of its very power over visible nature, representation is brought face to face with the limits that power sets. It thereby gestures toward horizons it can never fix or cross. Yet like Platonic shadows shifting on a wall, what it contrives to make us see is transfigured by the awareness of what it cannot.

Notes

1 On baroque visuality in general, see Christopher Braider, *Refiguring the Real: Picture and Modernity in Word and Image, 1400-1700* (Princeton, NJ: Princeton University Press, 1993), chap. 5, 'Idols of the Mind: Baroque Illusion, Theatrical Persuasion, and the Aesthetics of Iconoclasm in Jan Steen'. For standard accounts, see Germain Bazin, *The Baroque: Principles, Styles, Modes, Themes* (Greenwich, CT: New York Graphic Society, 1968) and Martin, *Baroque*. For a more complex interpretation endebted to Lacanian theory, see Buci-Glucksmann, *La folie du voir*.

2 What Buci-Glucksmann's *La folie du voir* calls the 'archéologie du Regard baroque' focuses on the typically exorbitant character of the visual experiences in which baroque beholders reveled: anamorphoses, saintly visions, the theatricalization of martyred bodies, scenes of 'wonder' (*mirabile*) and madness (*furore*), the portrait of darkness and abysmal 'nothingness' or the operatic excess of public spectacles like the pyrotechnical volcanic mountain created by Bernini and Thor to cap the celebrations of the birth of an heir to the French throne in 1661.

3 The massive scale and range of the production of images in seventeenth-century Holland are reviewed in Alpers's *The Art of Describing* and Schama's *The Embarrassment of Riches*. See too Campbell's *Wonder & Science*, one of whose leitmotivs is the insatiable appetite for pictures of almost anything from the new territories of America to the eyes of a fly as seen through Hooke's microscope and from forms of torture among the Iroquois of French Canada to craters and ridges on the moon.

4 Campbell, *Wonder & Science*, chap. 7, 'Anthropometamorphosis: Manners, Customs, Fashions, and Monsters'.

5 On the Pascalian theme of 'diversion' (*divertissement*), see *Pensées* 132-139/165-171. For an account of the more general problem of 'curiosity' and its both classical and Christian enemies from antiquity to the eighteenth century, see Blumenberg, *The Legitimacy of the Modern Age*, pt. 3, 'The "Trial" of Theoretical Curiosity'.

6 See *Refiguring the Real*, pp. 20-36. Also see Margaret R. Miles, *Image as Insight: Visual Understanding in Western Christianity and Secular Culture* (Boston: Beacon Press, 1985) and, with a feminist twist whose relevance will emerge in a moment, the same author's *Carnal Knowledge: Female Nakedness and Religious Meaning in the Christian West* (Boston: Beacon Press, 1989).

7 See the classic studies by Rensselaer W. Lee, *Ut Pictura Poesis: The Humanistic Theory of Painting* (1940; repr. New York: Norton, 1967) and Jean Hagstrum, *The Sister Arts: The Tradition of Literary Pictorialism and English Poetry from Dryden to Gray* (Chicago: University of Chicago Press, 1958). For a concise account, see Christopher Braider, 'The Paradoxical Sisterhood: *Ut Pictura Poesis*', in *Cambridge History of Literary Criticism* (Cambridge: Cambridge University Press, 1999), vol. 3, *The Renaissance*, ed. Glyn P. Norton, pp. 168-175.

The Vindication of Susanna

8   On the centrality of vision in the period, see the sources indicated in note 1 and Foucault, *Les mots et les choses*, Gilman, *The Curious Perspective*, Timothy J. Reiss, *The Discourse of Modernism* (Ithaca, NY: Cornell University Press, 1982) and Anthony J. Cascardi, *The Subject of Modernity* (Cambridge: Cambridge University Press, 1992). Martin Jay offers valuable insights in *Downcast Eyes: The Denigration of Vision in Twentieth-Century French Thought* (Berkeley, CA: University of California Press, 1993), chap. 1. But though he acknowledges how some baroque figures question the 'ocularism' they inherit from classical and Renaissance sources, his historiography is skewed by the case he wants to make for the uniquely 'anti-ocularist' attitudes of twentieth-century French writers from Bataille and the Surrealists to Levinas and Lyotard. This leads him to insist that the 'ancien scopic régime' enters a true 'crisis' only with the Impressionists and the philosophical vitalism of Bergson—a position whose untenability the present chapter aims to demonstrate.
9   William of Ockham, *Philosophical Writings*, ed. and trans. Philotheus Boehner (New York: Nelson, 1957), p. 41.
10 See Nicole Oresme, *De proportionibus, and Ad pauca respicientes*, ed. and trans. Edward Grant (Madison, WI: University of Wisconsin Press, 1966). I am endebted for this example to Barry Mazur, Professor of Mathematics at Harvard.
11 See Alpers, *The Art of Describing*, pp. 73-74, and Campbell, *Wonder & Science*, chap. 6, 'Outside In: Hooke, Cavendish, and the Invisible Worlds', both on Hooke's *Micrographia* and on Margaret Cavendish's *The Blazing World*, defending the perdurable spirit-life Hooke's microscopic exfoliation of animate nature discredits.
12 See Alpers, *The Art of Describing*, pp. 33-37, and more generally Martin Kemp, *The Science of Art: Optical Themes in Western Art from Brunelleschi to Seurat* (New Haven, CT: Yale University Press, 1990), esp. chap. 2, 'Perspective from Dürer to Galileo', and chap. 3, 'Perspective from Rubens to Turner'. Harry Berger, Jr., *Fictions of the Pose: Rembrandt against the Italian Renaissance* (Stanford, CA: Stanford University Press, 2000), chap. 1, 'Technologies: The System of Early Modern Painting', is also helpful, especially for the salutary corrective it administers to the tendency to read art's scientific impulse in reductive terms, as an unmitigated expression of the hegemonic 'monocularism' of the emerging 'bourgeois' order.
13 Descartes, *Œuvres philosophiques*, vol. 1, pp. 614-615.
14 For perspicacious critical commentaries, see Richard Rorty, *Philosophy and the Mirror of Nature* (Princeton, NJ: Princeton University Press, 1979), chap. 1, 'The Invention of the Mind', chap. 3, 'The Idea of a "Theory of Knowledge"' and chap. 4, 'Privileged Representations', and W.J.T. Mitchell, *Iconology: Image, Text, Ideology* (Chicago: University of Chicago Press, 1986), chap. 1, 'What Is an Image?' and chap. 5, 'Eye and Ear: Edmund Burke and the Politics of Sensibility'.
15 See Bal, *Reading Rembrandt*, pp. 141-48. Bal offers among other things a detailed *mise au point* of feminist cultural historiography. For a more general view of the feminist revision of Western art history, see Griselda Pollock, *Vision and Difference: Femininity, Feminism, and the Histories of Art* (New York: Routledge, 1988).
16 Bal herself follows this path in *Reading Rembrandt*, chap. 10, 'Dead Flesh, or the Smell of Painting'; so, more briefly and less emphatically, does Alpers, *Rembrandt's Enterprise*, p. 81. For an overview, see Jonathan Sawday, *The Body Emblazoned: Dissection and the Human Body in Renaissance Culture* (New York: Routledge, 1995). Barbara Stafford, *Body Criticism: Imaging the Unseen in Enlightenment Art and Medicine* (Cambridge, MA: MIT Press, 1991), chap. 1, 'Dissecting', examines comparable practices in the eighteenth century.

17 See Bal, *Reading Rembrandt*, chaps. 2 and 4. On gender in science, see Evelyn Fox Keller, *Reflections on Gender and Science* (New Haven, CT: Yale University Press, 1985); with specific reference to the age of Descartes, Erica Harth, *Cartesian Women: Versions and Subversions of Rational Discourse in the Old Régime* (Ithaca, NY: Cornell University Press, 1992); and for Bacon, José María Rodríguez García, 'Solitude and Procreation in Francis Bacon's Scientific Writings—The Spanish Connection', *Comparative Literature Studies* 35.3 (1998), pp. 278-300. See also Mary D. Garrard, 'Artemesia and Susanna', in Norma Broude and Mary D. Garrard (eds), *Feminism and Art History: Questioning the Litany* (New York: Harper and Row, 1982), pp. 147-171, and *Artemesia Gentileschi: The Image of the Female Hero in Italian Baroque Art* (Princeton, NJ: Princeton University Press, 1988). As Garrard explains, the life, work and unduly clouded reputation of Artemesia Gentileschi constitute an important test case in that she was both a major baroque artist and a victim of rape. For the broader cultural theory on which all of these writers draw, see Laura Mulvey, 'Visual Pleasure and Narrative Cinema', *Screen* 16.3 (1975), pp. 6-18, Teresa De Lauretis, *Alice Doesn't: Feminism, Semiotics, Cinema* (New York: Macmillan, 1983) and Kaja Silverman, *The Acoustic Mirror: The Female Voice in Psychoanalysis and Cinema* (Bloomington, IN: Indiana University Press, 1988).

18 Bacon, *New Organon*, pp. 21 and 23.

19 Ibid., p. 25. Also see Campbell's excellent analysis of this and related passages, *Wonder & Science*, pp. 71-85.

20 For the official autobiographical account, see *Œuvres philosophiques*, vol. 1, pp. 587-591. But also see pp. 52-61 for the more detailed version furnished by Descartes's contemporary biographer Baillet, including Baillet's translation of the now lost Latin text transcribing a series of dreams to which we will turn in chapter 4.

21 *Œuvres philosophiques*, vol. 1, p. 587. For a literary parallel, see Sidney's repression of the feminine in the *Apology for Poetry*, ed. Geoffrey Shepherd (New York: Barnes and Noble, 1973). Defined in classic *ut pictura* terms as a 'speaking picture' (p. 101), poetry feasts on its 'sister' (a loaded metaphor in the context of Sidney's biography) inasmuch as it is precisely by virtue of its power to present a 'perfect picture' of the 'particular truth of things' (p. 107) that it claims superiority over other forms of literary expression—history, philosophy or law. Nevertheless, despite its pervasive presence as a metaphor for poetry, painting as such is completely elided: an omission that goes hand-in-hand with the gesture by which, having begun by arguing poetry's cultural centrality as the 'nurse' of all arts and sciences, Sidney almost immediately replaces the, if not unambiguously maternal, at least clearly feminine figure of the nurse with a male personification. This seems moreover tellingly related to the repression of the moment of production in the attack on contemporary dramatists with which the *Apology* both reaches its close and reveals the true source of the anxiety in whose light poetry needs defence in the first place.

22 Bacon, *New Organon*, p. 130.

23 For a classic account of the distinction between primary and secondary qualities, see John Locke, *Essay Concerning Human Understanding*, ed. Alexander Campbell Fraser (1894; repr., New York: Dover, 1959), bk. 2, chap. 8, sections 7-10.

24 This is the central idea behind the 'Copernican revolution' accomplished in the *Critique of Pure Reason*, first introduced in the Transcendental Aesthetic with reference to the concepts of space and time defined as determining the basic form of all objects of experience and to that extent knowledge. What Locke, focused on objects themselves, calls 'qualities' Kant addresses from the viewpoint of the *subject* whose

'transcendental' form is determined by the 'concepts', 'categories', 'anticipations', etc., implicit in the logical structure of all acts of sense and cognition.

25 Cesare Ripa, *Iconologia*, repr. of the Roman edition of 1603 (Hildesheim: Georg Olms, 1970). I cite the digested version of Ripa's descriptive gloss in Edward A. Maser's ed. of the Hertel edition of 1758-60 (New York: Dover, 1971), emblem 50.

26 Rona Goffen notes the link between personified Truth and the *Venus Pudica* in her defence of Titian's treatment of female nudes against feminist charges. See, e.g., *Titian's Women* (New Haven, CT: Yale University Press, 1997), p. 130.

27 Sir Kenneth Clark, *The Nude: A Study in Ideal Form* (1956; repr., Princeton, NJ: Princeton University Press, 1984), p. 116. See too Goffen, *Titian's Women*, pp. 146-157, and the analyses assembled in *Titian's Venus of Urbino*, ed. Rona Goffen (Cambridge: Cambridge University Press, 1997).

28 For a complementary reading of Rubens more generally, see Margaret Deutsch Carroll, 'The Erotics of Absolutism: Rubens and the Mystification of Sexual Violence', in *Representations* 25 (1989), pp. 3-30.

29 For an important formulation of the general theory of reading (and thus of 'cultural texts') on which Bal and Pollock base their political interpretations of Western art history, see Bal's introduction to *Reading Rembrandt*. The central argument is that, since all readings are conducted from our particular, politically situated position in the social and historical world, they inevitably project our own choices, interests, perspectives and socio-historical experience on their objects. Reading is then always political since it constructs the works of past and present as a function of our strategic position relative to other readers and, through them, to the ideologies, institutions and conventions within which they and we are alike defined. A problem with this theory is that, though designed at one level to preempt criticism by assigning whatever flaws other readers may find to all readings as such, it tends at another level to undermine the truth claims Bal also wants to make—most explicitly in the section of the chapter on the 'semiotics of rape' entitled 'Real Rape: The Importance of Telling Stories'. Bal wants it both ways, demanding that stories of 'real rape' be accorded an objectivity she withholds from Rembrandt's work in order (among other things) to avoid having to answer objections she predefines as politically motivated. All of this strikes me as the more unfortunate in that, for the most part, Bal's readings of actual images need no such defence. Nor does the fact that it has taken feminism to make us acknowledge the canon's sexual violence mean that feminism *projects* that violence as a function of its own anachronistic viewpoint. Bal herself returns to all of these issues in *Quoting Caravaggio*, where her 'preposterous' grasp of the dynamic relation between creative past and interpretive present is far more supple, subtle and forgiving.

30 See Bal's discussion of what much of the art historical tradition regards as Rembrandt's 'ugly' female bodies, bodies she rightly sees as emancipated from the conventional male standards of beauty associated with the otherwise all-powerful male gaze (*Reading Rembrandt*, pp. 143-148). Alpers (*The Art of Describing*, pp. 223-224) makes a similar point with reference to Vermeer. Though comparable things arise in southern art, it is possible (and, in view of what I will say later about Baconian as opposed, say, to Cartesian science, even likely) that this reflects a major cultural difference as between Northern and Southern Europe: a difference in turn related to northern 'descriptive' practices as contrasted with the idealisms of southern painting. For a recent development of this thesis, see Berger, *Fictions of the Pose*, pt. 4, 'Rembrandt's Looking-Glass Theater', where Rembrandt's singular yet also distinctively Dutch rejection of Italian models comes to the fore. Especially illumin-

ating is Berger's trenchant critique of Kenneth Clark's sense of the deficiencies of the mere (and often revolting) 'nakedness' of Rembrandt's women as compared with their idealized counterparts in the noble 'nudes' of Italian art (*Fictions of the Pose*, chap. 21, esp. pp. 435-439). Berger's target in this chapter is Clark's *Rembrandt and the Italian Renaissance* (New York: New York University Press, 1966).
31 Roger de Piles, *Abrégé de la Vie des Peintres, Avec des reflexions sur leurs Ouvrages, Et un Traité du Peintre Parfait, de la connoissance des Desseins, & de l'utilité des Estampes* (Paris: François Muguet, 1699), p. 222. See also pp. 156-159.
32 This recalls Rembrandt's notoriously combative relations with his patrons. See Svetlana Alpers, *Rembrandt's Enterprise*, pp. 89-106, Schwartz, *Rembrandt*, and Berger, *Fictions of the Pose*, chap. 2, 'Politics: The Apparatus of Commissioned Portraiture' and pt. 3, 'The Embarrassment of Poses: On Dutch Portraiture'.
33 See Jonathan Brown, *Velázquez: Painter and Courtier* (New Haven: Yale University Press, 1986), pp. 182-183.
34 Bal, *Reading Rembrandt*, pp. 64-86. For congruent readings, see also Nancy J. Vickers,' "This Heraldry in Lucrece's Face" ', *Poetics Today* 6 (1985), pp. 171-184, and Norman Bryson, 'Two Narratives of Rape in the Visual Arts: Lucretia and the Sabine Women', in Sylvana Tomaselli and Roy Porters (eds), *Rape: An Historical and Cultural Enquiry* (Oxford: Blackwell, 1986), pp. 152-173.
35 Bal, *Reading Rembrandt*, p. 84.
36 Ibid.
37 This rebuttal of Bal's claims founders the moment we assume, as Alpers does, that the kind of appropriative violence associated with Rembrandt's portrayal of women is endemic to his art as a whole, whatever the subject. See, e.g., Alpers's discussion of Rembrandt's portrait of his patron Jan Six as an allegory of the sitter's resistance to digestion by the artist (*Rembrandt's Enterprise*, pp. 91-93). But see Berger's refutation in *Fictions of the Pose*, pp. 311-314, the more valuable for engaging the general hermeneutic issue Bal's book raises concerning what happens when the beholder undertakes narrative speculations designed to make a picture say what his or her argument wants it to. Compare Berger's analysis with Bal's overheated discussion of allegorization in the context of 'semiotic appropriation' (*Reading Rembrandt*, pp. 82-86), where interpretive violence figures both as the crime of which she accuses male representations of, e.g., the Rape of Lucretia and as the basis for her own refigurations of their treatments of that theme.
38 Compare this defence of Rembrandt's Lucretia with Goffen's of Titian's (*Titian's Women*, pp. 192-213). Goffen is content to counter charges writers like Bal, Vickers and Bryson make, showing Titian to have been more sympathetic and less exploitive than her adversaries claim. I add that Titian may also *identify* with Lucretia as embodying both a victimhood and a sense of interiority shared with his heroine.
39 For a recent reading of the politics of Lope de Vega's *Fuenteovejuna* that parallels my own, see Mithcell Greenberg, *Canonical States, Canonical Stages*, chap. 2. However, Greenberg's interest in the play is different from mine. Extending to Spain the psychoanalytic interpretation of literature's contribution to political institutions and ideologies he has worked out over the years for France, he sees the rapist (the evil Comendador) as a scapegoat whose sacrificial triangulation dissolves all conscious social difference in the symbolic corporate body of the absolutist monarch who replaces the Comendador. In my reading, by contrast, the villagers' response to the rape *emphasizes* social difference. Nor should we see the play's dénouement as mere repressive mystification. Rather, a quite deliberate bargain is struck, a social

contract Lope does not have to name precisely because the King's exemplary (but also clearly and consciously conventional) conduct conveys the point for him.
40 Bal, *Reading Rembrandt*, pp. 156-176.
41 See Alpers, *The Art of Describing*, pp. xxv-xxvi, and Schama, *The Embarrassment of Riches*, pp. 314-320 and pp. 619-620.
42 See Schama, *The Embarrassment of Riches*, chap. 3, 'Feasting, Fasting, and Timely Atonement'. On the tension between eroticism and moralism in Dutch art, p. 462.
43 This is the burden of the chapter in *Le Visible et l'invisible*, ed. Claude Lefort (Paris: Gallimard, 1964), devoted to 'L'entrelacs—le chiasme' (pp. 172-204), as of the annexed worknotes addressing the relation between *le voyant* and *le visible* (pp. 314-315) and the 'reversibility' inscribed in the chiastic structure by which visual subject and visible object are conjoined (pp. 316-318). Merleau-Ponty adumbrates features of earlier work in the *Phénoménologie de la perception* (Paris: Gallimard, 1945) on the 'intentional' structure of our corporal engagement in and experience of the world as indirectly revealed in the form of the objects of consciousness. The aim is to reverse Brentano's famous formula for intentionality, 'No hearing without something heard, no seeing without something seen', in order to yield the corollary: 'Nothing heard without a hearing, nothing seen without a seeing'. The essential reciprocity thus exposed is related to what leads Alberti, in the second book of *De pictura*, to define painting not merely as a 'mirror of nature', but as the 'fountain of Narcissus': the portrayal of nature is already, by implication, self-portrayal. Nor should we be surprised that the painter who has left us the chiastic gazes of the two Susannas should also be the greatest as well as the most inveterate of all self-portraitists, creating indeed the fundamental idiom of painterly self-portrayal. It is interesting further to observe what becomes of this chiastic structure, borrowed from Merleau-Ponty, in Lacan's work on painting in the chapter of *Les quatre concepts fondamentaux de la psychanalyse* devoted to the *regard* or gaze. Especially suggestive is the section entitled 'Qu'est-ce qu'un tableau?' (pp. 120-135), which opens with a graphic representation of the link between painting and beholder as the chiastic superimposition of opposed Albertian pyramids projected, on the beholder's side, from the position of the geometric 'sujet de la représentation' and, on the painterly side, from the position of the *regard* itself. The 'other' of each projection thus emerges as the base of an opposing pyramid, both pyramids being intersected at an exactly symmetrical point by the 'image' projected by the subject and the *écran* or 'screen' thrown up by the *regard*. But the crucial thing is just that, in this arrangement, the gaze belongs not to the 'subject' by which the image is projected, but instead to the Other placed as it were *en retrait*, on the far side of the image, with the result that it is in fact the beholder who emerges as the object of the gaze rather than the other way around. Buci-Glucksmann touches on this point in *La folie du voir*, pp. 93-95.
44 On iconoclasm in period science, see Braider, *Refiguring the Real*, pp. 169-172.
45 Bacon, *New Organon*, p. 92. The tag from Daniel also serves as the motto for the *Magna instauratio*.
46 For Rembrandt's treatment of this subject, see *Refiguring the Real*, pp. 17-19.
47 See, e.g., *An Essay Concerning Human Understanding*, bk. 2, chap. 11, section 10, where Locke denies animals the power of abstract thought on the grounds that 'we observe no footsteps in them of making use of general signs for universal ideas'.
48 Bacon, *New Organon*, p. 37.
49 William Shakespeare, *The Merchant of Venice*, in *Complete Works*, ed. W.J. Craig (Oxford: Oxford University Press, 1905; repr. 1966) 4.1.223. It is germane to Bacon's problem that, as Portia's notoriously ambiguous judgment emerges, the name

'Daniel' is taken up by other characters, who turn it into triumphant jeering at Shylock's expense.
50 Bacon, *New Organon*, p. 142.
51 Locke, *An Essay Concerning Human Understanding*, introduction, section 6.
52 See too Alpers's epilogue in *The Art of Describing*, where she tempers her hard Baconian interpretation of Dutch 'description' along the lines urged here.
53 On the registration of the beholder in the perspective art of the Renaissance, see Alpers, *The Art of Describing*, pp. xix-xx. It is significant that she raises this issue in the context of seventeenth-century Dutch 'descriptive' art: an at once non-narrative and anti-theatrical art closely related (as she herself observes) to the 'absorptive' art that, following Fried's *Absorption and Theatricality*, we are about to discuss.
54 Michael Fried, *Absorption and Theatricality: Painting and Beholder in the Age of Diderot* (Chicago: University of Chicago Press, 1980), p. 61. For a fuller discussion of the grounds on which I both amend and generalize Fried's insights concerning the aesthetico-philosophical force of 'absorption', see Braider, *Refiguring the Real*, pp. 257-265.
55 Michael Baxandall, *Patterns of Intention: On the Historical Explanation of Pictures* (New Haven, CT: Yale University Press, 1985), p. 102.
56 For Baxandall's complete discussion of the role of Locke's theory of perception in eighteenth-century French painting, see *Patterns of Intention*, chap. 3, 'Pictures and Ideas: Chardin's *A Lady Taking Tea*'. But see too the introduction, 'Language and Explanation', which proleptically extends the Lockean tact with which Chardin represents his lady to his own interpretive engagement with painting itself.
57 Bal, *Reading Rembrandt*, chaps. 8 and 9; on *The Blinding of Samson*, pp. 329-360.
58 Bacon, *New Organon*, p. 39.
59 See the discussion of 'ideas in general' in Immanuel Kant, *Critique of Pure Reason*, trans. Norman Kemp Smith (London: Macmillan, 1929; repr. 1976), pp. 309-314, and *Prolegomena to Any Future Metaphysics*, trans. Paul Carus, rev. James W. Ellington (Indianapolis, IN: Hackett, 1977), pp. 69-70, where the non-experimental character of ideas is directly related to the possibility of metaphysics.
60 Kant, *Critique of Judgment*, p. 185.

Chapter 2

The Fountain of Narcissus: The Ontology of St Paul in Caravaggio and Rembrandt

Conceived with enlightened 'reference to the universe' rather than idolatrous 'reference to man', what the baroque calls truth, the Naked Lady of scientific as well as artistic or allegorical desire, proves at best approximation—the vestige or trace, the image or sign, of something that by its very nature escapes. Truth itself is never so poignantly near as in those Susanna-like moments of ironic self-possession where its personified embodiments look back in token of their enigmatic remoteness.

One lesson to draw is the need to resist the temptation to take the monuments of baroque culture at what we imagine to be face value. The result complicates the revisions to which feminism, Foucaldian social criticism, new historicism or the new art history subject the baroque canon. Like Daniel decoding Nebuchadnezzar's dream or exposing the imposture behind the miracles attributed to the idol of Bel, a major point of contemporary method is to dismantle the cultural past, applying forensic styles of reading designed to unmask unpalatable truths concealed yet also fingered by the deluding appearances with which the artist's hand has cloaked them. But such readings risk engendering a deceptive self-evidence of their own. The naïve realisms of idolatrous projection are not the exclusive province of the pious. In arrogating to themselves the power of dismantling art's impostures, latter day iconoclasts manufacture idols no less coercive, and no less *imaginary*, than the slavish pieties they reject.

As Harry Berger argues in his recent book on Rembrandt, a salient feature of the self-consciously painterly art of the baroque is the often entirely deliberate publication of its own incriminating facture.[1] In a fragment on the one, elusive 'place' to which alone truth properly appears, Pascal (like Descartes before him) invokes the analogy of perspective:

> Thus paintings seen from too far away or too near. And there is only one indivisible point that defines the true place.
> The others are too near, too far, too high or too low. Perspective assigns it in the art of painting, but who will assign it in truth and in morality? (21/55)

As for Berger, the immediate danger Pascal describes is what happens if we get too close. The illusion falls apart: the faces, bodies and places composing the virtual world the artist intends us to see disintegrate to reveal the seemingly random brushstrokes and clots of paint that are in fact all painting is—a point James Elkins colourfully underscores by urging painters' consciousness that what painting is is *shit*.[2] But for an artist or connoisseur, the tension between what art shows and what art is—to use Berger's terms, between the graphic illusions art purveys and the densely textured means that create them—does not negate the artist's accomplishment. On the contrary, the icon's dissolution in the indexical traces of the painter's hand takes on an iconic grandeur whose measure is just the tension to which it witnesses.[3] As Berger observes for Rembrandt, the matter of his impasto is as central a theme as the visual effect it helps produce. Yet what makes the impasto matter is the illusionistic effect that overcomes it only to revert to impasto again.

The discovery that self-evidence is an artifact of at once self-ratifying and self-denouncing imagination is thus endemic to the baroque.[4] Consider, for instance, the era's pervasive fascination with the antinomies of trompe-l'œil. In Andrea Pozzo's spectacular *Allegory of the Missionary Work of the Jesuit Order* (1691-94) on the ceiling of the nave of the church dedicated to the Order's founder (fig. 2.1), the chiliastic mission of St Ignatius is enacted in the illusionistic flight that leads our astonished gaze up through the very matter of the church to the celestial kingdom whose redeeming light already breaks in on the world of yearning darkness here below. Pozzo's is an art of literal make believe: induced to see what is not there, we are persuaded to credit what cannot be true, taking the image *for* a truth that is itself purely imaginary. Yet for all we credit Pozzo's illusion, we never lose sight of the fact that it *is* an illusion: the very wonder such achievements produce underscores the antithetical art on which they trade. The euphoric exertions of the baroque imagination thereby endorse the notorious ambivalence evinced by the duplicitous force of the terms the era used to describe its representations—'likeness', 'image', 'semblance', 'counterfeit', 'art' itself. The hallmark of what contemporary observers conventionally identified as the truth of a given painting is just the illusion it induces and the craft of which that illusion is the index—formal aspects in turn addressed to the beholder's own both physiological and psychological predisposition to be deceived. It is indeed to this last constituent of the truth-effect art promotes that Pascal refers in invoking the need to discover the right perspective point. The truth we perceive in an image is a reflex of where we stand, psychically as well as physically. It is a mirage that dissipates the moment we change position, unmasking the factitiousness of what seems at first so real.

The present chapter aims to explore this ambivalence further in order to develop the underlying *ontology* it simultaneously expresses and informs. As we have seen, this ambivalence is encoded in the basic critical idiom the era deployed to describe the illusions of pictorial art. A logical place to start is accordingly with a parallel terminological dilemma at the heart of early modern aesthetics as a whole.

Fig. 2.1 Andrea Pozzo, *Allegory of the Missionary Work of the Jesuit Order*. S. Ignazio, Rome

One of the trickier problems facing students of early modern culture is the ambiguity surrounding the key term *imitation*. The word arises in a variety of contexts, from aesthetics to education and from the philosophy of language to the theology of Christ. But while the verbal form remains constant, encouraging us to imagine it refers to a single activity, the term has in fact two linked yet distinguishable meanings. On one hand we find what a wide range of both literary and art historians—Thomas Greene, Louis Marin, Michael Baxandall, Norman Bryson or, most recently, Berger—suggest we should consider the naïve or primitive notion of *imitatio naturae*.[5] In this view, obedience to Aristotle's *Poetics* and Horace's *Ars poetica* leads early modern theorists to insist that the primary 'rule of art' is the mirror-like replication of the external world canonically associated with painting. On the other hand, again in the wake of writers like Greene, Marin, Baxandall, Bryson or Berger, we meet the theoretically more sophisticated notion of imitation as the representation less of external nature than of other artworks. In this second view, reinforced by analysis of the early modern cult of classical *ekphrasis*, the fundamental engine of aesthetic creation becomes the Renaissance practice of poetic *aemulatio*, the simultaneously reverent and competitive reproduction of authoritative ancient example.

Both senses are abundantly attested by period sources.[6] Renaissance theorists of painting and poetry alike insist both that the spring of art lies in the imitation of nature and that *good* art (that is, successful imitation) must go to the school of time-honoured precedent. Poetry is consistently defined by a power of illusion theorized by analogy with painting: as Sidney puts it in his *Apology* (1595), voicing the central presumption informing the whole tradition, poetry is 'an art of imitation, for so Aristotle termeth it in his word *mimesis*, that is to say a representing, counterfeiting, or figuring forth—to speak metaphorically, a speaking picture'.[7] Yet what poets invent and compose must always be seen in the heroic 'light in Troy'—with an eye to the example of Homer and Virgil, Horace or (as time goes by) Tasso, Shakespeare and Racine. The work is measured against the standard literary ancestry sets. Similarly, painting is defined (rather more self-evidently) as the illusionistic reproduction of visible nature, a notion played out in the solemn recycling of classical legends about bunches of grapes so lifelike birds peck at them or women so ravishing beholders fall helplessly in love. Nevertheless, the perfection of pictorial art demands that painters learn to paint in every sense *after* the great masters of the past. Artists are thus expected to look to the achievements of Zeuxis and Apelles as recorded in Pliny or, once Vasari's *Vite* (1550; revised in 1568) establishes a modern canon of like stature, Michelangelo, Titian and Raphael as a guide to present practice.

Albeit with noteworthy exceptions and second thoughts, the naïve view of imitation prevailed among historians from the Romantics to the structuralist revolution of the 1960s and early 1970s. It was therefore taken for granted that the basis of early modern painting and poetry alike is *imitatio naturae*, aimed (in Sidney's words once more) at reproducing the 'particular truth of things'.[8] This did not prevent scholars from attending to formal values in the operation of models and precedents drawn from iconographic tradition or in the search for documentable sources and influences in painters' or poets' work. Yet when discussion turned from particular texts and images to their general theory, the ruling presumption was of a kind of transparency. Putting the case in Albertian terms, if with little sense of the complexity of Alberti's idea, image and text were perceived as a mirror or window in which painters and poets make life itself appear, reproduced in its phenomenal integrity.[9]

However, ever since the emergence of structuralist, semiotic and deconstructive models first of texts and then (through disciplinary diffusion of the sort Marin and Bryson embody) of images,[10] this presumed (or at any rate ideal) transparency has given way to a more thinglike opacity. Rather than theorizing images and texts relative to the external world rendered with more or less accuracy, directness and 'truth' in its extra-aesthetic integrity, the focus moved to the works themselves conceived in terms of their mediating formal, material and cultural conditions of possibility. Attention shifts from mimetic features inherent to the work itself as an expression of its supposedly unmediated relation to external nature in order to focus on the at once social and rhetorical codes to which art conforms, the systems of patronage and exchange in which it is enmeshed, the political as well as moral or aesthetic ambitions it serves and the sexual, sociological or confessional overdeterminations to which it is inevitably subject. Seen in this light, the first sense of imitation is bound to seem not only primitive or naïve, but an outright mystification.[11]

The gains this change secured are self-evident. The careful historical reconstructions performed by Greene, Baxandall and Berger, the more iconoclastic attentions of Bryson or, in an explicitly political vein, of W.J.T. Mitchell and Marin, and the accomplishments of feminist students of the early modern period like Griselda Pollock, Mary D. Garrard or Mieke Bal[12] have produced deep insights into the social and cultural negotiations of which images and texts form the deposits, instruments and theatre. Nevertheless, a certain discomfort with some consequences of recent scholarship, in particular as they affect the appreciation of painting, is not simply retrograde. We risk losing sight of something essential to early modern culture, a key to the specific historical difference it makes and to the peculiar witness it bears especially in the form of painting, if we simply collapse imitation as *imitatio naturae* into a version of poetic *aemulatio*. By refiguring what early moderns understood by and practised as natural imitation in terms of a work's relation to the evolving tradition to which it belongs, we neglect how the tradition is driven by just that problematic relation *to the world*—an irreducibly extra-aesthetic world undigested by painterly or poetic representation—theorized as *imitatio naturae*.

It may clarify the point to recall that the distinction between *imitatio naturae* and *aemulatio* largely overlaps that between painting and poetry. Our habit of emphasizing an underlying identity parallels a similar reflex in the period itself: the humanistic theory of art encapsulated in the doctrine *ut pictura poesis*, 'as in painting, so in poetry'.

As Baxandall has shown, inasmuch as *ut pictura* springs from an imitation of classical paradigms designed to recover the lost legacy of ancient literature by reconstructing ancient languages and the texts that preserved them, it was itself a product of humanist *aemulatio*. *Ut pictura* emerges as a controlling preoccupation and assumption in the first place because it was found so to be among the classics: a precedent reinforced by the occasions it offered, in the form of elaborate comparisons and contrasts, for composing model Ciceronian periods.[13] However, the doctrine was also inspired by the sense of painting's peculiar privilege as an expression of what Aristotle and Horace taught humanists to think of as the core of the ancient philosophy of art, namely, *imitatio naturae*. The same classical sources that induced early humanists to compare painting and poetry further urged the centrality of the imitation of nature as the fount of poetic as well as pictorial creation. And where was nature more vividly portrayed than in the work of Giotto and Botticelli, Michelangelo, Titian and Raphael, living reincarnations of the lost illusionistic art so tantalizingly evoked in Pliny's accounts of the legendary Zeuxis, Pamphilos and Apelles?

Yet to grasp *ut pictura*'s testimony, we must remember that, for all the doctrine argued painting's primacy, encoding poetry's subordination in the very syntax of the presiding trope, in practice painting answered to poetic example, and in particular to the idealized patterns of heroic conduct seen in the glorious light in Troy. One sign of this reversal is the universally acknowledged preeminence of 'history' painting: the representation, as Rensselaer Lee puts it, of 'significant human action', the exemplary deeds recorded in epic verse, classical mythology and holy scripture.[14] Another is the quibble in Roger de Piles's *Abrégé de la vie des peintres* (1699) about just what it is in nature painters are supposed to imitate. Piles rejects the inevitably defective particulars of ordinary experience, written off as 'the poverty of ordinary nature', in favour of what the tradition calls 'la belle nature'. The proper object of painterly imitation is thus nature 'rectified' in conformity with the creative 'principle' or 'intention' to which she attempts to adhere in accordance with standards of beauty, nobility and grace whose source lies wholly beyond the evidence available to mere natural sight—in free powers of insight, 'invention', judgment and creative 'design' for which poets supply the type.[15]

It is to quibbling of this sort that we owe the Aristotelian commonplace concerning the pleasure we take in the imitation even of 'distressful' things ('the basest animals and corpses') we would look on with horror in real life.[16] But such quibbles also yield interest in a second legend concerning Zeuxis, one that rivals (and contextualizes) the story about the image of grapes birds tried to eat. Commissioned to paint a picture variously identified as Helen or Venus—not merely the most beautiful woman who ever lived, but the very image of womanly beauty itself—Zeuxis avoided the course his picture of grapes would predict. Rather than portray the most beautiful woman he could find, he selected the finest features from a number of women in order to compose the closest possible approximation to a finally ideal and therefore inimitable loveliness.[17] The illusionistic skill the tale of grapes celebrates ultimately serves an idealism quite opposed to it—an idealism for which the work of Homer far rather than that of Zeuxis supplies the authoritative repository. To be sure, as David Summers explains, this emphasis on painting's 'ideal' power to surpass mere natural givenness is endemic not only to early modern discourse *about* art, but to the intrinsic language of art itself. By drawing on the painter's disciplined yet unconditional imaginative power to perceive and reproduce eternal patterns of beauty that, though artfully made available to visual sense, nonetheless wholly exceed the range of natural experience, painting expounds and extols its incontrovertible appeal. The move also explains the intellectual basis for the painterly practices that determine the prestige of Summers's hero Michelangelo.[18] The fact remains that, as Michelangelo's own dual status as painter and poet reminds us, the idealism painting embraces is not exclusively its own. By decreeing the essential 'sisterhood' of the arts, Renaissance aestheticians and their baroque and neoclassical epigones minimize differences inimical to the finally poetic moral purpose and canons of beauty to which both arts conform.[19]

Of course, the parallel reductions of painting to literary example effected in the aesthetic writings of the sixteenth and seventeenth centuries and in historical and semiotic theory today run in opposite directions. *Ut pictura* tends to sublimate the world encountered in everyday life. Whence not only the ambivalence informing Piles's double use of the word nature itself, but the materialist Hobbes's equivocation between the uppercase Nature that wills royalism as a way out of the impasse of political association and the state of 'meer nature' that engenders the anarchic 'war of all against all' from which royalism rescues us.[20] Conversely, by subjecting painting to the same iconoclastic referral to underlying conditions as it does poetry, contemporary criticism explodes the pretty delusions of aesthetic fiction to reveal the brute contingencies (social, sexual and political as well as formal and material) such fiction conceals. Still, diametrically opposed as the intentions behind *ut pictura* and contemporary cultural theory may be, the net effect is the same. By recasting painting as a version of poetry, each contrives to make painting invisible: the one by forcing painterly imitation to conform to the idealizing canons of poetic taste; the other by performing a deconstruction painting already effects not simply despite, but as a reflex of its mimetic force.

Against this background I propose to look at two pictures by painters famous precisely for their uncompromising resistance to poetic taste. The first is Caravaggio's *Conversion of St Paul* in the Cerasi Chapel in Rome. The second, by Rembrandt, also takes a Pauline theme: the late *Self-Portrait as the Apostle Paul*. That both should invoke Pauline example is doubly significant. At one level, the invocation attests to the continuing place of textual (more specifically, scriptural) imitation. Both images are history paintings, if iconoclastic ones, devoted (with an Albertian emphasis on the prefix) to representing antecedent writings, that is, making them present anew.[21] At another level, however, the iconoclasm both bring to this task reflects the iconoclastic force of the texts from which they draw inspiration. Attention to Paul's authority will then help us see how Caravaggio and Rembrandt's iconoclastic relation to historical imitation is grounded in the nature—better, the metaphysics—of painterly *as opposed* to literary, historical or poetic mimesis. In this sense, painting encodes a metaphysics of *immanence* that, far from underwriting canons of beauty allowing the image to transcend guilty identification with 'meer nature' in the name of aesthetic idealism, endorses commitment to worldly nature reproduced in the fallen state from which poetry would raise it. By challenging the reductions to which both the *ut pictura* tradition and our own more cynical sense of aesthetic expression subject pictorial art, these two paintings will enable us to acknowledge at once the aesthetic integrity and the philosophical force with which early modern painting is invested.[22]

Let us begin by recalling the powerful ambivalence that greeted Caravaggio and Rembrandt alike. Contemporary accounts of Caravaggio, from Van Mander's *Het Schilder Boeck* of 1604 through Bellori's *Vite de' pittori, scultori e architetti moderni* of 1672 to Piles's *Abrégé* of 1699, consistently describe him as at once the age's greatest exponent of naturalism and the man almost single-handedly responsible for destroying the art of painting. Caravaggio's outstanding *naturalezza* and his baleful influence on the art to come are in fact two sides of the same coin. Commentators thus granted that he helped painting recover from the excesses of the mannered, anti-naturalistic style inherited from Michelangelo, Parmigianino or Bronzino. By painting rigorously 'after nature', working (like Rembrandt) directly from live models in the studio,[23] Caravaggio brought painting back to earth. In the process, he restored a proper respect for the human body's native colours and attitudes. Further, through the revolutionary intensity of his *chiaroscuro*, he gave the human body a dramatic relief that fused a heightened sense of reality with expressive effects of great poignancy and power.

The problem, as Bellori observes, was that, in this laudable effort to revive the attentive study of nature, Caravaggio 'made no attempt to improve on [its] creations'.[24] On the contrary, taking nature as his only guide, he deliberately chose models for a visual interest rooted in the coarse irregularity of ordinary human beings, and then made a point of reproducing them exactly as he saw them. The procedure inspired the oft-told tale of painting people casually met in the street, first in the early genre scenes featuring cardsharps, fortunetellers and mischievous boys, and later in votive images. The scandalous potential of this procedure emerges in *The Death of the Virgin* (c. 1605-06; fig. 2.2), a painting shocking not only because Caravaggio's model was alleged to have been a prostitute, but also because he gave the dead Virgin the bloated features of a corpse, compromising the legend of the bodily Assumption the picture rehearsed.[25] Caravaggio's defiance of the legend of the Virgin's Assumption amplifies his notorious predilection for dwelling on the callused hands, dirty feet, bald heads and scruffy bearing of the peasants and laborers he posed in the roles of saints, martyrs or the heroes of classical mythology. And what was true of the choice and treatment of models was just as true of his practice of composition generally. Whence the constant complaints about the awkwardness of his subjects' attitudes and gestures, the want of grace, decorum or design, and above all the lack of *invenzione*, of a freely-imagined aesthetic *idea* going beyond the figures arranged before his eyes to capture the moral beauty it was painting's essential mission to make visible.[26]

The charges directed at Rembrandt mirror point for point those leveled at Caravaggio. Piles writes that Rembrandt

> owed such knowledge as he acquired of his profession to the sharpness [*bonté*] of his wit and to his reflections. One must nevertheless seek in his works neither correctness of design nor a taste for the antique. He himself said that his only goal was the imitation of living nature, making nature consist solely in created things as we see them.[27]

Piles does allow skill at portraiture: 'he made a large number of portraits endowed with surprising force, suaveness and truth'—paintings that resemble his exquisite etchings in the remarkable adroitness with which they 'express both

Fig. 2.2 Caravaggio, *The Death of the Virgin*. The Louvre, Paris

the flesh and the life'. Piles further concedes that, despite a failure 'to choose what is beautiful in Nature', Rembrandt 'displayed wonderful art in the imitation of present things', and most notably in his portraits that, 'far from fearing comparison with any Painter, often eclipse, by their presence, those of the greatest Masters'. Yet the very thing that made for the remarkable 'presence' of his portraits—their uncanny power to confront us with autonomous individuals grasped in their unique and irreducible singularity—fatally flawed his art: the refusal to rise above the world as he saw it, sacrificing the claims of beauty on the altar of fidelity to mere 'present things'.[28]

The alleged causes for these failings are themselves instructive. In Caravaggio's case, the deliberate ugliness he cultivated was adduced to his troubled melancholic temperament: it was seen to spring from the same source as the infamous hubris and paranoia evinced by his incessant quarrels with patrons, his dubious sexual proclivities and the violent behaviour that led him to kill a man in a tavern fight.[29] Piles's Rembrandt is likewise a sorry object-lesson ('une preuve tres-sensible') of 'the power that habit and education exert over natural gifts'. Despite possessing tremendous native talents, Rembrandt had the misfortune of being Dutch, a citizen of a nation proverbial for its phlegmatic *pesanteur* and lack of imaginative vivacity—traits compounded by association with the riff-raff of the lower middle classes and the Jewish quarter rather than nobler spirits from more exalted orders of society.[30] However, what was never alleged in either case was something inherent to painting itself, something precisely linked to that awesome presence no one could help acknowledging. And it is just here that attention to the inspiration both Caravaggio and Rembrandt draw from the New Testament tradition of Paul proves illuminating. For the ambivalence with which contemporary observers responded to their paintings is shared by the painters themselves as reflected in the choice of texts informing the paintings I have singled out for a closer view.

The Cerasi *Conversion of St Paul* (1601; fig. 2.3) is a compendium of Caravaggiesque traits. There is the weary attendant with his worried wrinkled brow and large workman's hands, looking down in amazement at the prostrate Paul while holding the head of a plain piebald horse quite unlike the noble purebreds other painters use. There is the strained muscularity of the general composition, bodies packed into a space whose claustrophobic exiguousness is emphasized by the elimination of all distance between image and beholder, in effect dumping the fallen saint into the viewer's lap.[31] The painting also creates powerful *chiaroscuro* effects, generating a stark contrast between the ambient darkness and the strong light descending at a sharp angle from the right to illuminate the attendant's head, the horse's flank and the ecstatic saint. Finally, there is the wrenching anamorphosis dictated in part by the painting's location, adjusting the figures to allow for the position of a beholder kneeling before the altar in the side chapel where the image hangs, but also expressing what all of the picture's features derive from their source in Acts 22.5-11.

The painting's anamorphic effect reenacts the conversion it helps depict by requiring a physical displacement parallel to the spiritual turn it portrays.[32] In the text from Acts, knocked from his horse by the sudden burst of celestial light, the saint is driven from the road of his persecutory intent—both stopped in his tracks and turned in the entirely new direction of devoted apostleship. In keeping with this text, Caravaggio now redirects the *beholder* by reconfiguring our physical relation to the canvas. Forcing us to foresake our normal, frontal posture relative to the image in favour of one dictated by the painting's placement,

Fig. 2.3 Caravaggio, *The Conversion of St Paul*. Cerasi Chapel,
S. Maria del Popolo, Rome

above us and to the right, on the side wall of the chapel where it hangs, the painting underscores the position we need to adopt in order to see it properly: that, precisely, of kneeling before the altar, and so of abandoning our daily pursuits in an act of humble supplication. And what makes for the dramatic necessity of this turn is our 'place' in the broadest sense: not just our position relative to the altar, but our home in the fallen world of carnal darkness that both image and beholder share.

As Howard Hibbard argues, the powerful contrast the *Conversion* sets up between breaking light and choking darkness reflects growing theological conflicts of great contemporary moment. Oriented by the downward, incomprehending gaze of the unenlightened attendant, the painting inscribes the severe Pauline and Augustinian theology of original sin soon to take shape in the unyielding Jansenist opposition to the crypto-Pelagian doctrine of 'efficacious grace' fathered by the Jesuit Luis de Molina.[33] Endorsing the austere, misanthropic contempt for mere 'worldy' things (*contemptus mundi*) that Pascal later champions, the *Conversion* portrays the gratuitous and unmerited gracine intervention alone capable of saving creatures like us from the hell of our carnal natures. This produces a profound paradox: the painting represents a light whose origin is wholly hidden. Paul may once have seen that light, becoming a spokesman and martyr for its sake. But the light Paul saw is now as invisible to beholders of Caravaggio's picture as to the bewildered attendant looking down at his sprawling master, away from the source concealed to the right above his head.

The sense of paradox surrounding the picture's light source suggests that, beyond lending dramatic weight to the story of Paul's conversion, Caravaggio's refusal to surrender to the idealizing prettiness of conventional art receives a Pauline sanction. We could of course cite many places in Paul's writings as keys to Caravaggio's interpretation of the instigating passage in Acts. The dominant theme of Paul's teachings, hammered out in all of the Epistles, is the unceasing contest between Godly light and worldly darkness. Paul expresses this contest in many different ways, and in particular as a series of cosmic oppositions pitting the living spirit of Christian love against the mortal letter of Hebrew law, the true righteousness of inner faith against deluded reliance on outward carnal works or the freedom granted by obedience to Christ against the bondage of unillumined human will and desire. But perhaps the clearest text, one moreover whose mirror conceit speaks directly to baroque sensibility, is 1 Corinthians 13.12: 'For now we see through a glass, darkly; but then face to face: now I know in part; but then shall I know even as also I am known.'[34] This verse articulates the tension figured elsewhere as the contrast between the 'invisible things of God' (Romans 1.20) and the idolatrous practices of the 'carnally minded' (Romans 8.6), those whose perspective on the otherwise plain text of creation is occluded by selfish reference to fleshly understanding. It thereby expresses not only the nature of the world of 'visible' as opposed to 'invisible' things, but also the absolute limits set on the visible world as a condition of natural vision. These limits are the dominant theme of Caravaggio's *Conversion*, rehearsed and confirmed by the very realism with which the painting so forcefully projects the story from Acts into the carnal world we inhabit. The presence Caravaggio brings to the portrayal of Paul's conversion becomes the antithetical index of our alienation from the truth this presence evokes, a loss as total and incontrovertible as the dramatic immediacy that denounces it.

The Cerasi *Conversion* thus tells its story in such a way as to comment on, and condemn, at once the art that rehearses it and the hellish carnal nature that requires such a rehearsal to image the light that escapes worldly nature. To this extent, the picture expounds the self-loathing evinced elsewhere in the self-directed erotic violence Caravaggiesque painting makes its own. One of the more disquieting features of *The Death of the Virgin* is the central figure's sexual availability: the literally prostituted model enacts a doubly illicit desire as representing both the Virgin and a corpse. But still more emphatic, and characteristic, are the mingled horror and relish expended on the beheading in the *Judith and Holofernes* of 1599 (fig. 2.4): a narrative that enfolds a barely concealed castration-strangulation fantasy legible not only in the ambiguous intensity of Judith's expression, but in the fact that Caravaggio casts himself in the

Fig. 2.4 Caravaggio, *Judith and Holofernes*. Galleria Nazionale d'Arte Antica, Rome

role of Holofernes. Decapitation is in fact a compulsory theme of Caravaggio's self-portraits. He returns to in *David and Goliath* (c. 1609-10), where the model (and presumed 'catamite') who poses as the youthful Biblical hero brandishes his master's severed head. Above all is the self-portrait worked into the infinitely recursive *Medusa* (c. 1597; fig. 2.5) whose face, frozen in the moment of petrified self-recognition when she meets her own countenance in the reflecting surface of Perseus' burnished shield, offers a spectacle we should not see since to see it is to be likewise turned to stone. The *Medusa*'s uncanny specularity

Fig. 2.5 Caravaggio, *Medusa*. The Uffizi, Florence

condenses the entire argument of Carvaggiesque self-portraiture, which is of course an argument about the nature of painting itself. Seen for what it truly is, in its native lineaments, the art of painting indulges a monstrous appetite (both the painter's and the beholder's: the picture presents the Medusa's mirror image rather than her severed head as such) that would destroy us were we to gaze on it directly, undisguised by heroic displacement.

Such is the spirit in which Caravaggio can be seen to incorporate a Pauline interpretation of the art he brings to bear in the Cerasi *Conversion* and the self-portraits alike. But what of Rembrandt? Rembrandt *being* Rembrandt, it will come as no surprise that for him, too, the key lies in a self-portrait—indeed, the late *Self-Portrait as the Apostle Paul* (1661). Paul's is hardly the only likeness Rembrandt assumed; yet the theme has a special relevance, revealing something deep about his conception of the nature of his art. To see this relevance, however, we must grasp the import not merely of this particular self-portrait, but of self-portraiture in general. In the form in which it has come down to us from the

Renaissance, the genre of the self-portrait is a kind of precipitate of the naturalism it exploits. That Rembrandt should portray himself at all, let alone as the apostle Paul, is thus in the first instance an expression of the broader naturalist goals his painting serves.

The commitment to self-portraiture reflects what has been a commonplace of Western art history since the inception of the discipline in Leon Battista Alberti's *De pictura* of 1435: namely, that both a major achievement and central precondition of Renaissance art is a certain appropriation of space.[35] What most obviously and immediately sets Renaissance painting apart from its medieval precursors, devoted as these remain even in Giotto to the planar surfaces they adorn, is mastery of the techniques of three-dimensional representation, miming the prospective structures of natural visual experience. As Berger insists with some heat, combating the kind of iconoclastic consensus we met with in chapter 1 concerning the presumed monolithic oppressiveness of early modern visual culture, the techniques involved are multiform and produce a wide variety of moods and effects.[36] In addition to an increasingly supple command of the projective geometry required to induce a coherent sense of apparent distances, we find shading and foreshortening designed to model the volumes and proportions of living persons, the objects and accessories with which they surround themselves and the rooms and landscapes they inhabit. The successful modeling of bodies and environing spaces is in turn enhanced by a regular treatment of light sources and the minute description of the reflective properties of the different materials painters portray and of the media (tempera, oils) used to portray them. Further, as Baxandall and, from a somewhat broader viewpoint, the cultural historian Lisa Jardine have shown, the art involved draws deeply on collateral habits and interests that are not strictly artistic: an eye trained in discriminating the intrinsic qualities of distinctive individuals, whether human, animal or the products of skilled workmanship; a growing taste for (and access to) worldly goods both of the sort paintings increasingly depict and of the sort paintings constitute in themselves; or adroitness at gauging volumes or assessing the relative price of different metals, stones and textiles.[37] But however rich and multifarious its sources and components, what distinguishes Renaissance art as a whole, making a decisive threshold that justifies our insistence on the advent of a clearly demarcated period, is a single dominant effect. We are, from an art historical viewpoint, finally and unmistakably in the Renaissance the moment painters succeed in methodizing the construction of a convincing graphic simulacrum of 'real' non- or extra-pictorial space. Nor is this merely a matter of method. The illusion of three-dimensional space becomes routine, prescribing not just a consistent aim, but a normative visual discourse to which painters automatically conform regardless of genre, theme or intent—the essential and universal presumption of Western artistic production.

To paint at all means to paint in three dimensions, with the result that, once past the heroic experimental age of the Netherlandish and Italian fifteenth century, the art it takes to do so, the fact of aesthetic mediation, goes curiously out of focus. Many scholarly quarrels stem from this lack of focus. To take one weighty example, in denouncing the prevailing 'replication' theory of art, Bryson is certainly right to claim that what passes for replication is a semiotic *art*: what tradition has tended to conceptualize as neutral reproduction is in fact an illusion. But the illusion was just the point; and so was the art it took to create it. The ideal of replication *made* the art, which is indeed why replication was so highly valued *as* an art, independent of what it represented. The naïveté Bryson assumes is of his own making. What is more, in foisting on the Renaissance a facile notion of an extra-verbal image supposed to escape the reach of signifying words, he constructs an equally facile account of its semiotic alternative, as though image and word, imitation and signification, did not intimately shape each other as twin faces of a single problematic. By claiming a suppression of art as semiosis, Bryson not only obscures the early modern semiotics of art; he masks a productive tension integral to the early modern sense of what imitation consists of and demands, symbolically as well as formally. In recalling the spatial illusionism on which Renaissance art depends, I aim thus to recover something of the remarkable intelligence that pervades it as an expression of the special kind of self-conscious symbolic experience naturalism provides.

A necessary correlate of the painterly projection of three-dimensional space is the imposition of a specific point of view inhabited by an incarnate human observer. It is a mistake to identify this point of view too closely with the strict mathematical constructions favoured by Italian art. As codified by Alberti, defining the standard procedure applied in Italy from the fifteenth century on, the key to the effect of three-dimensional space is indeed the geometry of linear perspective. Yet other models exist, some of them, like those adopted by Alberti's Netherlandish contemporaries, Jan van Eyck and Roger van der Weyden, far looser and more 'empirical' than their Italian counterparts.[38] Moreover, landscapes, large-scale architectural interiors and historical panoramas often orchestrate multiple perspectives in order to accommodate the variety of views and points of focus such themes entail.[39] Nor can Albertian geometry adequately account for the range of moods and postures individual paintings assign their beholders. The specialized roles observers perform in the presence of a given image and the corresponding characters or identities they may be led to assume are subject to a wide spectrum of variation and nuance, depending on the kind of scenes or persons a painting portrays, the genre to which it belongs, the moral, votive or political function it serves, where it is placed, how it is hung or (as in Rembrandt's *Susannas*, royal portraits, images of Christ as the sacrificial Man of Sorrows or Jan Steen's *Oyster-Eating Girl*) the intensity with which it directs viewers' attention back on themselves by making them the self-conscious objects of pictorial scrutiny.[40] Nevertheless, all of these modes and effects are grounded in a single fact: the adoption of an incarnate viewpoint demanded as a condition of three-dimensional art.

It is this necessary formal feature of Renaissance art that justifies speaking of an *appropriation* of space construed as an act of seizure or usurpation—a more or less violent making one's own. Such is the motive underlying Alberti's otherwise baffling characterization of painting, in the second chapter of *De pictura*, as the pool or fountain of Narcissus. Painting, he claims, is not only the highest, but the *original* of all the arts:

> Indeed, hardly any art, except the very meanest, can be found that does not somehow pertain to painting. So I would venture to assert that whatever beauty there is in things has been derived from painting. Painting was honoured by our ancestors with this special distinction that, whereas all other artists were called craftsmen, the painter alone was not counted among their number. Consequently I used to tell my friends that the inventor of painting, according to the poets, was Narcissus, who was turned into a flower; for, as painting is the flower of all the arts, so the tale of Narcissus fits our purpose perfectly. What is painting but the act of embracing by means of art the the surface of the pool?[41]

What initially recommends the Narcissan metaphor is paranomasia: Alberti is seduced by the pun on 'flower' that drives the pseudo-syllogism (or enthymeme) ornamenting the hubristic claims he makes on painting's behalf. Painting is the flower of all the arts; Narcissus (so Ovid reports at *Metamorphoses* 3.509-10) turned into a flower; the inventor of painting was therefore Narcissus. But the syllogism's failure to equate already warns us that more is at stake than painting's priority as the original, the highest and therefore the flower of the arts. The deeper point is what *grants* it this preeminence, and for a start its new-found (or, as Italian humanists liked to insist, newly recovered) status as *imitatio naturae*. Painting is a mirror of nature, offering the world a reflecting surface of the sort in which Narcissus lost his soul in misdirected self-contemplation. The analogy's appropriateness is thus keyed to the power of illusion granted by the art of linear perspective it is Alberti's historic mission to codify.

But even this fails to keep pace with Alberti's free associations; and it fails precisely because it neglects the *artfulness* that sustains painterly imitation. For all it is said to mirror external nature, painting is not in fact a mirror at all. More specifically, to address a point Leonardo raises in his notebooks, art does not mechanically reproduce, as an actual mirror must, whatever happens to stand before it. It will (and can) only 'reflect' what the artist consciously chooses to represent in it.[42] But this is where the otherwise stretched allusion to the legend of Narcissus comes into its own. What most fundamentally determines Narcissus' relevance is the work of art conceived in Heidegger's punning spirit as at once the product of the artful hand that makes it and the workly process the completed artwork sets in train.[43] Painting's very success as a self-forgetful mirror of nature, effaced by the vivid visual presence it bestows on the things it portrays, invokes a corollary notion of *self*. For it takes an artist to convert nature into representation, and nowhere more centrally than in the kind of art Alberti's treatise undertakes to codify: the art of one-point linear perspective. If, as Alberti supposes, the primary aim is to create the illusion of a natural world unfolding in the three dimensions of natural optical experience, the projective geometry involved affixes to the world so portrayed a negative impression of the artist's face as a formal precondition. Insofar as the illusion of a third dimension implies the adoption of a definite perspective, the world that arises in the shape this prescribes implies the person of the artist from whose angle we imagine we see it.

The ultimate thrust of Alberti's Narcissan metaphor is that portraiture and self-portraiture are inextricably linked as twin facets of a single phenomenon: the one entails the other as its counterpart and consequence. One index of this link is a commonplace to which Summers alludes in an important discussion of the two-faced 'spiritual' reference of physiognomic truth in Renaissance Italian portraiture: *ogni dipintore dipinge se*—every painter paints himself.[44] In part because he invokes the formula in the context of Quattrocento art, the ideology with which Summers identifies the commonplace is Neoplatonism. The point then, for him, is the way in which the aphorism draws attention to the imaginative gifts and rational intelligence by which each painter distinguishes him or herself as the source of a specific style, a characteristic vision, a personal power of insight, judgment and design, a self-determined moral identity and the at once inimitable and transcendental *idea* of which all of these constitute material expressions.[45] We do not in this sense need to see the artist's face in order to grasp the essential character of his or her inspiration since the painted face is the correlate of the Neoplatonic idea that lies both behind and beyond it. Still, as Summers concedes by locating the origins of Quattrocento Neoplatonism in the rise of painterly naturalism and thus in the pragmatics of point of view on which naturalism depends, the idealism he highlights is as such the byproduct of its opposite. Summers is certainly right to suggest, echoing Erwin Panofsky's early monograph on 'perspective as a symbolic form', that the 'definition of point of view' integral to naturalist art 'raised a paradox: that the "objective" world is only visible from the standpoint of a subject, that we may only see how things "really are" from a point of view'.[46] And he is just as right to see in this subjectivity the licence for the idealist turn that Michelangelo and Raphael give painting in the high Renaissance. Yet the corollary also applies: the subjective structure required as a paradoxical condition of naturalist objectivity entails the reciprocal objectification of the subject of naturalist portrayal.

All of which explains why the moment we have the sensation of real three-dimensional space, whether in the free, empirical mode of the Netherlands or in the more strictly geometric constructions of Italy, we get the convention of the 'signature portrait'. The depiction of a three-dimensional world initiates the tradition of artists peering back from unexpected corners of the world they depict.[47] As attested by the mirror registering Jan van Eyck's testamentary presence in *The Wedding Portrait of the Arnolfini* (1434; figs. 2.6 and 2.7) or Raphael's slyly sidelong likeness in the right foreground of *The School of Athens* (1510; figs. 2.8 and 2.9), to look at a painting *by* van Eyck or Raphael already virtually amounts to looking *at* van Eyck or Raphael since it is from their viewpoint that the painting's spatial illusion wells up, like water from a fountain or pool.

Latent then in the Renaissance appropriation of space is the logic of implication through which space and the appropriating person—through which space as a personal *proprium* and the person whose implicit property it is—invoke each

The Fountain of Narcissus

Fig. 2.6 Jan van Eyck, *Wedding Portrait of the Arnolfini*. National Gallery, London

Fig. 2.7 Jan van Eyck, *Wedding Portrait of the Arnolfini* (detail with artist's self-portrait)

Fig. 2.8 Raphael, *The School of Athens*. Stanza della Segnatura, The Vatican Palace, Rome

other as complements. But I want to indicate something more: not only how space promotes person as a necessary condition of its own appropriative realization, but also how person itself, as a condition, is in turn productively (because dialectically) called in question.

Fig. 2.9 Raphael, *The School of Athens* (detail with artist's self-portrait)

Renaissance art appropriates space by indexing it to person. But person is itself a byproduct of the appropriative form, as dependent thereon as the space that emerges as its property. Self-portraiture (whether in visual or verbal form, as indexed to a Rembrandt or, as Joel Fineman shows in his book on the 'invention of poetic subjectivity' in the Sonnets, to a Shakespeare) is where the incipient chiasmus described by the relation between visual object and visualizing subject comes explicitly to light.[48] However, the discovery or (to play, as Fineman does, on the term's dual register in classical rhetoric) the *invention*, that is, both the creation and the retrieval, of the person of the artist is inevitably belated.[49] It is only when working back from the appropriated world that we meet the face its form implies; and this belatedness reveals an asymmetry we have to reckon with.

Consider the case of Rembrandt. Rembrandt's face, available in some seventy-five versions in multiple guises and media composed over four decades,[50] is of interest not simply in its own right, but because it is perceived to be the source of other, prior images in which it does not nominally figure. Some self-portraits are composed in the service of something else, where Rembrandt uses his face as a model for pictures whose ostensible subjects are not Rembrandt himself, but the Prodigal Son (c. 1636; fig. 2.10), the laughing Democritus (late 1660s; fig. 2.11),[51] or indeed St Paul. All of them can, moreover, be appreciated simply as portraits, the kind of picture even so otherwise severe a critic as the neoclassical Piles admired. But the existence of quite so many self-portraits also suggests a response to contemporary demand—the emergence of a market for

Fig. 2.10 Rembrandt van Rijn, *Self-Portrait with Saskia, as the Prodigal Son*. Staatliche Kunstsammlungen, Dresden

likenesses of Rembrandt himself. As Svetlana Alpers caustically reminds us, Rembrandt was unusually quick to grasp the mechanisms determining the financial value of his work, leading him at one point to buy back as many of his prints as he could lay hands on in order to drive up the price.[52] If Rembrandt turned out so many self-portraits, it is surely in part because Dutch patrons wanted them. But why should patrons want them if not for the sake of his other pictures, as images of the author of the sort of work they prized? They are the fruit of speculation in a double sense: paintings born of an interrogation of his art aimed at turning a profit on their association with the kind of pictures we have come to value as 'Rembrandts'.

Rembrandt's face thus depends *from* images we recognize as depending *on* it. But this means that we can never properly grasp the face in the form in and as which it genuinely interests us. The self-portrait marks a displacement it can never overcome not just because self-portraiture implies an infinite regress, the endless succession of yet further portraits of the artist portraying himself, but because of the indelible belatedness of its own self-discovery. And it is finally just to his fascinated and uncompromising awareness of this fact that we owe Rembrandt's status as the archetypal self of modern, post-Renaissance self-portraiture—along with the poetic subjectivity of Shakespeare and the philosophic

Fig. 2.11 Rembrandt van Rijn, *Self-Portrait as an Old Man Laughing*.
Wallraf-Richartz Museum, Cologne

subjectivity of Montaigne or Descartes, one of the three major sources of Western self-understanding. Rembrandt paints his own face so often, so searchingly and in so many modes, moods and guises precisely because the task is hopeless. Many things contribute to this hopelessness, from the inevitable mediations of convention, form and material expression to the simple (yet fundamental) elusiveness or, to borrow Joseph Margolis's term, 'intransparency' of truth itself.[53] But the deepest reason lies in the relational and differential, in a word *dialectical*, character of self inscribed in its emergence as entailment—as arising quite literally beside itself, in the space implied by the forms it makes.

The philosophical articulation of this dialectical predicament has to await Hegel's *Phenomenology of Spirit* or *Mind* (1807). Early modern philosophers get closer than we are accustomed to think. Though deeply opposed in the means they use as in the ends they hope to achieve, Pascal's apologetic *Pensées*

(1670), Spinoza's naturalistic *Ethics* (1677) and the sensualist Locke's pragmatistic *Essay Concerning Human Understanding* (1690) all point to the chiastic reversal at the heart of critical thought.[54] In each of these works, the traditional analysis of knowledge from the standpoint of the known turns inside out to produce a preparatory discussion of its enabling conditions in the self-conscious structure of knowing. It nevertheless remains for Hegel to make the crucial step announced in the preface to the *Phenomenology* when he notes the paradox involved in what was by his time the well-established convention of affixing a preface to the account of philosophical truth. If truth is indeed *truth*, the timeless exposition of the immutable order of things, it should need no prefatory explanation of 'the end the author had in mind, the circumstances which gave rise to the work and the relation in which the writer takes it to stand to other treatises on the same subject'.[55] Yet from Descartes's carefully propaedeutic *Discours* (1637) to the *Prolegomena* (1783) with which Kant prepares the completion of his critical system in the *Critique of Judgment* (1790), philosophy increasingly locates itself in the history of its own discipline as an indispensable preliminary to the work of philosophy as such.[56] If this is the case, it is not just because philosophy is the literary record of other thinkers' thoughts that each new generation is called on to correct; it is because the philosophers of the past *think otherwise* as a reflex of the historical unfolding of thought itself. Philosophy has a history because consciousness is an *act* called forth by a world it both reflects and transforms in the historical works and institutions by which it is expressed.

Yet the philosophical uncovering of thought's incorrigible historicalness is a belated phenomenon: Hegel's critical *anagnorisis*, the moment of chiastic self-consciousness in which he turns the history of philosophy into the philosophy of history, merely explicates what is already latent in Rembrandtesque self-portraiture. This is partly a function of Rembrandt's agonistic sense of his place in the history of art. Rembrandt exhibits indeed an acute historical awareness most exhaustively explored in Berger's *Fictions of the Pose*, where deliberate opposition to the idealist norms of Italian painting is shown to yield a complex second-order practice of his medium. To adopt the Peircean terms Berger favours, because he paints not only from or after, but against the models the Italian Renaissance sets, Rembrandt transforms the art of painting into its own interpretant. In Rembrandt's hands, the self-portrait becomes an at once iconic and indexical discourse that, by challenging, subsumes the systems of meaning in which the environing culture embeds it.[57] But the decisive source of the historical self-consciousness Rembrandt's self-portraits evince is the uniquely intimate relation their unregenerate naturalism sustains with the world as Rembrandt portrays it.

Rembrandt's self-portraits enact the movement of dialectical return that Maurice Merleau-Ponty calls 'l'entrelacs': a chiastic 'interlacing' or criss-cross pattern of reciprocal implication to which Jacques Lacan reverts in the famous seminars on *le regard*.[58] In Merleau-Ponty as in Lacan, self—the 'subject'—arises as *object*, an incorporated precipitate of the world implicitly apprehended in the form that it gives the world in order to have one. What Rembrandt thus tirelessly pursues while remaining unfailingly conscious of his inability to overtake it is the perplexing absence self becomes as a reflex of the visibility it confers on the things it perceives. As Hegel insists, self's innermost meaning stems from its relation to *non*-self, and more specifically to its status as that by which non-self comes to conscious light, as *other*. The first step in knowledge of what I am is then to ask what the *world* looks like, for I am just that point from which the world looks just like that. Yet this in turn implies that all I am is whatever that thing is at which the world *looks back*: I am that embodied being *for* the world implicit in the form in which the world becomes visible *for me*. But if this is so, then the gesture by which self poses the question of its own nature alienates the very thing that makes it matter: its character as the ground of a relation most fully realized solely in the self-evidence it accords its other as such. The project of self-portraiture is defeated by a double mistake: the attempt to see what only the world can see, namely, the thing I am when engrossed in the act of seeing; and self's usurpation of the place of the images that alone reveal its true nature and value since, unlike self, they alone abide and to that extent truly exist.

As a downpayment on the demonstration this thesis requires, we now turn, as promised, to the late *Self-Portrait as the Apostle Paul* (fig. 2.12). What retains our attention is a twofold displacement. We note first of all the displacement caused by the 'as' of the conventional title, an adverb repeatedly used to denote self-portraits. For each 'young Rembrandt with face in shadow' or 'old Rembrandt in a linen cap', there is at least one 'Rembrandt as the Prodigal Son' or 'Rembrandt as an old man laughing'. Insofar as this is a self-portrait as opposed to, say, a depiction of St Paul for which Rembrandt used himself as a model, Rembrandt arrives at the truth of his own face along the bias of analogy. He does not (and it is a telling point of grammer that he cannot) portray himself 'as Rembrandt'. Each pictorial statement of Rembrandt turns out to be an interrogative. The route back to Rembrandt, as origin of the picture we are looking at, is of necessity oblique, tacking here by way of scriptural allusion just as elsewhere it navigates among the multiform queries even his most straightforward self-portraits become as an expression of their temporal and numerical as well as modal multiplicity.

But there is also a second displacement, commenting on the first, which comes by way of the Pauline text (1 Corinthians 13.12-13) that we drew on for Caravaggio's Cerasi *Conversion*: a text that enables us to gloss the light source whose thematic invisibility points the moral of the tired old face the painting proposes in its author's stead, as Paul.[59] As before, I cite the King James Bible, closely modeled here on William Tyndale's revised translation of 1534, with the important doctrinal concession of rendering Tyndale's Lutheran 'love' as a version of the Vulgate's *caritas*:[60]

12 For now we see through a glass, darkly; but then face to face: now I know in part; but then shall I know even as also I am known.

13 And now abideth faith, hope, charity, these three; but the greatest of these is charity.

Fig. 2.12 Rembrandt van Rijn, *Self-Portrait as the Apostle Paul*.
Rijksmuseum, Amsterdam

Already pointing beyond the picture's subject as a self-portrait is the artful care expended on the natural truth of the old man's face: the bulbous nose and oddly pursed lips; the deep wrinkles and folds of the aging skin; the unkempt beard and ungovernable curly hair; the weariness that comes from decades of attentive labor. To begin with, then, there is just this man, 'Rembrandt', emerging from the penumbral ground in all the poignancy of his lonely singularity. Yet however true his appearance may be in purely human terms, this old man, whom we take for Rembrandt, is also the apostle Paul, identified by the turban he wears in token of the Biblical past, the conventional baldness of the furrowed brow, the Hebrew book he holds in his hands and the typological sword protruding from the folds of his cloak in token of the decapitation he suffered for Christ's sake. Even setting aside the fact that, true as it may be, what Rembrandt depicts remains a *pose*, forasmuch as the aged Rembrandt doubles as St Paul, we find cause for further thought.[61]

The direction of the sitter's Pauline gaze provides the focus for deeper reflection. Placed at a slight distance from the plane, the saint (or artist) lifts his tired myopic eyes from his reading. But where does he look? Toward whom, or what, does he transfer his glance? At the moment in which he is portrayed, his eyes turn vaguely in our direction; but the movement begun on the right when he lifts his eyes from his book carries his gaze beyond the painting's spectators toward the source of light behind him, hidden in some indeterminate space off to the left. It is this detail above all that authorizes us to specify the picture's text in the first of Paul's two verses, inscribing the gesture by which the saint turns from the dark glass of this life toward the momentous *then* when, after death, we shall at last gaze on truth face to face. (And let us note in passing how our own gaze now enacts this very death, in the face-to-face encounter prepared for us by a picture more than three-centuries old.) This places Paul's truth in a realm to which no image has access—not only because no painting could ever depict the light that Rembrandt designates as the ultimate source and subject of his work, but also because no human eye could see that light even if it could be represented. The image does not finally speak to our *eyes*, but rather to something other, and inner, to which Paul appeals in the next verse: faith of course, and hope; but above all *charity*—the curious sensation Tyndale calls love.

In the guise of a self-portrait, Rembrandt explores a dilemma that speaks to the essence of Paul's apostolic mission. Paul is a teacher assigned the task of exhibiting Christ's reality as Saviour and as the paradoxically incarnate Word in a world of carnal darkness whose inhabitants will inevitably fail to see, believe and understand—a world where every attempt to represent truth transforms it into a now tragic, now comic travesty. This problem has a special relevance to 1 Corinthians inasmuch as what impels Paul to write the letter is the Corinthians' failure to remember what he had told them during his original visit, face to face, concerning the need to embrace even those sinners whom, on a visit subsequent to Paul's own, the belligerent Peter has excluded from Christ's church.[62]

Love, the Greek *agape* or Latin *caritas*, is invoked at several levels: as the attitude Christ's example enjoins toward outsiders as well as the faithful; as the grounds for Paul's claim versus the hard, unloving Peter; but also, in a transposition St Augustine lays at the very basis of Christian doctrine,[63] as the key to grasping both Paul's original spoken words, the Hebrew text he holds in his hands and the written words sent in an epistle whose necessity and fragility are alike confirmed by the events to which they respond and belatedly try to remedy. Both the contrast asserted in verse 12 (between the now of the dark glass and the later then when, after death, we finally see face to face) and the appeal launched in verse 13 (to faith, to hope and to the loving charity alone capable of helping us sense even now what will only then be truly known) say the same thing: to see what stands before us means looking with eyes other than carnal ones. And what is true of Paul's endlessly iterated words—the ones spoken in Corinth, those of the first epistle supplementing them in his absence, those of the second epistle supplementing the first, and so on down to Augustine's injunction that love is the one true way to Christian doctrine—is all the more applicable to the image Rembrandt sets before us. To understand it—whether as a doctrinal statement in the guise of a self-portrait or as a self-portrait in the guise of the pictorial exposition of a doctrinal dilemma—means sensing in it something other than whatever it is we think we see. For what we see is the mark of something as invisible as the light source that makes the figure in the painting visible in the first place. The painting offers a portrait whose multiform identity inscribes the infinite deferral of the face-to-face encounter it invites. And what is this if not the *true* self it contracts to portray?

As hinted earlier, however, it is crucial to bear in mind that this truth remains *dialectical*. Self surfaces as the belated correlate of its other; the subject is an implicate of the objects it represents and by which alone its creative activity makes itself known and valued. But this means that the face's truth cannot be determined except as lodged beyond itself—not only in the radiance Paul's text locates in the unimaginable light that awaits us after death, but also in the realm of carnal darkness from which the portrait springs as a likeness and token. We have seen how self-portraiture is a reflex of painterly imitation. We now see how this commits it to an appeal to the world of which Rembrandt's naturalism is the symbiotic register: the world it shapes, as Rembrandt's, the uniquely self-designating product of his hand and eye; but, equally, the world it shapes as part of the wider experience in which it finds matter and place. Self-portraits are always at some level interrogations of the art identified with the artist whose image they yield. But this art questions the world to which the artist gives characteristic form. Rembrandt *invents* the world according to Rembrandt, but in the double sense of forging and finding, patenting and coming across.

So it is to the world as Rembrandt finds it—even if, in the end, it takes just the historically determinate figure Rembrandt to do so—that the self-portrait turns in search of the answer to the question it asks. Yet the world the self-portrait meets—what even Pilès acknowledges as the unique mode of presence Rembrandt achieves—is itself a question: the deep ontological question figured as the infinite deferral Paul calls love. It is a truism of our post-Freudian age, though one with which the artists of the baroque were also acquainted, that love is merely the sublimated and therefore mystified form of a darker power: the greedy, destructive erotic drive that at once animates and distorts the art of Caravaggio. Certainly, the reminder underscores the contrast in temperament that, for all tradition has joined them as parallel object-lessons of the excesses to which unenlightened naturalism leads, sets Rembrandt and Caravaggio radically apart. Caravaggio voices the question of love in the angry tones of tortured ambivalence while Rembrandt sounds the gentler note of the quiet Christian charity with which Paul revises the picture of faithless and hopeless estrangement framed in 1 Corinthians 13.12. Still, more significant than the contrast is what Rembrandt shares with Caravaggio: the ontology both see as performatively embodied by the form of painting as such. Paul's text enables the image to espouse not merely authoritative speech about, but the very form of fallen human experience.

This in turn suggests something of what was at stake when artists like Caravaggio and Rembrandt violated the aesthetic norms enshrined in poetic *aemulatio* in the name of an apparently more naïve and primitive sense of imitation: the nature of nature as at once illumined and occluded by the characteristic early modern doubletalk about nature and imitation alike. As hinted earlier, resistance to *ut pictura*'s sublimation of imitation as *imitatio naturae* and, by that means, of certain insights into the nature thus imitated enacts an important shift that gathers speed as the era of the Counter Reformation approaches its apotheosis fand catastrophe in the baroque. And at the heart of this shift lies the problem of immanence—what Heidegger has in mind in saying both that metaphysics remains philosophy's central task and that the world has no outside.[64] There is, in other words, a deep affinity between the defiant version of naturalism found in Caravaggio and Rembrandt and what Spinoza and Pascal aim at, now in an historical exegesis of scripture in the interests of a deified nature that is also a radical naturalization of divinity, now in the Jansenist's simultaneous refusal of the world and assertion of an irremediably hidden God. As Spinoza and Pascal ironically insist, the very ideals in whose name human beings strive to transcend fallen historical experience themselves express that experience.

Poetic *aemulatio* encounters an absolute ontological limit, inscribed in the *imitatio naturae* it aims to rectify and surpass. The only authentic representation of the ideal, of *truth*, is one that espouses the form it transcends, gesturing toward the light as an emergent property of the darkness that obscures it. But where the high aesthetic orthodoxy emanating from Italy sees this as loss, Caravaggio and Rembrandt enable us to recognize a new authority, grounded in the deep philosophical content, and indeed *vocation*, of the art of painting. Nor does this merely substitute a new verbal discipline for the older one, *ut pictura philosophia* taking over where the more conventional *ut pictura poesis* leaves off. The embrace of the Pauline text sets painting free to explore and expound the message for which its innermost formal nature frames it—a message philosophy itself only barely brings to light.

Notes

1 See Berger, *Fictions of the Pose*, pp. 53-58. But note the distinction Berger draws between 'facture', used to 'denote the traces of what the painter did then', and 'texture', designating 'the representation of those traces now visible as part of the painting' (p. 53). The point (developed in more detail in pt. 4, on Rembrandt's self-portraits) is to distinguish the merely instrumental fact of Rembrandt's work as painter, indexed by the physical traces it leaves behind, from the second-order act by which he thematizes those traces. '*Facture* denotes the work of the hand and its traces in the genetic frame of the *énonciation*, "I am painting," while *texture* denotes the represented traces in the fictive frame of the *énoncé*, "I have painted." The distinction lexically sustains and reinforces the severance and alienation of the second from the first. My interest is in the texture that represents the facture rather than in the facture that produced the texture' (pp. 391-392).

2 See, e.g., James Elkins, *What Painting Is: How to Think about Oil Painting, Using the Language of Alchemy* (New York: Routledge, 1999), pp. 136-137.

3 This underlies Berger's distinction between facture and texture. For a broader theoretical-cum-taxonomic discussion to this effect, see Berger's analysis of the four fundamental 'modes' of early modern painting: the 'decorative', where art adorns the culturally prescribed physico-symbolic locales in which it appears and to whose liturgical or political decorum it loyally submits; the 'graphic', where art exceeds its decorative brief for the sake of an illusionistic 'windowing-out' of the picture plane focused on persons, objects and the scenes they inhabit as they 'really' and 'objectively' are in themselves; the 'optical', where representation of things as they are yields to that of how they are seen, a shift in which 'the way they are shown and seen modifies, obscures, or conflicts with their objective structure and appearance'; and the 'textural', where 'the qualities of paint and the traces of the painter's hand are interposed between the eye and the image', *Fictions of the Pose*, pp. 42-58. See, too, the related adaptation of Peirce's 'icon', 'symbol' and 'index', notions on which my own analysis draws, pp. 20-31. For comparable remarks, see Alpers, *Rembrandt's Enterprise*, chap. 1, 'The Master's Touch'.

4 Also see Braider, *Refiguring the Real*, chap. 5, 'Idols of the Mind: Baroque Illusion, Theatrical Persuasion, and the Aesthetics of Iconoclasm in Jan Steen'. Buci-Glucksmann's *La folie du voir* knocks on this door, esp. in her chapter on baroque 'palimpsestes de l'irregardable' (pp. 199-232), focused on the variously 'unregardable' absences with which baroque art is preoccupied. Still, her Lacanian commitments determine an exclusively spectatorial viewpoint, stressing the effects art produces rather than the means deployed in producing them. While this yields a generously aesthetic approach grounded in formal properties (*tenebroso*, trompe-l'œil, flamboyance, etc.), the Lacanian emphasis neglects the *art* involved. Characteristic in this context is the chapter on 'le travail du regard' (pp. 67-89). Vital though the work to which the beholder's eye is called may be in baroque art, more fundamental still is the hand that frames the forms that put the eye to work. In accordance with the pun on which Heidegger's 'The Origin of the Work of Art' trades, I would urge that Buci-Glucksmann's focus on the baroque *artwork* occludes a sense of the equally baroque emphasis on art *as work*. We will return to this idea.

5 Beyond Berger's *Fictions of the Pose*, see Thomas Greene, *The Light in Troy: Imitation and Discovery in Renaissance Poetry* (New Haven, CT: Yale University Press, 1982); Louis Marin, *Etudes sémiologiques: Ecritures, peintures* (Paris: Klincksieck,

1971), *Détruire la peinture* (Paris: Galilée, 1977) and *Des pouvoirs de l'image: gloses* (Paris: Seuil, 1993); Michael Baxandall, *Giotto and the Orators: Humanist Observers of Painting in Italy and the Discovery of Pictorial Composition, 1350-1450* (Oxford: Clarendon Press, 1971); and Norman Bryson, *Word and Image: French Painting of the Ancien Régime* (Cambridge: Cambridge University Press, 1981) and *Vision and Painting: The Logic of the Gaze* (New Haven, CT: Yale University Press, 1983). See too David Quint's amplification of Greene's views in *Origin and Originality in Renaissance Literature: Versions of the Source* (New Haven, CT: Yale University Press, 1983).

6   This is a staple of the literature on *ut pictura*. For a concise survey of the primary literature, see Braider, 'The Paradoxical Sisterhood'.
7   Sidney, *An Apology for Poetry*, p. 101.
8   Ibid., p. 107.
9   A striking example of this double tendency is the work of the great historians associated with the Warburg Institute—Erwin Panofsky, Fritz Saxl and Rudolf Wittkower.
10 Bryson's trajectory from English studies to art history parallels that of his early method, which applies literary theory (Barthes, Bloom, Lacan) to the interpretation of art historical relations. Similarly, Marin is a philosopher whose literary and historical interests led to investigations in early modern theories of representation that eventually inspired a turn to painting.
11 For a wonderfully balanced overview of this shift, see Berger, *Fictions of the Pose*, pt. 1, 'Early Modern Technologies and Politics of Representation and Their Consequences'. The 'consequences' alluded to form a theme cashed out in the analysis of Rembrandt's self-portraits in pt. 4, 'Rembrandt's Looking-Glass Theater'.
12 See Mitchell, *Iconology*, Broude and Garrard (eds.), *Feminism and Art History*, Carroll, 'The Erotics of Absolutism', Michael Ann Holly, *Panofsky and the Foundations of Art History* (Ithaca, NY: Cornell University Press, 1984), Pollock, *Vision and Difference*, and Bal, *Reading Rembrandt*.
13 Baxandall, *Giotto and the Orators*, pp. 121-139.
14 See Lee, *Ut Pictura Poesis*, pp. 9-23.
15 On the 'poverty of ordinary nature', see Piles, *Abrégé de la vie des peintres*, p. 222; on the imitation of nature's 'principle' or 'intention', pp. 21-22; on the 'rectification' of nature, esp. by means of comparison with the canonic works of the past, p. 17.
16 Aristotle, *Poetics* 1448b; trans. James Hutton (New York: Norton, 1982), p. 47.
17 The principal source for these legends is Pliny's *Historia naturalis* 35.61-66; *The Elder Pliny's Chapters on the History of Art*, ed. and parallel trans. K. Jex-Blake (1896; repr. Chicago: Argonaut, 1968), pp. 106-111. Bryson's omission of the legend of the Helen/Venus painted for the Temple of Hera Lakinia, retaining only the story of Zeuxis' illusionistic grapes, points to the one-sidedness of his picture of the early modern theory of painterly imitation.
18 David Summers, *Michelangelo and the Language of Art* (Princeton, NJ: Princeton University Press, 1981). Summers generalizes the analysis of Michelangelesque idealism in *The Judgment of Sense: Renaissance Naturalism and the Rise of Aesthetics* (Cambridge: Cambridge University Press, 1987).
19 The doctrine *ut pictura poesis* may be seen as implicitly fueling the anti-visual discourse Jay's *Downcast Eyes* misleadingly ties to the apotheosis of modern critical thought in twentieth-century France. Jay's wholehearted embrace of the 'ocularcentric' hypothesis propounded by his French sources concerning the 'scopic' régime in force prior to the advent of Western modernity in the late eighteenth and early nineteenth centuries overlooks the profound ambivalence attending vision during the

apogee of visual culture in the fifteenth to seventeenth centuries. For an encyclopedic (and very angry) survey of the iconoclasm dogging visual art from antiquity to the present, see David Freedberg, *The Power of Images: Studies in the History and Theory of Response* (Chicago: University of Chicago Press, 1989). For a more relaxed account, see Jacqueline Lichtenstein's *La Couleur éloquente: rhétorique et peinture à l'âge classique* (Paris: Flammarion, 1989), which not only anchors ambivalence toward images in early modern culture, but relates mistrust of the visual to the parallel suspicion of rhetoric, and both to the emergence of Platonic 'dialectic'.

20 See Thomas Hobbes, *Leviathan* (London: Everyman, 1965), p. 66 and p. 82.
21 See Leon Battista Alberti, *De pictura* 2.25; *On Painting*, ed. and parallel trans. Cecil Grayson (London: Phaidon, 1972), pp. 60-61.
22 Unpacking painting's philosophical potential as evinced by the continuity between Michelangelo's theory of art and Kant's *Critique of Judgment* is the central task of Summers's *Judgment of Sense*. However, Summers's sense of what this amounts to is limited by the idealism dictated by his view of Michelangelo as the preeminent exponent of what his earlier book calls '*the* language of art'. Because he endorses Michelangelo's idealist interpretation of the naturalist engagement with sense, Summers proves unresponsive to those anti-idealist practices (epitomized by Caravaggio and Rembrandt) through which painting participates in the ontological shift behind philosophical as well as aesthetic modernity. So while Summers is right to see Kantian aesthetics as a logical outcome of the historical evolution to which painting contributes, he is wrong to identify this with unmediated idealism. On the contrary, the evolution's fundamental engine is the naturalist reduction to which idealism fundamentally *reacts*—which is why, in Kant as in the contemporary Lessing of *Laokoon*, the system of aesthetics promoted by German idealism relegates painting to a secondary status in relation to both poetry and the poeticized version of nature associated with the simultaneously 'subjective' and 'universal' character of aesthetic judgments. For a fuller account of my alternative to Summers's historical scheme, see Braider, *Refiguring the Real*, esp. the conclusion, 'The Poetry of Absorption and the Ontology of the Modern in Lessing, Greuze, and Kant'.
23 On Rembrandt's studio practices, see Alpers, *Rembrandt's Enterprise*, chap. 3. Much of Alpers's case for Rembrandt could be profitably applied to Caravaggio.
24 Giovanni Pietro Bellori, *Le vite de' pittori, scultori e architetti moderni*, ed. Evelina Borea (Turin: G. Einaudi, 1976); see Howard Hibbard, *Caravaggio* (New York: Harper and Row, 1983), p. 362.
25 See Hibbard, *Caravaggio*, pp. 202-203. The contemporary source for the claim that Caravaggio's model for the Virgin was a prostitute is Giulio Mancini's *Considerazioni sulla pittura*, an unpublished ms. of c. 1617-21. See Hibbard, pp. 347-349.
26 Bellori makes the charge of want of invention explicit. See the text in Hibbard, *Caravaggio*, p. 364. We have already noted the ambiguity of the term invention. We now see how it maps the ambivalence toward painterly naturalism.
27 Piles, *Abrégé de la vie des peintres*, p. 433.
28 Ibid., pp. 433-435.
29 Caravaggio's character as art history's favourite bad boy has received fresh currency in Helen Langdon, *Caravaggio: A Life* (New York: Farrar, Straus and Giroux, 1998), Peter Robb, *M* (Sydney: Duffy and Snellgrove, 1998) and Desmond Seward, *Caravaggio: A Passionate Life* (New York: William Morrow, 1998).
30 On how Rembrandt's education and associations spoiled his natural gifts, see Piles, *Abrégé de la vie des peintres*, pp. 435-436. On contemporary attitudes toward the proverbially 'phlegmatic' Dutch, see Schama, *The Embarrassment of Riches*, pp.

257-288. For their special relevance to the scandal of naturalism, see Lessing's *Laocoön: An Essay on the Limits of Painting and Poetry*, trans. Edward Allen McCormick (Indianapolis, IN: Bobbs-Merrill, 1962), p. 1 and Kant's *Observations on the Feeling of the Beautiful and Sublime*, trans. John T. Goldthwait (Berkeley, CA: University of California Press, 1960; repr. 1981), p. 105.

31   See Svetlana Alpers, 'Describe or Narrate?: A Problem in Realistic Representation', *New Literary History* 8, pp. 15-41, who draws on this feature to underscore Caravaggio's commitment to representation as opposed to narrative. By dumping the hero in our lap, obliterating the distance between image and beholder, Caravaggio rubs our noses in the brute fact of representation as such, cut off from flight into the idealized realm of 'significant human action'.

32   This develops an insight derived from Gilman's commentary on the elder Hans Holbein's *The Ambassadors* in *The Curious Perspective*, pp. 98-104. See too Braider, *Refiguring the Real*, pp. 115-119.

33   See Hibbard, *Caravaggio*, pp. 130-131. For a classic study of the Pauline-Augustinian theology of grace, esp. as pushed to the limits by Jansenism, see Goldmann, *Le Dieu caché*, chap. 7, 'Jansénisme et vision tragique' and the whole of pt. 3, devoted to Pascal. For a more recent commentary, see Marie-Florine Bruneau, *Racine: Le jansénisme et la modernité* (Paris: Corti, 1986), one of whose major sources is Blumenberg's *Legitimacy of the Modern Age*. While Blumenberg does not comment on Jansenism per se, Bruneau is right about the general relevance of his central theme, i.e., the contest between Christian gnosticism and growing faith in meliorism and human self-determination.

34   See, e.g., Gilman, *The Curious Perspective*, chap. 6, esp. pp. 167-175.

35   The notion of a Renaissance 'appropriation of space' was suggested by the late Albert Cook, who set it as the theme for a conference panel to which he invited me to contribute.

36   See Berger, *Fictions of the Pose*, chap. 1, 'Technologies: The System of Early Modern Painting'. Berger's reference to a 'system' (and *a fortiori* '*the* system') of early modern painting is partly ironic since he ultimately resists the idea. What makes the phenomenon of Rembrandtesque portraiture (and *self*-portraiture) possible is the at once aesthetic and political act of painting 'against' the Renaissance (more specifically, the *Italian* Renaissance) and so against whatever in Renaissance art encourages the illusion of systematicity. This is also a theme in Alpers, for whom the anti-Italian descriptiveness of seventeenth-century Dutch art goes hand-in-hand with a rejection of the geometric procedures of monocular perspective Albertian Italy transmits to the rest of Europe. See *The Art of Describing*, chap. 2, ' "Ut pictura, ita visio": Kepler's Model of the Eye and the Nature of Picturing in the North'.

37   See Michael Baxandall, *Painting and Experience in Fifteenth-Century Italy: A Primer in the Social History of Pictorial Style*, 2nd ed. (Oxford: Oxford University Press, 1988) and Lisa Jardine, *Worldly Goods: A New History of the Renaissance* (New York: Doubleday, 1996).

38   See Erwin Panofsky, *Early Netherlandish Painting: Its Origins and Character* (1953; repr. New York: Harper and Row, 1971), vol. 1, p. 3.

39   For accounts of many of these alternatives, see Alpers, *The Art of Describing*, chap. 2, ' "Ut pictura, ita vision" ', and chap. 4, 'The Mapping Impulse in Dutch Art'.

40   On how painting constructs beholders' relation to pictures, the role they are accordingly called on to assume and thus their socially determined character as conscious subjects, see Jonathan Crary, *Techniques of the Observer: On Vision and Modernity in the Nineteenth Century* (Cambridge, MA.: MIT Press, 1990). However, as Berger

108 *Baroque Self-Invention and Historical Truth*

(*Fictions of the Pose*, pp. 35-41) argues, Crary's picture is remarkably narrow and reductive. Not only does he subscribe to the mistaken view that there is only one system of visual construction, that of Albertian perspective; he also believes that this type of construction produces a single kind of subject, i.e., the historical personage we call '*the* subject', i.e., the 'bourgeois' subject of modern social rationality. Quite apart from the anachronism involved in the cavalier assumption that bourgeois canons of identity are unproblematically continuous with precursors in the fifteenth, sixteenth and seventeenth centuries, Crary overlooks the wide variety of moods, modes and postures in which paintings may interpellate their beholders.

41   Alberti, *De pictura* 2.26; *On Painting*, pp. 60-63.
42   'The painter who draws merely by practice and by eye, without any reason, is like a mirror which copies every thing placed in front of it without being conscious of their existence.' *The Notebooks of Leonardo*, ed. and tr. Jean Paul Richter (1883; repr. New York: Dover, 1970), p. 18. Despite his otherwise resolute defence of painting versus poetry on the strength of the empirical truth (*sperientia*) afforded by its superior naturalism, Leonardo remains committed to the ideology of painterly invention. This commitment is nonetheless tempered by a more faithful imitation of nature than poetry accommodates. So Leonardo's point here is a double one. Painting is no mere mechanical replication because the painter must bring something (an invention) to the representation of nature. Still, even as replication, painting demands recognition as an art, i.e., as requiring a conscious activity the mirror metaphor fails to register.
43   See again Heidegger's 'The Origin of the Work of Art'.
44   Summers, *The Judgment of Sense*, pp. 110-112; but also see Berger's critical commentary, *Fictions of the Pose*, pp. 80-84.
45   The indelible link between the artist's inner moral, psychological and intellectual identity and the works of art he or she imagines and produces is the fundamental theme of both of Summers's books, as it was of the classically-based Italian art theory at the centre of his researches. But while Summers's insistence on the idealist construction of the relation between mind and art is entirely appropriate to the Michelangelo of his first book, and thus to 'the language of art' as Michelangelo and his contemporaries conceived (or idealized) it, it provides too narrow a basis for the more general philosophy of art that *The Judgment of Sense* aims at.
46   Summers, *The Judgment of Sense*, p. 6. See too Erwin Panofsky, *Perspective as a Symbolic Form*, trans. Christopher S. Wood (1927; New York: Zone Books, 1991).
47   See Pascal Bonafoux, *Les Peintres et l'autoportrait*, translated as *Portraits of the Artist: The Self-Portrait in Painting* (New York: Skira/Rizzoli, 1985), pp. 17-21. Bonafoux touches on an interesting counterexample in the self-portrait the twelfth-century mystic Hildegard von Bingen has left in the margin of a manuscript. Hildegard distinguishes herself from the nuns in her charge (also portrayed in the margin) by enlarging the figure that represents her, as befits her status as their superior. The image is thus doubly non- or pre-perspectival: there is no regard for natural proportion, and correspondingly no point of view. But there is no self-portrait either: the image inscribes not an individual being, but a generic Mother Superior.
48   Joel Fineman, *Shakespeare's Perjur'd Eye: The Invention of Poetic Subjectivity in the Sonnets* (Berkeley, CA: University of California Press, 1986). The main lines of Fineman's historico-formal argument are staked out in the introduction, esp. pp. 44-48, where he defines the 'chiasmic' structure of desire inhabiting the Sonnets.
49   For the base sense of the term invention as an inventorial finding, see, e.g., Cicero, *De partitione oratoria* 31. This (what Fineman's Shakespeare might call 'cross-coupled') notion of invention informs the place Fineman assigns Freudian 'repeti-

tion' in conditioning the Shakespearean sense of person and subjectivity. See, e.g., *Shakespeare's Perjur'd Eye*, p. 47.

50   For an official count, see H. Perry Chapman, *Rembrandt's Self-Portraits: A Study in Seventeenth-Century Identity* (Princeton, NJ: Princeton University Press, 1990), p. 3.

51   This painting is usually designated as 'Rembrandt' or 'Self-Portrait as an Old Man Laughing', which has the merit of aiming at neutral description. However, as I recall elsewhere (*Refiguring the Real*, p. 217), the subject (and consequently the title) is moot since various clues (both internal and external) suggest it may also be identified as 'The Laughing Democritus' (opposed to the 'Weeping Herakleitos', represented by the frowning effigy in the left background) or as the ancient Zeuxis, who, it is claimed, painted at the end of his life the portrait of an old woman of such comical ugliness he died laughing at his image of her. See Chapman, *Rembrandt's Self-Portraits*, pp. 101-104, who favors this last reading. For another reading, which opts for an identification with Democritus as a proto-Lacanian 'Joker', see Berger, *Fictions of the Pose*, pp. 505-511. The point (one Berger would endorse) is that the choice of title is finally and inevitably a polemical matter destined to call attention to the painting's exemplary (and delightful) indeterminacy.

52   Alpers describes Rembrandt's speculation on his own works in *Rembrandt's Enterprise*, chap. 4, 'Freedom, Art, and Money'. Alpers's thesis contrasts Rembrandt's practice with that of Rubens, the quasi-industrial scale of whose workshop makes him look like Rembrandt's rival for the honour of inventing the artwork as commodity. According to Alpers, what distinguishes Rembrandt from Rubens, leaving the latter on the pre-capitalist side of the developing art market, is Rembrandt's deliberate *originality*. For all their uniqueness, Rubens's paintings continue to 'cleave to pictorial tradition'. Thus, what identifies Rubens as a great painter is his power to turn out what tradition readily regards as *great paintings*. With Rembrandt, on the other hand, we get something altogether new: paintings quite unlike anything anyone had ever seen before, whose hallmark is that they could only be *by Rembrandt*. '[T]his', Alpers concludes, 'was where Rembrandt's peculiarity and innovation lay. It was the commodity—the *Rembrandt*—that Rembrandt made that was new. And it is he, not Rubens, who invented the work of art most characteristic of our culture—a commodity distinguished among others by not being factory produced, but produced in limited numbers and creating its market, whose special claim to the aura of individuality and to high market value bind it to basic aspects of an entrepreneurial (capitalist) enterprise.' (p. 102) For a comparable (if more critical) analysis, see Schwartz, *Rembrandt*, pp. 226-227.

53   On 'intransparency', see Joseph Margolis, *Interpretation Radical but Not Unruly: The New Puzzle of the Arts and History* (Berkeley, CA: University of California Press, 1995), p. 2. For those who have yet to encounter him, Margolis may be characterized as Stanley Fish for philosophers. Like the Fish of *Is There a Text in This Class? The Authority of Interpretive Communities* (Cambridge, MA: Harvard University Press, 1980), Margolis explores how interpreters of literature and art constitute their objects in the process of finding something to interpret. The truth of works (the target of a 'correct' interpretation) is therefore intransparent in the sense that it is only accessible through the labor of construction required for it to exist as an object of interpretation in the first place. But, also like Fish, Margolis wants to demonstrate that this process is neither gratuitous nor capricious ('unruly'). Where Fish invokes the steadying influence of 'interpretive communities', Margolis sets out to show that constructivist theses possess both a greater logical coherence and a far wider epistemic and ontological reach than analytic philosophy is prepared to credit.

54 It is crucial that all three writers focus not merely (like Bacon or Descartes) on the methods required to arrive at knowledge, but on knowledge's conditions of possibility as a function of its form, springs and 'originals' as a specifically human endeavour. Pascal, Spinoza and Locke all thereby anticipate the 'Copernican revolution' performed a century later in Kant's response to the scepticism Hume derives from the critical turn inherited from their common forebears in seventeenth-century thought.

55 Georg Wilhelm Friedrich Hegel, *The Phenomenology of Mind*, trans. J.B. Baillie (rev. ed., 1931; repr. New York: Harper and Row, 1967), p. 67.

56 The phenomenon of philosophical prefaces and introductions merits further attention, and not least for its relation to the parallel emergence of philosophical treatises written for or toward philosophy itself ('prolegomena', 'groundworks', etc.).

57 On Berger's use of Peirce's notions, see *Fictions of the Pose*, pp. 20-31. On how Rembrandt's opposition to cultural norms shapes those general features of his painting that determine what Fish might call its 'self-consuming' tendency to serve as its own interpretant, see Berger's discussions of the painter's agonistic engagement with 'mimetic idealism' (chaps. 2 and 4).

58 See Merleau-Ponty, *Le visible et l'invisible*, pp. 172-204 and the annexed worknotes devoted to the reversible relation tying 'le visible' to 'le voyant' (pp. 314-318) and Lacan, *Les quatre concepts fondamentaux de la psychanalyse* (pp. 120-135), a discussion of painting in the context of Lacan's famous analyses of the gaze. Berger (*Fictions of the Pose*, pp. 158-165) offers a particularly useful commentary, summing up the current state of play in the context of 'the narcissism of orthopsychic desire', i.e., the desire to see ourselves not merely as we imagine (or would *like* to imagine) ourselves, but as others see us—a desire that leads us (among other things) to represent ourselves *to* ourselves in the form in which we desire to be seen.

59 Note that, while the Catholic Caravaggio quotes 1 Corinthians by osmosis, as a text distilling the Pauline mood infusing so much post-Tridentine devotional art, the Protestant Rembrandt surely read Paul for himself. Further, as I hope to show later, Paul's verses adhere so closely to the details of Rembrandt's self-portrait as to suggest we have good reason to think Rembrandt had them specifically in mind.

60 On Tyndale's contribution to the idiom that would eventually yield the King James version of the Bible, and thus to the temper of the English language as a whole, see Daniell, *William Tyndale*. Daniell returns to the theme throughout, but see in particular the discussion of the language of the New Testament of 1526 (pp. 134-142).

61 The following analysis revises an earlier one in *Refiguring the Real*, pp. 217-218.

62 See 1 Cor. 1.10-31, where Paul notes the 'contentions' between Jews and Greeks following the Corinthians' breakdown into rival parties pitting those 'of Apollos [Paul]' against those 'of Cephas [Peter]'. The source of these contentions (the accusations of 'sin' with which Jews and Greeks seem to have taxed each other) covers a lot of ground—everything from the 'touching of women', fornication and incest to conflicting dietary concerns, dealings with 'idolators', law suits and circumcision.

63 For Augustine's key definition, see *De doctrina christiana* 3.10-16.

64 This insight frames the whole argument of *Sein und Zeit*. The disclosure (or 'unconcealment') of our 'thrownness' into a world of pure facticity eliminates metaphysical value or meaning as a given of human experience, except as a need (or reflex) of consciousness (*Dasein*) itself. The 'horizonal' and 'ecstatic' temporality of *Dasein* thereupon substitutes for the verticality its own advent as the source of meaning calls in question, reinstating metaphysics as a dimension of conscious being as such.

Chapter 3

Hercules at the Crossroads: Image and Soliloquy in Annibale Carracci

In chapter 1, we explored the rhetoric of mastery and possession, the semiotics of violence and rape, informing the at once aesthetic and epistemological motif of the Naked Lady. We found that, even in its capacity as an icon of desire, subsuming natural truth in an image that expresses representation's prehensile power to expose and grasp the underlying order of feminized nature, the Naked Lady betokens nature's finally indigestible otherness. It thereby symbolizes the ambiguities in which representation both meets and expounds its insuperable limits. This led us in the next chapter to examine the peculiar ontology of baroque art: a Pauline ontology of fallen flesh one of whose entailments is the dialectical problem the artist's self becomes as a source of light that mirrors the very darkness it claims to dispel. The latent 'I' of baroque representation, the image of identity set forth in baroque self-portraiture, turns out to be far more complex than we tend to imagine. In particular, it not only proves vulnerable to contesting forces overtaking it from without; contestation inhabits it as an indissociable condition of its inner mode of being.

Our new aim is to unpack this complexity further by shifting from the mode of human *being* to the sense of human *agency* self-portraiture incorporates. To this end, we will focus on a painting one of whose many merits is its status as an epitome of the Roman baroque, a pictorial style of which it constitutes an early (and crucial) exemplar. I propose to read Annibale Carracci's *Hercules at the Crossroads* (1595-97) as an emblem of the collective historical personage we call the modern subject. In portraying the ancient Hercules, the painter supplies a blueprint for self-conscious agency at large, an inward turn whose most characteristic literary expression is a figure we will take up near the end of the present chapter: the ego of dramatic soliloquy. Carracci's *Hercules* is, then, the image of still other images that together frame the political, moral and discursive agent whose consolidation in the sixteenth and seventeenth centuries is commonly held to mark the onset of the modern West.[1]

To the extent that the modern self combines authority and power, the Greek demigod is well suited to the role. Both god and man, Hercules unites the higher consciousness of the ideal with the muscular concreteness of practical life. Hercules is, first and foremost, a force of nature whose heroic deeds firmly anchor him in the secular world—a world that, in one memorable episode, he rescued from primeval chaos by bearing the sphere of the encroaching heavens on his back. But this force of nature is also Jupiter's son, the human child of cosmic mind. In the natural body of Hercules, the Jovian principle of order visits the sublunary world of human experience not merely as militant might, but as personified justice in search of monsters to slay, crimes to avenge, deep-seated wrongs to right.

This already locates Hercules' political significance as a persistent metaphor of secular sovereignty. Revered in the Middle Ages as one of the Nine Worthies, a chivalric mirror of the moral as well as martial virtues of true knights, Hercules becomes a proxy for the Renaissance prince before evolving, in the Hapsburg Empire, Bourbon France or Stuart England, into a prosopopeia of the modern state.[2] Such is the at least official spirit in which Carracci uses him to decorate the Camerino, the small study for Cardinal Odoardo Farnese in the palace his great ancestor Alessandro, later Pope Paul III, had built in Rome to advertise his dynasty's learning, magnificence and power.[3] But Hercules also speaks in the early modern era to the conception of humanity in general, the rational as well as material being whose distinctive vocation it is to redeem the inchoate contingency of profane experience by binding it up in thought. The trope of Hercules bearing the heavens on his back symbolizes not merely political might, but the reach of human intellect, mind and muscle guided by the simultaneously divine and natural light of reason. Francis Bacon alludes to this attribute in deploying the Pillars of Hercules as the emblem for the frontispiece of the *Magna instauratio* (1620), framing the proud motto, *Multi pertransibunt & augebitur scientia*—'Many will pass through and knowledge will be increased'.

Hercules thus belongs to the family of mythographic figures Hamlet (1602) has in mind in the parodic 'praise of man' that underlies his sneering explanation of his politic uncle's motives in sending for the hapless Rosencrantz and Guildenstern:

> What a piece of work is man, how noble in reason, how infinite in faculties, in form and moving, how express and admirable in action, how like an angel in apprehension, how like a god: the beauty of the world; the paragon of animals.[4]

Taken out of context, these opening words give no hint of the prince's satiric intent. Yet the personification's very doubleness as god and man, mind and body, rational might and carnal appetite, refutes its pretensions, leading Hamlet to round on the boast with a sardonic snap the sharper for the smutty *double entendre* it occasions:

> and yet to me, what is this quintessence of dust? man delights not me, no, nor woman neither, though by your smiling you seem to say so. (2.2.311-14)

Even (if not especially) as an epitome of modern self, Hercules is subject to alternate readings: the very thing that shapes his exemplary interest defines him as a focus of ambivalence. The humanation that makes his godlike attributes seem at once so admirable and attainable undercuts the grandeur he embodies. Symbol of humanity's more than merely mortal nature, he also enacts the mortal fall that constitutes our humanity. Though his Olympian father subsequently grants eternal afterlife, even Hercules dies, poisoned by a jealous wife enraged at adulterous liaisons that recall the irregularities attending his inception. Sired by Jupiter on the unwitting wife of the pious Amphitryon, the hero's nativity is an episode of such sleazy venery that only low Plautine farce can accommodate it.[5]

As appropriate as Carracci's fable may be to portraying the modern subject as the hubristic embodiment of autonomous self-assertion, rational certainty and temporal power, it is to the legend's underside, the sneaking *envers* of the boastful *endroit*, that I now direct attention. The modern self does indeed adopt the rhetoric of mastery and possession that Bacon and Descartes notoriously associate with natural philosophy, avatar of a sovereign rationality to which the monarchic head of the new secular state gives authoritative political expression. What nonetheless ultimately defines the subject, making the specific historical difference it registers, is the way it twins certainty with doubt, power with impotence. Though Descartes may picture it as a radically self-determined origin or ground, the modern ego remains a site of tragic indecision, personifying the anxiety that accompanies not only the power to act and choose, but the pressing need to do so under conditions that conceal where our acts and choices lead. Contrary to the assumption so curiously shared by intellectual left and right alike—a Burckhardtian view embraced as unquestioningly by Theodor Adorno and Michel Foucault as by the more conservative Richard Popkin and Hans Blumenberg[6]—we cannot, then, take the sovereign modern subject at face value. The moment of radical scepticism that Popkin chronicles is not just a heroic break with the prejudices, fantasies and superstitions of the past. But neither is it simply a mystified image of the new discursive and ideological order by which, in the oppositional version of the story, the rationalist doxa proclaims a tyranny epitomized by Foucault's favourite icons of the modern hegemonic state—the insane asylum, the panoptic prison and the school. The essential point is the doubleness, and that of which this doubleness is the correlate: the new sense of self indexed to a new (and radical) experience of time.

In exploring how Carracci depicts the legend of Hercules at the Crossroads, our focus is less the meaning he was expressly commissioned to convey than the one that, deviating from the entire tradition of such depictions before him, he happens on without necessarily planning to—a chance discovery possible just because the legend represents a moment of transition in which the hero's double nature moves to the fore. The prideful emblem indicts its own catastrophe. For all the sovereign mastery and power, the rational dominance and secular might, that Carracci's painting claims on Odoardo Farnese's behalf, its deepest motives echo not only the sardonic disillusionment informing Hamlet's parodic encomium of the 'paragon of animals', but also Montaigne's portrayal of the labile instability of human identity or the intermittent insistence even in Bacon, even in Descartes, on the limits of human insight and authentic self-awareness.

But the painting goes on to expound the modern self's irrevocable *engagement*. The very autonomy the subject claims ironically confirms its radical implication in and yet unshiftable responsibility for the wider realm of interests, passions, creeds and customary prepossessions in which it moves. The actions it undertakes reveal its enthrallment to the unlooked for and unplottable events of which it is the plaything. What makes the modern subject does not in fact lie in self as such at all, except insofar as self is the theatre of dark coercive forces that transcend and condition it: the world of which it is a part and the Herakleitian or (as Joseph Margolis prefers to say) Protagorian flux of which that world is the contingent product and counterpart.[7] Put another way, what makes the modern subject is the incipience of history in the dawning consciousness of history as the at once deterministic and fortuitous history of consciousness itself. Of all this then, *per hypothesi*, I take Carracci's *Hercules* to be the symbol.

Not that I believe Carracci himself meant his *Hercules* to be so taken. There is nothing in the documentary record, as first assembled in Bellori's *Vite* of 1672 and enriched by art historians since, that permits us to assert that Carracci was aware of, still less that he deliberately concerted, what I discern in this image. Moreover, art history offers little help here since the questions I raise are not of the kind that even 'new' art historians are in the habit of asking. The traditional picture of artistic agency confines us, in the main, to assigning two types of meaning: those adduceable to a personal intent of the sort a painter could confide on paper and those defined as narrowly 'aesthetic'. Few painters have left a verbal record as extensive as the notebooks of Leonardo, the correspondence of Poussin or the academic lectures and treatises of Le Brun. This encourages us to embrace the familiar image of 'mute' artists engendering 'pure' artistic forms—forms incapable of thought independent of the immediate visual expression of the feelings or emotions appropriate to the subjects prescribed for them and to the explicit cultural understandings those subjects encode.[8] This is in fact what Bellori sees in Carracci's *Hercules*. Bellori describes it as a conventional allegory confected in accordance with an iconographic programme dictated by the humanist Fulvio Orsini at the behest of Cardinal Agucchi in order to commemorate (rather than question) the period idea of civic heroism.[9] Nor, really, could it have been otherwise, given the implicit terms of Carracci's commission. Hired to ornament the Farnese palace with pictures trumpeting the presumptive merits of its rich and powerful occupant, the painter was obliged to reproduce the moral commonplaces his patron's ambitions and self-image commanded.[10] The play of Carracci's genius was to this extent limited to how he chose to express in visual terms an invention defined by others—that, and the eclectic ideal of beauty to which that formal expression attests.

One need not question the adequacy of notions of intent circumscribed by demands for explicit conscious formulation to understand that images register far more than their creators can be shown to have meant them to.[11] Like any other product of human endeavour, whether word, deed or artifact, a painting may bespeak, betoken or betray far more than its author can be shown to have consciously had in mind. Further, as significant as the content of the idea that an image deliberately expresses is the content of the wider public sensibility to which it is addressed and by which it is appreciated. In the case of Carracci's *Hercules*, we must assess and interpret not only the explicit programme, but also the underlying taste of which both the programme and the form are correlates. We must ask what it means that patrons and beholders should prize an image that *looks like that*, and so the deeper meaning of the look itself. This procedure seems all the more needful given the curious disjunction that Denis Mahon and Charles Dempsey note between the classical theory surrounding Carracci's work and the baroque proclivities informing his stylistic practice: the peculiar divorce between what contemporary observers said they liked and what pictures like Carracci's *Hercules* actually gave them.[12]

Finally, like any other human word, deed or artifact, a painting is subject to the ironies inflicted by what the Feste of Shakespeare's *Twelfth Night* (1601) calls 'the whirligig of time', the logic of sheer successiveness by which time 'brings in his revenges'.[13] One of the many exemplary features of detective stories (and as a Foucaldian archaeology bent on excavating the monuments the past has left us, cultural history is nothing if not a detective story) is that we do not read the true text until the second time around, in the perspective of our knowledge of the end.[14] It is only once the mystery has been solved that we know what to look for, or even quite what we are looking *at*: what is a clue, and what a red herring; what the evidence really tells us; what indeed the evidence really is. I take this to be true of all texts (visual as well as verbal) in a still wider sense. Even a conscious act looks different in the retrospective light of what follows, metamorphosed by the combined forces of supervenience and consequence. We change the world (if only *numeriter*, because there is now more *in* the world than before) by what we ourselves do, but also by what happens beyond and yet owing to our doings, as an unintended byproduct of our deeds. And with this new world, new faces or aspects appear, new properties and meanings unavailable in the original moment of composition or performance.

This wider cultural process accounts, moreover, for the innovative (and therefore transformational) relation Carracci's *Hercules* (fig. 3.1) entertains with its own past.[15] The painting recapitulates an ancient legend descending chiefly from the sophist Prodikos of Chios as reported in Xenophon's *Memorabilia* (2.1.21ff). Setting out on his adventures, the young Hercules comes to a crossroads, where he pauses, uncertain of the way to turn. Two women approach. One urges him to take the sweet highway of sensuous pleasure, the other the steep and arduous track of heroic virtue. And while, as noted earlier, Hercules' career is not without regrettable lapses—he is nothing if not susceptible to carnal appetite and weakness—on this occasion he chooses virtue's path. The story thus explains how a certain youth named Hercules becomes the hero *Hercules*, the exemplary justicer charged with setting the world to rights.

As one might expect, the story is important to Stoics as an image of civic duty and of the self-overcoming that duty enjoins. But it is also important to the 'higher philosophy', yielding, through the image of parting roads, a narrative embodiment of the *Littera Pythagorae*, the arcanic upsilon figuring the divorce

Fig. 3.1 Annibale Carracci, *Hercules at the Crossroads*. Museo Nazionale di Capodimonte, Naples

between the upward way of true reality and the lower road of shifting appearances to which worldly satisfaction consigns us. Further, thanks notably to the language of the Lord's Prayer (Matthew 7.13), with its contrasting roads of 'temptation' and 'deliverance from evil', seconded by Luke's image of the 'narrow door' that leads to salvation (Luke 13.24), the legend finds a place in Christian soteriology and the dualist cosmology it too endorses. Indeed, this Christian appropriation yields our earliest visual portrayal of the theme, in the woodcuts adorning Jacob Locher's Latin adaptation and expansion of Sebastian Brant's *Narrenschiff* (1494), the *Stultifera navis* of 1497 (fig. 3.2).

Fig. 3.2 *Judgment of Hercules*. From Jacob Locher, *Stultifera Navis* (Strasbourg, 1497)

The first thing we notice is the departure from the Prodican model. Instead of an encounter with the legend's female personifications, we have an allegorical dream: the hero confronts his choice not in the world of unmediated events, but in the timeless dimension of vision. The women stand off near the horizon, distanced from both the recumbent hero and each other to form a pattern that reproduces the Pythagorean Y of parting ways. There is accordingly no action of the sort the legend relates: the image overleaps the dramatic choice the hero makes in order to portray the distant ends to which Hercules' companions invite him to direct his steps. Finally, in the woodcut's clarified because abstract landscape, we meet a scrupulously disambiguated depiction of the true nature of the alternatives. Naked Voluptas stands before a bed of roses among which Death skulks beneath the sulphurous rain of the *Dies Irae*, the final day of wrath and judgment. Nun-like Virtus, by contrast, stands before a briar of thorns, clutching the humble distaff of patient labor; and yet, behind and above, we already discern the effulgence of celestial glory, crowning the strenuous life that Virtue enjoins.

The design marks the crossing of the Hercules legend with later parallels. One is ancient and Stoic: the famous Dream of Scipio transmitted by Cicero (*De republica* 6.9.29) and Macrobius (*Comentarii in somnium Scipionis*), in which the future destroyer of Carthage, Scipio Africanus, is granted a prophetic vision of the victorious career his espousal of civic duty will grant. The other is medieval, deriving from the frame narrative for the compendium of morally improving tales set forth in Geoffroy de La Tour Landry's fourteenth-century *Livre pour l'enseignement de ses filles*, a text available to Locher and his associates in Marquard vom Stein's fifteenth-century translation, *Der Ritter vom Turn*. This same scheme resurfaces later in a Raphael that is still often known as the *Dream* or *Vision of a Knight* (1504; fig. 3.3) but that Erwin Panosky convincingly identified as *The Dream of Scipio*.[16] Still, much as it owes to such parallels, the very

Fig. 3.3 Raphael, *The Dream of Scipio*. National Gallery, London

clarity that the Locher *Hercules* achieves more deeply reflects its generic character, reinforced by the absolute claims of Christian dualism. In focusing on the story's status as an exemplum, it accords it a frankly emblematic as opposed to dramatic force.

It is worth stressing the legend's dramatic potential. The episode takes the form of a debate, pitting Pleasure against Virtue in a dispute for Hercules' soul. It thus contains the basic Hegelian minimum for drama: dialogue and conflict in the collision of two irreducibly compelling subjective perspectives from which the same set of circumstances may be interpreted. We note also that, though vouchsafed both perspectives, Hercules may choose only one, and the making of this choice forms the matter of the fable. However, the tradition down to Carracci's generation eschews this dramatic aspect. What counts is not the choosing, but what is chosen, and the fact that Hercules chose aright. Hercules is in the end less depicted than cited as an example whose interest lies in the fact that he already is the heroic 'Hercules' and has therefore already made the exemplary choice. So the legend unfolds not in the time of events, but in that of 'historical', that is figural or allegorical precedent—a feature that becomes still clearer in later, more sophisticated and aesthetically satisfying images just because, despite their greater suppleness and finish, they too adopt the same figural pattern. The elder Lucas Cranach, for instance (c. 1536-37), takes up the story not at the moment of decision, but when Hercules announces his choice by offering modest Virtue the open hand of fealty and election. Similarly, in Dürer (c. 1498-99) we get not the scene of choice, but the moment when the hero rises at Virtue's side in a disciplinary act that proleptically recapitulates (a telling oxymoron) the content of an heroic career that has only just begun.

The emblematic form and meaning latent in Cranach and Dürer emerge explicitly in the thirty-ninth of Christoff Murer's posthumous *Emblemata* (1622; fig. 3.4), where, for all the centrifrugal mannerist energy, the allegorical programme asserts full control. Though the personifications now occupy the dramatic foreground, they sit passively to either side of an erect and martial Hercules. The hero in turn not only extends an approbatory hand toward Virtue, but, in the cock of his head, the authoritative fist planted on his hip, and the stern expression of his massive face, seems to harangue a downcast Pleasure. The personifications are moreover accompanied by diacritical insignia that spell out their unequivocal natures. In addition to a distaff, the modestly clad Virtue holds a Bible to whose title she emphatically points; and at her feet lie a terrestrial globe, a compass, a square and a mason's hammer in token of the practical arts and sciences. Pleasure, on the other hand, voluptuously naked, holds a goblet of wine and a lascivious lute, with a viol, grapes and a pot of coins at the ready. Meanwhile, in a background framed by the drawn curtains of allegorical discovery, we meet the familiar Pythagorean Y of parting roads, each path obligingly labeled to make certain of its character, the *Via Vitae* on the heraldic right (the viewer's left) and the *Via Mortis* to the sinister left (the viewer's right).

Or consider a later, more refined and exuberant pair of engravings by Johann Sadeler on designs by Friedrich Sustris, celebrating the accession of Maximilian I of Bavaria on 1 January 1595. Here, the debate format is at last asserted. In the first image (fig. 3.5), the young hero stands, his club resting on his shoulder, between contesting personae urging him to turn in their rival directions. We also observe a great deal of dramatic activity. Virtue takes Hercules by the arm with one hand while pointing out the road that leads to his heroic destiny with the other. Pleasure for her part, dressed for the shameless yet seductive delights of a ball, waves the pretty fan of vanity in the opposite direction. Next, in the sky

Fig. 3.4 *Judgment of Hercules*. From Christoff Murer, *XLI Emblemata Miscella Nova* (Zurich, 1622)

overhead, convulsed by cosmic happenings, a flying angel blows the trumpet of both fame and impending revelation, while mustering soldiers, the Olympian gods and the winged Time of undying glory gather to mark Hercules' impending choice. Finally, in the background, landscapes open to one side on a Parnassus inhabited by still riderless pegasi and, to the other side, on a lightning-struck region of darkness and death. However, despite the image's obvious activity, we see no real action: the engraving portrays a triumphant truth whose invariant hieroglyph, the upsilon of Pythagoras, is firmly fixed to the rock behind Hercules' head. And in the second version (fig. 3.6), where Hercules receives the features of Sustris's princely patron Maximilian himself, the hero candidly returns the beholder's gaze, breaking the picture plane in order to drive the moral home.

Not all versions of the legend are so relentlessly moralized; especially in Italy, we discern a less judgmental image of the world of pleasure and a correspondingly greater tension. In a coffer-lid decoration attributed to the Florentine artist Niccolò Soggi (c. 1512-15; fig. 3.7), the contrasting landscapes to which the divergent paths lead underscore the soteriological lesson far less vehemently

Hercules at the Crossroads 121

Fig. 3.5 Johann Sadeler, after Friedrich Sustris, broadsheet commemorating the accession of Maximilian I of Bavaria, 1 January 1595

Fig. 3.6 Johann Sadeler, after Friedrich Sustris, detail of second treatment

122 Baroque Self-Invention and Historical Truth

Fig. 3.7 Niccolò Soggi (?), *Judgment of Hercules*, decorated coffer lid. The Ca d'oro, Venice

Fig. 3.8 Girolamo di Benvenuto, *Judgment of Hercules*, decorated coffer lid, whereabouts unknown

and without the by now familiar eschatological prospect on final things. Hercules accordingly appears full of poignant regret: while the nun of Virtue already draws him away, genteel Pleasure tries to hold him back as he honours her with a last, rueful glance in parting.[17] The apocalyptic scheme in a decorative box-cover executed at around the same time by the Sienese painter Girolamo di Benvenuto (fig. 3.8) is more muted still. The background landscapes offer little contrast; and since the artist has replaced Hercules' club and lion-skin with a costume of transparent gauze, the militant hero becomes a graceful boy. Relieved of the martial iron required for his legendary deeds, the hero seems a potential conquest of earthly concupiscence in his own right.

These Italian pictures illustrate a development intensified in the baroque as evidenced by a version produced by the Rubens workshop (c. 1635; fig. 3.9).

Fig. 3.9 Workshop of Pieter Paul Rubens, *Hercules at the Crossroads*.
The Uffizi, Florence

Here again the balance clearly falls on virtue's side. Despite the look of longing that he shares with the goddess of love and beauty who symptomatically supplants the more abstract Pleasure of yore, and despite the coaxing *amor* clinging to his leg, Hercules already turns toward martial Minerva, who stoops to draw him to his manly feet. A page holds a restive steed at the ready, and the central group is dominated by an urgent Time, both stressing the imminence of departure and embodying the fabled history the hero is about to make. Yet the heart of the picture is clearly the erotic tension in the wonderful mingling of eyes and lips; and the hero's melting loins are discreetly pointed by the amusingly vestigial and, here, pacific lion-skin that barely covers Hercules' groin. The choice the hero has made was clearly agonizing. Nevertheless, in the form in which Rubens's assistants report the event, Hercules has already made it. So while we witness, in Rubens and the Italians, a less uncompromising view of worldly pleasure, one that heightens the tension and the sense of choice, it is nonetheless only with Carracci (fig. 3.1) that the choice itself moves squarely to the centre as the theme. And, by the same token, it is only with Carracci that the topic's dramatic potential is fully realized.

To be sure, drama is not what most of us would immediately notice: our first impression is surely of classical quiet, clarity, harmony and balance. Especially when contrasted with the busy Rubens, Carracci's scheme appears to reduce the elements to a near minimum. Hercules is seated at the centre, flanked by Virtue, face forward as she pivots on her axis toward the left, and by the echoing inverse figure of Pleasure, her back toward us while she pivots enticingly to the right. A poet sits at Virtue's feet, ready to immortalize the deeds to which his mistress enjoins Hercules by pointing up the steep road to where a distant Pegasus awaits its lofty rider. In answer, to our right, are masques for dancers, a viol and a book of music, marks of the lewd measures that accompany the opulent promise of Pleasure's thinly veiled body as she prepares, with a dancing sway of her hips, to lead the hero to delights concealed in the shadowy woods beyond.

These features comprise the key to Carracci's innovation as Erwin Panofsky sees it, and the reason for the selection of Carracci's *Hercules* as the model to which virtually all subsequent treatments turn. Panofsky refers to the painting's remarkable 'reconstruction' of an 'ideal Antiquity' latent in the 'real' one of both legend and artistic precedent.[18] In this sense, what determines the painting's significance is its embodiment of the eclectic programme by which the early, anti-Caravaggistic baroque already points to the classical ideal of art that will later reform and then supersede it. Carracci's *Hercules* distinguishes itself by a 'scientific' naturalism, as Dempsey calls it, but a naturalism that, for all the emphasis on natural forms and colours shared with the harsher, more agonistic Caravaggio, is guided less by nature than by the clarified and corrected *ideal* of nature discovered in the classical art of the past.[19] And yet, important as all these interpretations are, they miss what is truly central to the painting and what its 'scientific' idealism brings into sharper focus: Hercules engaged at last in the actual moment of choosing.

True, here too the theme of choice is inevitably projected against the background of what we know the choice to have been. Hercules remains 'Hercules', an exemplary personage whose legendary deeds determine what we take the image to represent—a circumstance underscored by the fact that this particular image originally formed part of a series of three devoted to the overarching theme of civic virtue. In addition, as Bellori reports in his *Vite*, though Carracci (under Orsini's direction) replaces figures like Sadeler's eschatological angel and Pythagorean Y or Rubens' urgent Time with a mere tree, the tree in question is a palm, promising the pious triumphs to come.[20] However, the peculiar visual and dramatic interest of Carracci's painting, the invention by which it refines on iconographic tradition so as to become the standard to which future artists turn, lies in effacing what the moral histories tell us, returning us to a moment *before* history, when the hero's deeds remain as yet unwritten. Though the beholder knows who this hero is, and thus what he chose, Carracci's Hercules, engrossed in the decisive yet still unconsummated act of choice, does not.

This new focus makes all the difference. The first thing that it yields is the visible discomfort that circularly communicates the agony of choice to us. Perched edgily on the central rock, Hercules throws his left arm awkwardly back across his torso, where it clutches the handle of the club down whose barrel the right arm idly dangles. The hero's attitude precludes his wonted militant self-assertiveness: tangled up in his own limbs, he is incapable of directed outward action, his energies blocked by the contrary claims on his will. The impression of wavering powerlessness is amplified by his isolation. While Virtue and Pleasure address him, they do not, as in earlier versions, *touch* him; and left to himself, naked yet curiously sexless and vulnerable, he stews in painful indecision, producing an effect concentrated, finally, in his expression. The face offers the very portrait of moral constipation. Turned slightly to one side, and lacking all external focus, the eyes look inward in token of the woeful effort to decide.

In Carracci's version, Hercules is not yet 'Hercules', but a sort of *ébauche*, hesitant and incomplete. Carracci dwells on the demigod's mortal half, portraying him in the act of gauging the magnitude of the labors to come, the sacrifice to which the immortal in him calls, and recoiling at the sight. True, this painful assertion of his mere human nature measures the dimensions of both the sacrifice and the heroic achievement, providing a classical analogue for the picture of Christ at Gethsemane, wishing away the cup of sorrow so as to underscore sufferings that his divine nature might induce us to minimize or doubt. Yet while the image enables us to appreciate the magnitude of Hercules' exemplary sacrifice, thereby bringing a new perspective to bear on a very old story, the hero here remains forever on the near side of his heroic destiny. Carracci suspends him in a solution of anxious introspection at a moment when not only his decision, but his own heroic identity hang in the balance.

This analysis reminds us of the special temporal force that Heinrich Wölfflin long ago associated with the dynamic 'painterliness' of baroque art.[21] Despite Carracci's eclectic sorting through models in search of classical dignity and refinement, studying what Wölfflin terms the tactile, plastic, sculptural 'objectivity' of classical friezes or the Roman Raphael,[22] and despite the signal inaction to which his Hercules is reduced, the picture is remarkably open and mobile, instinct with a tension owed precisely to the dramatic incompletion of the hero's attitude and gaze. Indeed, the picture's subtle dynamism authorizes giving as it were a baroque spin to the selection of classical models: what makes Carracci eclectic is the inability to decide which models to use, resulting in the uneasy multiplicity of which this image is a particularly acute example. We notice, for instance, that, in addition to representing the opposing claims of pleasure and duty, the painting's female personae embody rival pictorial styles. The dancing figure of Pleasure expresses a baroque mobility echoed in the mixed palette Carracci uses to portray her, and in particular the pinkish orange gold of her dress. On the other hand, the classical stillness of Carracci's austerely rectilinear Virtue receives emphasis from the primary red and blue in which she is clothed.[23] The hero's indecision is thereby enacted at the level of line and tone as well as posture and expression, producing in the process an underlying imbalance expressed in the sense of time the image conveys. The more consummately classical Poussin (c. 1636-37; fig. 3.10) deploys Carracci's design in such a way as to restore the self-confirming temporality of the heroic example by replacing the focus on the moment of logical finality.[24] Though the melancholy introspection of his face registers the cost the decision exacts, Poussin's Hercules has already made up his mind. By contrast, the tense of Carracci's painting is an unstable

Fig. 3.10 Nicolas Poussin, *Judgment of Hercules*. Stourhead, The Hoare Collection (The National Trust)

compound of present and future perfect: an indicative now unsettled by the consciousness of what has not yet but only *will* have happened—the coming instant, impending, imminent, when the hero's choice will at last have been fixed.[25]

The effect is clearly related to the dramatic impetus characteristic of baroque narrative, as in, say, Guido Reni's *Massacre of the Innocents* (c. 1611; fig. 3.11), whose traumatic stilleti hover in the dreadful instant immediately preceding the murderous plunge: a momentum still more marked in Bernini's *David* (1623), coiled on the brink of releasing the lethal stone, or his *Daphne* (1622-24), caught in the very second in which her metamorphosis begins, or, most famously, his *St. Theresa* (1645-52; fig. 3.12), where the ecstatic nun orgasmically anticipates the thrusting lightning bolt the angel holds on the point of driving it home. But

Fig. 3.11 Guido Reni, *Massacre of the Innocents*. Pinacoteca Nazionale, Bologna

the effect is also linked to the unique temporal dynamism that characterizes baroque inwardness. Carracci's *Hercules* shares the elusiveness of Rembrandt's second *Lucretia* (1666; fig. 1.11), where foreknowledge of the story enables us to dwell, with the heroine, on the self-administered death that even now overtakes her; and it also recalls that of the Louvre *Bathsheba* (1654; fig. 3.13), in which Uriah's desolate wife already revolves the tragic consequence of King David's letter declaring his adulterous passion. Or again, it shares the complex introversion of La Tour's *Magdalen with a Night Light* (c. 1625; fig. 3.14), where eager response to the inviting ripeness of the penitent's youthful beauty is subtly checked by her moody contemplation of the emblems of faith, mortality and remorse.

In all these ways, then, Carracci's innovation consists in giving his theme a form and force that epitomize baroque style. Yet it is important that the change he introduces is not merely stylistic, a matter of the 'language of art' in a reductively aesthetic sense. It further enacts a new *ontology* in whose light the representation of Hercules' choice indexes a deeper and more pervasive transmutation in the conception of human being and human destinies.

128 *Baroque Self-Invention and Historical Truth*

Fig. 3.12 Gian Lorenzo Bernini, *Ecstasy of St. Theresa*. S. Maria della Vittoria, Rome

Fig. 3.13 Rembrandt van Rijn, *Bathsheba at Her Bath*. The Louvre, Paris

Fig. 3.14 Georges de La Tour, *Magdalen with a Night Light*. The Louvre, Paris

Consider one final contrast, with a painting as notable for its classical stability, tactility and objectivity as Carracci's is for its labile baroque painterliness: a picture drawn from the parallel iconographic tradition Panofsky calls the 'Signum Triciput' or 'Three-Headed Sign' of human rationality, Titian's *Allegory of Prudence* (c. 1565-70; fig. 3.15).[26] Prudence is not the universally acknowledged subject of this picture. In the National Gallery in London, where it hangs, it has until fairly recently borne the title *Allegory of Time*. The preliminary evidence in either case is the same. Scanning from left to right, the three human heads in the upper register denote the three Ages of Man: old age, maturity and youth. These identifications are underscored by the animal heads in the lower register: a wolf for the ravening past that devours all things, a lion for the courage to meet present need and the ever trusting, ever sanguine dog for wholehearted pursuit of future hopes and goals. Yet the attitude of the central human figure, the mature male, already indicates that what matters is less time itself than the human *experience* of time defined by the figure's living place in it. It is significant here that the mature man does not return the beholder's gaze in a visual apostrophe fixing us in the present of our viewing. His glance turns rather to the right, giving him over to abstracted thought or, more precisely, to *fore*-thought, absorbed in meditations binding past and future together in prudential calculation. The painting is then only about time insofar as time is the medium of concerted conduct, the element in which we deliberate, calculate and act.

Fig. 3.15 Titian, *Allegory of Prudence*. National Gallery, London

We should also note that, as an allegory, devoted to portraying eternal verities, the image finally *annuls* time. Such is in fact the cardinal office of the virtue it extols. Unlike the majority of human beings, condemned to move in the dark and therefore to experience time as blind fortuity, the prudent overcome time by anticipating it. Rather than act on reckless impulse, prudence holds itself in check, subjecting its projects and desires to sceptical scrutiny. Indeed, as Victoria Kahn has shown in analyzing the Machiavellian cynicism to which early modern rhetoricians are led by growing awareness of the critical divorce between the moral ends their art at least nominally espouses and the amoral means it exploits in their service, prudence and scepticism are twins.[27] What more than anything sets the prudent apart is the studious cultivation of a habit of mistrust, the calculated refusal to take appearances at face value. In particular, the prudent control for the self-deceiving fantasies engendered by their own motives, biases and assumptions, whether in the shape of the fears the minatory memory of the past inspires, symbolized by saturnine age and the devouring wolf, or in the form of their hopes and ambitions for the future, symbolized as youthful optimism and the eternally sanguine dog.

It is moreover just this sceptical sifting of appearances that grants the mature man at the centre of Titian's image mastery not only over himself, but over unfolding events. The central head in Titian's picture occupies the temporal midpoint. To one side, in the figure of the past, sits memory, both 'natural' and 'artificial': the single head that the three heads together form is indeed a 'theatre' or 'palace of memory', stocked with an experience of the past drawn both from a private store and from the reserves of history—that reservoir of examples to which the present may be compared in order to determine its true character.[28] And yet prudence is not slavishly bound to the past; history's lessons must ultimately be oriented toward the forward-looking youth on the right. Prudence deploys the past as the instrument of present decision-making in pursuit of future goals—a procedure that suggests to Titian not only the direction of the central figure's glance, but also the face's leonine resoluteness. Reining in hopes and fears alike, the central figure overcomes both memory and impulse in order to give the whole design a determination of which his own highly individuated, tactile objectivity is the warrant.

Titian's painting displays a remarkable coincidence of visual and moral objectivity, clinched in the way the allegory cashes out as a type of picture in major respects opposed to it, namely, the portrait. The symbolic abstraction wears a concrete face. As Panofsky explains in a postscript updating his original essay on the painting's iconography, the central figure is Titian's devoted second son and heir, Orazio Vecelli, flanked by the aged Titian himself and (since neither of Titian's sons produced an heir) the distant relative he adopted as Orazio's successor, Marco Vecelli.[29] Prudence thus triply overcomes time: through Titian's choice of his second son as a worthy heir; through the heir's exhibition of the deliberative gifts that make him worthy; and through the fortitude and sobriety of the adoptive grandson, whose mien augurs well for the future of the painter's house.

The *Allegory of Prudence* is a family portrait elevated to the status of a general truth. Both portrait and truth are underwritten by an at once moral and aesthetic decisiveness that confirms not only the cardinal virtue the painting represents, but also the sense of time that makes the representation possible. And this sense of time is in turn grounded in a particular sense of history: history as a source of examples whose value and efficacy are assured by their adduction of an enduring state of nature. What holds the three-headed sign together is faith in the constant, self-replicating order of things. If the prudential calculus works, if the as yet formless future is infallibly guided and shaped by the memory of the past operating through present rationality, it is because at the most fundamental level—directly accessible only to the divine mind of which the *signum triciput* is commonly invoked as a symbol, yet mediately accessible to humanity thanks to the God-given light of reason—past, present and future are one and the same. The past offers the good counsel of precedent because, however difficult to foresee or calculate, the future will always be a version of the past, just as the past will always be an accurate mirror for the future. The mature face of prudence expresses an empowering conviction in the immutable sense of historical identity and truth—of history, in short, as its major literary exponents, the moralist Plutarch, the sententious Tacitus or the cynical Machiavelli, invariably portray it: as the record of transcendental constants transmitted in the form of the concrete particulars of the past, particulars as such redeemed by the universal laws of which they provide the instances and exemplars.

Titian's *Allegory* glosses the faith that informs pre-baroque versions of the story of Hercules at the Crossroads. Hercules himself is one of the exemplary constants on which the pre-baroque historical imagination draws. Before Carracci, Hercules is always 'Hercules', a characteristic embodiment of the heroic virtue proclaimed by the choice history records him as having made. And so long as faith in history as emblematic sameness—as self-replicating and self-confirming nature—endures, no real choice is possible since the choice he makes, the right and exemplary one, is forever the same. But to the extent that Carracci's Hercules succumbs to an agony of indecision, he bespeaks a sense of historical time that marks a radical departure: a world in which the future has become literally incalculable because its form is no longer determined by the exemplary, mythological and allegorical past.

Which brings me at last to my real concern. As promised at the start of this chapter, my theme is the advent of the modern subject as attested by the emergence of another baroque innovation, historically coincident with Carracci's *Hercules*: baroque drama as characterized by the perfection of the soliloquy.

There is no particular mystery about the distinctive internal features of the perfected soliloquy of the late sixteenth and early seventeenth centuries. Despite a renewal of interest in such matters, scholars still underestimate the form's debt to deliberative rhetoric.[30] Early modern dramatists represent consciousness less as a living stream, a spontaneous upwelling of unmediated thoughts, impressions and feelings, than as an essentially verbal phenomenon—a conceptual habit reinforced by the nature of the medium inasmuch as dramatic characters can only privately *think* what the dramatist contrives to make them publicly *say*. But the linguistic emphasis also reflects deeper psychological assumptions. Like their medieval predecessors in the Aristotelian schools, and like the humanists from whom they receive their literary training, early modern playwrights imagine the psyche itself in dialectical terms. The mind reasons; but to reason is to discourse—whence *Hamlet*'s pleonastic 'discourse of reason' at 2.1.150. And especially when the mind meets alternatives, discourse properly conducted is a process of weighing, debating, deliberating—that is, of exercising one's powers of rhetorical analysis and speech. In composing soliloquies, dramatic poets not only imitate deliberative or forensic models, drawing on the conventional stock of rhetorical devices and patterns of argument as an external means of rendering mental life. They also picture inner experience itself as a rhetorical situation: a kind of Ciceronian tribunal before which the speaking subject is summoned by its own deliberative faculties, there to debate both within and against itself the *sic et non* or *pro et contra* of whatever course of action the dramatic circumstances dictate.

The humanist model of the mind underscores more clearly the link between theatrical practices and the iconographic tradition to which Carracci's *Hercules* belongs. More specifically, it gives sharper relief to the role that the debate format plays in the pictorial dramatization of the act of choice on which the tradition focuses. For in addition to personifying the rival moral principles between which Hercules is called to choose, the personae of Virtue and Pleasure externalize the conflicting urges that define the hero's inner psychic state. But this in turn highlights how the change Carracci's version of the legend introduces relates to a comparable shift both in the use to which the baroque soliloquy puts rhetoric and in the form of life rhetoric voices. What sets Marlowe, Shakespeare and the Jacobeans apart from Tudor predecessors like the Sackville and Norton of *Gorboduc* (1561) or the Kyd of *The Spanish Tragedy* (1592), or what distinguishes Mairet (1604-86), Rotrou (1609-50) and Corneille (1606-84) from Jodelle (1532-73), Garnier (1534-90) and Montchrestien (1575-1621), is how they naturalize the deliberative patterns of soliloquistic speech.

Earlier soliloquies retain the tang of the lawyerly cask from which they are habitually drawn—and we must remember that, as a class, early modern dramatists generally come from (and often continue to inhabit) the legal circles from which most non-clerical intellectuals are recruited in the early modern era.[31] We encounter orations rather than monologues, set-piece displays of rhetorical virtuosity rather than spontaneous acts of dramatic self-expression. The result is a formal and tonal character emphasized in the French context by the typographical convention of putting the especially good bits (sentences, *pointes*, apologues, epigrammes) in quotation marks, prepackaged in readily citable form.[32] No similar device emerges on the English scene, but the tendency survives there too well into the Jacobean age. With a dramatically gratuitous loquacity later parodied in *Hamlet*'s Polonius, *Richard II*'s (1595) 'time-honoured' John of Gaunt delays the opening of the famous 'this England' speech with an interminable string of windy commonplaces on the prophetic virtues of the words of the soon-to-die:

> O, but they say the tongues of dying men
> Enforce attention like deep harmony:
> Where words are scarce they are seldom spent in vain,
> For they breathe truth that breathe their words in pain:
> He that no more must say is listened more
> Than they whom youth and ease have taught to glose,
> More are men's ends marked than their lives before:
> The setting sun, and music at the close,
> As the last taste of sweets, is sweetest last,
> Writ in remembrance more than things long past.
> Though Richard my life's counsel would not hear,
> My death's sad tale may yet undeaf his ear. (2.1.5-16)

Where even Shakespeare is not immune to the sententiousness he elsewhere parodies, other playwrights frankly congratulate themselves for writing what Shakespeare's epigone John Webster calls his own *White Devil* (c. 1608; published 1612): 'a most sententious tragedie' as laudable for its accumulated pithy sayings as for its properly dramatic qualities.[33]

The major internal innovation consists then in heeding Gertrude's impatient injunction to Polonius, demanding 'more matter, with less art' (2.2.95), thereby curtailing the rhetorical set-piece for the sake of crisper dramatic flow. But more important than this internal change, or more precisely its fundamental point and condition, is the new external relation to the surrounding action. In earlier drama, the action is in large part a pretext, an occasion for speeches that become a focus in themselves, quite apart from their contribution to advancing or elucidating the plot. By contrast, baroque playwrights firmly anchor the speeches in the plot even if their immediate function remains to meditate or comment on the meaning of the action. What carries the change, bringing the soliloquy its characteristically baroque shape and momentum, is the fact that the commentary arises as the work of the actors themselves, conceived as direct participants in the action. Soliloquistic speech becomes a dramatic reflex of the events it explicates; and as such, it obeys aesthetic imperatives most fully articulated, in what only looks like a paradox, by the neoclassical theorist François Hédelin, abbé d'Aubignac.

As worked up in d'Aubignac's *Pratique du théâtre* (1657), the principle commanding the new aesthetic system is *immanence*. Working from the Aristotelian distinction between *mimesis* and *diegesis*, the demand that drama be envisaged as the imitation of events unmediated by epic or historical narration, d'Aubignac proclaims that the poet's 'principal aim' is to 'elaborate the action as represented',[34] thus confining what the audience or reader perceives to what is seen and heard directly and exclusively on stage. In part 1, chapter 8, explaining 'in what manner the poet must make known the setting and actions necessary in a theatrical play', d'Aubignac insists that the information required to understand who the characters are, where the action takes place and in fact every detail of costume, ethos and décor must be expressed by the characters themselves: our instruction must arise 'naturally', as a spontaneous outgrowth of the action whose comprehension it assures. D'Aubignac is so uncompromising on this point that he goes on to proscribe stage directions as the superfluous crutches of a cloddish want of art. Not only should the poet eliminate all didascalic scene descriptions ('For example: Here appears an open temple; here is discovered a palace ornamented by diverse columns and superbly constructed. Here the actors must sit in such an order') (pp. 47-48), but 'he must make his actors speak with such art, that it will not even be necessary to mark the division into acts and scenes, or even to give the interlocutors' names' (p. 48).

Dramatic representation should then ideally be wholly self-announcing, self-explicating, self-contained. And what is true of the action at large is still more so of soliloquy. Soliloquy retains the traditional function of commenting on the action in a way that helps the spectator or reader to absorb the global design and invention of the play as a whole. It thereby contributes to what we might call the mnemonic office of Aristotelian unity: the aim of giving spectators and readers a total unitary picture of the action and of the dramatic logic that structures it. But soliloquy performs this role by the strictly immanent means of dramatic verisimilitude. Soliloquy is an attempt, in the form of deliberative speech, and more specifically in the form of rhetorical *hypotyposis* or verbal picturing, to arrest the time of events. But it does so as a reflex of the speaker's engagement in the resistlessly necessary development of events themselves.

Soliloquy is a product of the surrounding action, precipitated by the events it tries to picture, events moreover the speaker advances in the act of trying to gain distance on them by deploying soliloquy to picture them. The opening of the final speech of Marlowe's precocious *Dr. Faustus* (produced c. 1588, but unpublished till 1604) illustrates the point:

> Oh, Faustus,
> Now hast thou but one bare hour to live,
> And then thou must be damned perpetually!
> Stand still, you ever-moving spheres of heaven,
> That time may cease, and midnight never come;
> Fair Nature's eye, rise, rise again, and make
> Perpetual day; or let this hour be but
> A year, a month, a week, a natural day,
> That Faustus may repent and save his soul!
> *O lente, lente currite, noctis equi!*
> The stars move still, time runs, the clock will strike,
> The devil will come, and Faustus must be damn'd. (5.1.274-85)

Faustus's desperate plea for time to stay its course and save him from impending damnation not only registers his horror before approaching fate; it *hastens* that fate. The very effort to stop the accelerating time of the action brings the action to a head. The speech takes its form from—indeed takes form *as*—the gathering crisis it tries to hold off.

Or consider *Hamlet*. It is not merely that, in Shakespeare's play, the hero's meditations are themselves an integral part of the action; they feed back into the events Hamlet labors to grasp and control by their means, and not least because, for all their wit and shrewdness, Hamlet's soliloquies show him to be forever in the dark. As he observes to Horatio at 5.2.10-11, a moment tellingly late in the play when he tacitly acknowledges the fruitlessness of the art of soliloquy that he now abjures, 'There is a divinity that shapes our ends, / Rough-hew them how we will.' The soliloquies of the Renaissance develop truths that stand as much apart from the immanent experience that yields them as the speeches themselves do from the developing plot. By contrast, baroque soliloquies have an inevitably ironic cast that expresses their blind engagement in an unfolding truth they cannot encompass precisely because they are part of it. They advance an end all the more implacable for their inability to foresee it.

It might appear that what we have in baroque soliloquy is a new sense of time grounded in a new sense of truth, but, on closer scrutiny, the reverse proves to be the case: we meet a new sense of truth springing from a new experience of time. For the tradition relative to which the baroque marks a break, truth is autonomous and self-sufficient, timeless, immutable, transcendent. It may well be that creatures like ourselves, committed to the fallen dimension of immanent temporal sequence, will inevitably fail to rise to direct knowledge of the true nature of things. Whence, in ironic counterpoint to the ongoing faith in the intercessory power of creative imagination that Italian art notably exhibits, the radical distinction the sceptical Montaigne draws between nature conceived as truth's projective self-expression in the space-time of concrete experience and the distorting fantasies inherent to shifting human custom.[35] Nevertheless, truth itself, and what Montaigne still sanguinely calls nature along with it, remains constant, whatever we fondly imagine it to be. And this faith in turn makes the Renaissance rhetorical set-piece possible, as the enunciation of a truth independent of acts, events and experience—in a temporal mode uncompromised by who pronounces it, when, why and how.

In the baroque, however, we witness a revolution in perspective to which Pascal gives memorable utterance in a fragment of the *Pensées* (126/159) alluded to in passing in our introduction. Contemplating the sorry spectacle of fathers dismayed by the erosion of the 'natural love' their children owe them, Pascal remarks on the (to him) more puzzling question of why anyone should think this unnatural. 'What', he asks, 'is then this nature that is subject to wearing away?' 'Custom', he continues, 'is a second nature that destroys the first. But what is nature? Why is custom not natural? I am very much afraid that this nature is itself only a first custom, just as custom is a second nature.' It is not simply that, as Montaigne understands, mere fallible human beings are incapable of telling the difference between nature and custom; there may in fact be no difference to tell. And if this is so, then acknowledging who speaks, when, why and how becomes of the essence because truth is adapted to the consciousness that frames it. Truth is no longer an autonomous Platonic form awaiting us on the timeless plane of transcendence; it clings to the shifting course of consciousness itself, a deliverance defined less as an object of the human mind than as its perspectival lining—the reverse side of human insight, endlessly turning with the restless thoughts that vainly grasp for it.

But beyond losing faith in a stable present reliably illumined by the light of truth, we find the fixity of the future changing too. The characters of baroque drama continue to be drawn from myth, legend and history—whether classical or recent European or, in a development that would merit a fuller commentary, Byzantine and Turkish.[36] Such characters are of course 'fated' to do what the annals record them to have done. Still, the representation of their deeds and choices in the immanent experience theatre affords is infused with a paradoxical sense of openness that makes these characters entirely and inalienably responsible for the fate that overtakes them. The broadly Augustinian anxiety prompted by the interweaving of the themes of predestination and free will—an anxiety indexed not only by the Jansenist Pascal and the more indelibly because conflictually Jansenist Racine, but also by the Puritan Milton of *Samson Agonistes* (1677), celebrating a darkness that is its own light—has a far wider currency than its explicit confessional associations would allow. Fate is, in baroque drama, the form the future takes from what its protagonists decide in the scenic here and now: what they are destined to endure is of their own making as the consequence of the choices we watch them perform. Fate is predestination experienced in the temporal register of free will, as the freely chosen yet blind embrace of a doom that, for all that it may be foreordained, could still have been different had the protagonists succeeded in choosing otherwise than they historically did—had their characters been other than they historically proved to be.

Walter Benjamin powerfully formulates this sense of fate, in *The Origin of German Tragic Drama*, as the moment of radical 'indecision' at the heart of the German baroque 'sorrowplay', and more specifically at the root of the German baroque conception of agency expressed in the figure of the royal tyrant.[37] But it is also precisely what Carracci brings to his portrayal of Hercules at the Crossroads. Like Shakespeare's Hamlet, Carracci's Hercules is a man who cannot make up his mind; and just as Hamlet's almost comic indecision prompts his tragic destiny, in Carracci, the happy fate we know to have been Hercules' takes on a strangely tragic tone. Even though Hercules is historically fated by his legend to make the right decision, the mere fact of representing him in the grip of agonized deliberation, when his happy heroic identity still hangs by a thread, recasts him in the image of the tragic hero we know that he was not.

The contrast between Renaissance and baroque expositions of Hercules' exemplary choice accordingly maps the change that, at the turn of the seventeenth century, comes over European drama as it begins to express both this new experience of time and the concomitant awareness of the nature of human consciousness as an irrevocably temporal (blind because perspectival) mode of being. But, by the same token, Carracci's *Hercules* also helps us visualize the psychological, epistemic and ontological entailments of this change: entailments whose privileged instrument, object and theatre is the figure we have come to call the modern subject. In focusing on the reality of Hercules' choice, Carracci's picture produces a powerfully temporal image in which the hero's identity *as* a hero is forever in doubt. And this focus images what Benjamin proposes as the mainspring of soliloquy in the sister art of drama: the anguished indecision that conditions the soliloquized sense of selfhood, self-knowledge and agency.

Further, precisely in its status as an image, and thus (despite its 'painterly' dramatic features) as a finally spatial rather than temporal mode of representation, Carracci's picture throws new light on the related triumph of the Aristotelian unity of action. The connection in turn resolves the apparent paradox involved in invoking d'Aubignac's dogmatically neoclassical *Pratique du théâtre* as an authoritative commentary on baroque dramatic art. Certainly, at one level, the Aristotelian classicism that d'Aubignac champions aims to expunge the excesses, irregularities and generic indiscriminateness we normally associate with baroque as opposed to the kind of classical drama d'Aubignac's treatise inculcates. To this extent, the aim is to eliminate what French classicists regard as the barbarous promiscuity, the irrational intermingling of high and low, noble and common, tragic and comic, that is so prevalent in Shakespeare and the Jacobeans, in Lope de Vega and Calderón, or in Gryphius, Hallmann and Lohenstein, Benjamin's touchstones for the belated German efflorescence of the baroque. And yet, looked at more carefully, the unity of action and the intimately related poetics of immanence demanded by French classicism announce and enact the advent of an aesthetico-ethical economy no less baroque for shaping the more polished products of the classical reform that d'Aubignac expounds.

D'Aubignac's sense of immanence registers the transition from the economy of *deeds* that characterizes both epic poetry and High Renaissance visual art to an economy of *action*: a kind of art in which the hero is no longer the autonomous author of events, but rather a creature whose acts and choices are determined by their dramatic occasion and by their involuntary intermeshing with the acts and choices of others. The dramatic action is henceforth conceived as an organic whole the rigorous logical necessity of whose unfolding defines the independent identities of its heroic agents as the ironic fruit of the choices that the encompassing plot forces those agents blindly to make. In the desolate synopsis that Horatio provides at the end of *Hamlet*, filling in the astonished Danish court and its new Norwegian master Fortinbras on what both the actor and the audience have just witnessed, the dead prince's survivor speaks

> Of carnal, bloody and unnatural acts,
> Of accidental judgments, casual slaughters,
> Of deaths put on by cunning and forced cause,
> And, in this upshot, purposes mistook
> Fall'n on th'inventors heads. (5.2.379-83)

Put thus baldly, and angrily, the tragedy Horatio describes looks far more like comedy than French classicism would tolerate. Still, the essential mechanism involved is no different from what we encounter as the very acme of classical purity in Racine's *Phèdre* of 1677. The ultimate cause of *Phèdre*'s tragic end is silence: the silence in which Hippolyte buries his embarrassed shame at being the object of his stepmother's lawless passion; the silence to which Phèdre herself is driven both by the humiliating guilt her at once adulterous and incestuous desires inspire and by the furious jealousy provoked when she discovers Hippolyte's love for another; and the silence with which the play's callous gods fulfil the arrogant Thésée's paranoid prayer that his son be punished for a crime of which he is innocent. The concatenation of blind deeds and blinder motives that kills all of *Hamlet*'s leading characters by mistake is thus the same as the one Racine's tragedy orchestrates. Both the explicit taste to which Racine ministers and the underlying sensibility of which that taste is the public expression demand a polish that the baroque impatiently brushes aside. Yet both ultimately answer to the same deep structure. And the key to that structure is *history* in the fully modern sense: not the timeless record of exemplary achievements to which the Renaissance gives that name, but rather the process of blindly mechanical, godless yet irresistible and unforgiving chance of which both the baroque soliloquist and Carracci's Hercules are the at once contingent and inevitable embodiments.

Notes

1   For samples of the critical and historical literature directly or indirectly devoted to the advent of the modern subject, representing both traditional and more recent, oppositional interpretations, see Max Horkheimer and Theodor Adorno, *The Dialectic of Enlightenment*, trans. John Cumming (New York: Continuum, 1990); Hans Blumenberg, *The Legitimacy of the Modern Age*; Pierre Bourdieu, *La distinction: critique sociale du jugement* (Paris: Minuit, 1979); Jacob Burckhardt, *The Civilization of the Renaissance in Italy*, trans. S.G.C. Middlemore, 3rd ed. (London: Phaidon, 1950); Anthony J. Cascardi, *The Subject of Modernity*; Michel Foucault, *Histoire de la folie* and *Les mots et les choses*; Stephen Greenblatt, *Renaissance Self-Fashioning from More to Shakespeare* (Chicago: University of Chicago Press, 1980); Paul Hazard, *La Crise de la conscience européenne, 1680-1715* (Paris: Fayard, 1961); Timothy J. Reiss, *The Discourse of Modernism*; and Taylor, *Sources of the Self*. I should also mention Jonathan Dollimore's *Radical Tragedy* and John D. Lyons's *The Tragedy of Origins: Pierre Corneille and Historical Perspective* (Stanford, CA: Stanford University Press, 1996) and *Kingdom of Disorder: The Theory of Tragedy in Classical France* (West Lafayette, IN: Purdue University Press, 1999), which make a case for tragic drama similar to the one urged here.
2   See the helpful survey in Stephen Orgel, 'The Example of Hercules', in Walther Killy (ed.), *Mythographie der frühen Neuzeit: Ihre Anwendung in den Künsten* (Wiesbaden: Otto Harrassowitz, 1984), pp. 25-47. To add to Orgel's list of representative examples: Hercules appears in a fresco in the Vatican Council Chamber and in a triumphal arch that Rubens designed for the Cardinal-Infant Ferdinand of Austria in 1635; Hercules (as 'Alcide') is one of the heroic personae for Louis XIV in Boil-

eau's Epistle VIII, 'Au roi'; and, as noted in the introduction, the legend of Hercules at the Crossroads is the minatory subject of the fourth interlude in Lohenstein's political tragedy, *Sophonisbe*.

3   On the composition and programme of Carracci's Camerino series, see John Rupert Martin, *The Farnese Gallery* (Princeton, NJ: Princeton University Press, 1965), pp. 21-48 and Donald Posner, *Annibale Carracci: A Study in the Reform of Italian Painting around 1590* (London: Phaidon, 1971), pp. 77-79.

4   William Shakespeare, *Hamlet*, ed. John Dover Wilson (Cambridge: Cambridge University Press, 1936) 2.2.307-11. I identify subsequent references by act, scene and verse in the text.

5   For an account of the Amphitryon legend and its dramatic career from ancient Greece to the twentieth century, see the historical introductions to the three plays presented in verse translation in Charles E. Passage and James H. Mantinband, *Amphitryon: The Legend and Three Plays (Plautus, Molière, Kleist)* (Chapel Hill, NC: University of North Carolina Press, 1974). The reader should also consult the concluding essay on the legend's fortunes after Kleist.

6   The striking consensus between left- and right-wing assessments of the modern subject is not universal, however. See, e.g., the neo-pragmatist Rorty's *Philosophy and the Mirror of Nature*, where the subject ('mind') is challenged from a strictly analytic perspective as a pure invention of early modern thought and Taylor's *Sources of the Self*, which critiques the early modern model of 'disengaged reason', i.e., of dualist autonomy and agency, from the standpoint of its nefarious moral consequences. Taylor is a liberal Catholic, but other moral philosophers mount comparable attacks. See, e.g., Bernard Williams, *Moral Luck: Philosophical Papers 1973-1980* (Cambridge: Cambridge University Press, 1981) and *Ethics and the Limits of Philosophy* (London: Fontana, 1985), both of which focus on the descriptive inadequacy of traditional notions of ethical standards, moral choices and thus moral agents. Of particular interest are Williams's analyses of the 'thickness' of moral concepts (a notion Taylor links to what he calls their unavoidable 'inarticulacy') and of the role played by sheer 'luck', i.e., the multifarious and unpredictable contingencies surrounding moral estimation and choice. Much of Williams's argument bears on the ways in which the unpredictable consequences of moral acts affect the evaluation of the acts themselves, as in the test case he calls 'Gaugin', where the painter's selfish abandonment of wife and children is retrospectively justified by the fact that he turns out to have been a great artist.

7   Radical notions of flux are of course commonly associated with Herakleitos, but I follow Margolis's lead in preferring to identify them with Protagoras. As Margolis notes, if Protagoras is the arch-antagonist of the philosophical absolutism descending from Plato and Aristotle, it is because he argues the case for an insight his great predecessor is content to conjure up by imagistic means. See Margolis, *Interpretation Radical but Not Unruly*, chap. 2, 'Interpretation at Risk', esp. pp. 63-71, and chap. 3, 'Prospects for a Theory of Radical History'.

8   See, e.g., Charles Dempsey, *Annibale Carracci and the Beginnings of Baroque Style* (Glückstadt: J.J. Augustin Verlag, 1977), pp. 1-7, who, commenting on Posner's *Annibale Carracci* and Denis Mahon's *Studies in Seicento Art Theory* (London: The Warburg Institute, 1947; repr. Westport, CT: Greenwood Press, 1971), challenges the 'anti-intellectual stance' Carracci is supposed to assume as a painter ('stop talking and start painting'). The source of the difficulty lies in professional habits notably evinced by Mahon. In the volume just cited, Mahon argues (convincingly yet misleadingly) that the actual practice of baroque artists other than Guercino bears no

relation to what contemporary theorists described. However, this view is supported less by appeal to what artists did in fact think than by analyzing what they painted, in Mahon's view, without thinking, as a bare reflex of the 'general methods of expression' that provided them with the 'qualitatively neutral constituent elements' of their art (p. 1).

9 Giovanni Pietro Bellori, *The Lives of Annibale and Agostino Carracci*, trans. Catherine Enggass (University Park, PA: Pennsylvania State University Press, 1968), p. 17. See also Posner, *Annibale Carracci*, p. 79.

10 The image's flattering connotation is the more needful given the Farnese family's notorious venality and ambition as chronicled, notably, in Paolo Sarpi's angry *Storia del Concilio Tridentino* (1619), ed. Giovanni Gambarin; repr. with intro. by Renzo Pecchioli (Florence: Sansoni, 1966). Though the Council was initially convened by the Farnese pope Paul III, in whom contemporaries saw a genuine reformer, his efforts to overcome Curial resistance to reform were fatally compromised by his desire to enhance papal control while simultaneously promoting the political ambitions of his numerous relatives, for whom he appropriated the duchies of Parma and Piacenza. But the implicit flattery involved in Carracci's choice of subject and iconographic programme is more generally a reflex of the relationship between early modern painters and their patrons. For a concise evocation of the complex transactions between artists and clients, see Baxandall, *Painting and Experience*, chap. 2, 'Contracts and the client's control'. For an overview focused chiefly on developments in papal Rome and the Republic of Venice, see Francis Haskell, *Patrons and Painters: A Study in the Relations between Italian Art and Society in the Age of the Baroque*, rev. & enl. ed. (New Haven, CT: Yale University Press, 1980). Chap. 1 analyzes the basic 'mechanics of seventeenth-century patronage' as a whole.

11 The problem of what counts as intent has been central to cultural and literary as well as psychological reflection since Freud. But both Hegel and Marx placed it at the heart of historical interpretation as well, a point the present chapter develops.

12 See Mahon, *Studies in Seicento Art Theory*. A similar point can be derived from Dempsey's *Annibale Carracci* by noting the tension between the propagandistic programme Carracci undertakes on his patron's behalf and the 'scientific naturalism' that informs his style.

13 William Shakespeare, *Twelfth Night, or What You Will*, ed. Sir Arthur Quiller-Couch and John Dover Wilson (Cambridge: Cambridge University Press, 1949) 5.1.376. Lyons discusses the relevance of what I call the logic of successiveness to Corneille in *The Tragedy of Origins*. See esp. the introduction, which cites Arthur Danto's *Analytical Philosophy of History* (Cambridge: Cambridge University Press, 1965) as an authority.

14 On the temporal structure of detective fiction, see Dennis Porter, 'Backward Construction and the Art of Suspense', in Glenn W. Most and William W. Stowe (eds), *The Poetics of Murder: Detective Fiction and Literary Theory* (New York: Harcourt Brace Javonovich, 1983), pp. 327-340. Though Porter does not explore it, the 'backward' direction of time in detective fiction has obvious Œdipal parallels examined by other essays in Most and Stowe's collection, esp. those of Geraldine Pederson-Krag, Geoffrey H. Hartman and Albert D. Hutter. For Foucault's archaeological model, so central to New Historicism, see, in addition to the works cited in note 1, the theoretical account offered in *L'archéologie du savoir* (Paris: Gallimard, 1969).

15 The following necessarily selective review of the tradition within which Carracci's painting is situated relies heavily on the typically thorough compilation in Erwin Panofsky, ' "Hercules Prodicius": Die Wiedergeburt einer griechischen Moralerzäh-

lung im deutschen und italienischen Humanismus', *Hercules am Scheidewege und andere antike Bildstoffe in der neueren Kunst* (Leipzig: B.G. Teubner, 1930; repr. Berlin: Edition Logos, Gebr. Mann Verlag, 1997), pp. 37-196.
16   Ibid., pp. 37-40.
17   For an introduction to Soggi's work, see Nicoletta Baldini, *Niccolò Soggi* (Florence: EDIFIR, 1997). On Soggi's *Hercules*, pp. 59-62.
18   Panofsky, *Hercules*, p. 126.
19   Dempsey, *Annibale Carracci*, p. 56.
20   Bellori, *Lives*, p. 21.
21   See in particular the discussions of baroque 'painterliness' and the baroque preference for 'open forms' in Wölfflin, *Principles of Art History*, pp. 18-32, pp. 41-53 and pp. 124-148.
22   On the sources for Carracci's *Hercules*, see Panofsky, *Hercules*, pp. 127-28.
23   I owe this insight into the dueling styles at work in Carracci's *Hercules* to responses by colleagues at Stanford University to a public lecture based on the material presented here.
24   See Anthony Blunt, *Nicolas Poussin* (New York: Bollingen, 1967), p. 129.
25   For a valuable analysis of the 'future perfect', see Lacan, 'Zeitlich-Entwickelungsgeschichte', in *Les Ecrits techniques de Freud*, esp. pp. 180-182.
26   Erwin Panofsky, ' "Signum Triciput": Ein hellenistiches Kunstsymbol in her Kunst der Renaissance', *Hercules am Scheidewege*, pp. 1-35. For Panofsky's reading of Titian's *Allegory* in this essay, see pp. 1-9. He returns to it later in 'Titian's *Allegory of Prudence*: A Postscript', *Meaning in the Visual Arts* (Chicago: University of Chicago Press, 1955; Phoenix paper ed.), pp. 146-168.
27   Kahn, *Rhetoric, Prudence, and Skepticism in the Renaissance*. It is interesting to note that, in a discussion of the role prudence plays in Italian Renaissance art generally—a discussion keyed, like the present one, to Titian's *Allegory*—Summers entirely overlooks the darker implications that Kahn's link to Machiavellian scepticism suggests. Prudence thus figures in his account as an at once moral and intellectual discipline aimed at enabling art to achieve the golden mean of liberal imagination. See *The Judgment of Sense*, pp. 266-282.
28   On the 'palace' or 'theatre of memory', see Frances A. Yates's classic *The Art of Memory* (Chicago: University of Chicago Press, 1966). On history as a reservoir of examples, see Lyons, *Exemplum* and Hampton, *Writing from History*. While both books focus on the rhetorical function of examples, Hampton proposes a more highly developed analysis of how recent historical events (the discovery of America, the Reformation, the political chaos of Renaissance Italy as chronicled by Guicciardini) undermine the value of examples by confronting them with unprecedented circumstances for which no historical equivalent may be found.
29   See Panofsky, 'Postcript', 165-167. See too the commentary in Francesco Valcanover et al., *Titian, Prince of Painters* (Munich: Prestel, 1990), pp. 347-348.
30   A signal exception to this rule is Fumaroli. See especially *Héros et orateurs*, which documents how far Corneille's dramatic practice is shaped by rhetorical methods and models acquired from his schooling with the Jesuits in Rouen.
31   Though we possess a fair amount of anecdotal information for England relating to individuals (e.g., Thomas Nash or Christopher Marlowe), the only systematic sociological study I know is that for France by Alain Viala, *Naissance de l'écrivain* (Paris: Minuit, 1985). In a table on p. 247 summarizing data on social provenance derived from contemporary censuses of *gens de lettres*, we discover that 189 writers are 'advocates'. This is the single largest category, followed by 'gentlemen' (188),

'Jesuits' (163), 'priests' (147) and 'parliamentarians and members of courts' (103). When we recall that 'parliamentarians' are legislators and administrative officers, and that 'members of courts' are legal as well as administrative officers, 292 writers come from legal circles.

32   See Jacques Schérer *La Dramaturgie classique en France* (1950; repr. Paris: Nizet, 1986), p. 321 and his 'notice' to Montchrestien's *Hector* in *Théâtre du XVIIe siècle*, vol. 1, p. 1152.

33   For John of Gaunt, I cite William Shakespeare, *Richard II*, ed. John Dover Wilson (Cambridge: Cambridge University Press, 1939). For Webster's self-gratulation, see *The White Devil* in Gamini Salgado (ed.), *Three Jacobean Tragedies* (Harmondsworth: Penguin, 1965), p. 139.

34   François Hédelin, abbé d'Aubignac, *La Pratique du théâtre* (1657). I cite a facsimile of the Amsterdam edition of 1715 (Munich: Wilhelm Fink Verlag, 1971), p. 33. Subsequent references appear in the text.

35   These are constant themes in Montaigne's *Essais*, but see in particular 'De la force de l'imagination' (1: 21), 'De la coutume' (1: 23) and above all the 'Apologie de Raimond Sebond' (2: 12). Montaigne's deeply sceptical picture of imagination may be productively set beside the idealization to which the same faculty is treated in Italian aesthetic theory as chronicled by Summers. See *Michelangelo and the Language of Art*, pt. 1, 'Fantasy'.

36   For a helpful introduction to 'orientalist' developments in the context of French drama, see Michèle Longino, *Orientalism in French Classical Drama* (Cambridge: Cambridge University Press, 2002).

37   Benjamin, *The Origin of German Tragic Drama*, pp. 70-72. But see also the later discussion of fate (pp. 128-138), which returns to the question of agency via the comic characteristics of the 'intriguer' (pp. 125-128), and the celebrated analysis of *Trauer* as mourning and melancholy (pp. 138-158).

Chapter 4

Imaginary Selves: The Trial of Identity in Descartes, Pascal and Cyrano

Like the dramatic soliloquies it mirrors, Carracci's *Hercules* enacts the baroque's exemplary awareness of the historical fate encoded in its protagonist's ironic self-entanglement. But while baroque art may image the historical condition shared with other modes of expression, it cannot *conceptualize* it. Nor, consequently, can it marshal reason in defence of the truth whose defeat it portrays. This is the task philosophers undertake on the strength of the special rationality their profession boasts. We have already discussed, in chapter 1, some aspects of what becomes of truth in the natural philosophy of baroque Europe. This led us indeed to the Pauline ontology of light-in-darkness that informs baroque self-portraiture and to the 'painterly' temporality embodied in the principle of immanence shaping the soliloquistic thrust of both visual and dramatic art. But though truth may prove as elusive and intractable for philosophers as for painters and dramatists, it does so with a difference that repays closer attention; and it is to this difference that we now turn.

The key is the privileged instrument that philosophy devises to counter the historical pressures the environing culture exerts, namely, the *mind*—an 'invention', as Richard Rorty rightly calls it, specifically designed to secure its own inner operations through disciplined self-possession.[1] But can mind in fact rescue truth from the historical wreck that prompts its efforts? To answer this question, we must leave Shakespearean England and baroque Italy for Cartesian France since it is in France, and more particularly the France of Descartes, that modern philosophy of mind receives its first systematic formulation. Yet the move to France raises problems of its own. For in keeping with the 'geometric' rationality Descartes epitomizes, the hallmark of seventeeth-century French culture is a calculated self-consciousness that seems to set it apart from the wider European context.

As we noted in the introduction, a peculiarity of the French seventeenth century is the signal absence of the otherwise pan-European phenomenon of the baroque. As Jean Rousset argued back in the 1950s, this absence is more apparent than real.[2] Dazzled by the prestige of the 'siècle' or 'temps de Louis XIV', the French have constructed a short, 'classical' century confined to the decades between the foundation of the Académie Française in 1635 and the Revocation of the Edict of Nantes in 1685.[3] Even Corneille—as Marc Fumaroli has shown, the brilliant exponent of the quintessentially baroque art of rhetoric incorporated in the Jesuit *ratio studiorum*—tends to be read in an Aristotelian light he disdained and pointedly resisted.[4] The apparent absence of the baroque is to this extent an artifact of French reading habits rather than a feature of period culture. The fact nonetheless remains that French culture is in the main inhospitable to baroque inspiration.

It is noteworthy that the baroque is one of the few historical fields in which French scholars spontaneously set their national tradition alongside others. Victor-Lucien Tapié, Pierre Charpentrat and Christine Buci-Glucksmann all look mainly to Italy for the visual arts; Jean-François Maillard's book on the 'spirit' of baroque heroism gives greater weight to English and Spanish than to French examples; and the Leibniz of Gille Deleuze's *Le pli* is not only a German, but the personification of nothing less than the 'German soul' itself as Germany makes its 'entry' on the philosophical stage.[5] One reason for this unwonted internationalism is the international character of the baroque itself; like Renaissance humanists before them, baroque painters and poets are intensely aware of developments in other parts of Europe. But the chief reason is that the clearest exemplars of baroque style almost always come from non-French sources. It is not just that—apart from the lyrics of Théophile de Viau or the younger, free-thinking Saint-Amant, the dramas of Corneille and Rotrou, the romances of d'Urfé and Madeleine de Scudéry or the extravagant science fictions of the legendary Cyrano—the French baroque has little to compare either with its Spanish and Italian counterparts or with homegrown products of the neo-classical reaction that displaces it. The baroque is exposed from the outset to the merciless light of an ironic urbanity that destroys the heroic trompes-l'œil and remedial allegories of baroque idealism.[6]

Whence, in an issue of *Littératures classiques* symptomatically devoted to 'the baroque in question(s)', an essay by Pascal Dumont that plots the evolution of seventeenth-century French philosophical prose along a teleological continuum in which the ornate baroque periods of Descartes's *Discours de la méthode* (1637) and *Méditations métaphysiques* (1641) give way to the 'attic' severities of Pascal's *Pensées* (1670). As we will see, Pascal's vaunted 'classical' austerity incorporates a deeply baroque perspectivism closely allied to equally baroque anxieties about the deluding rhetorical 'persuasiveness' that defines the limits of human rationality. Nor should we forget the 'asiatic' turn of texts like Bossuet's funeral orations or the same author's *Discours sur l'histoire universelle* (1681), monuments of the Ludovican era habitually marginalized in conventional accounts of French literary history. Dumont's essay still espouses a majority view that, in taking the urbane decorum of high classical rationality as its standard, leaves little room for the passionate irregularities of baroque feeling.[7]

I do not pretend to explain why this should be so—though a major marker is surely the complex of social, aesthetic and political forces focused through the censorship exerted by the Académie, a body that, in the notorious 'querelle du *Cid*' of 1637, punished Corneille just for those features of his dramaturgy that are most baroque.[8] However, I do urge that we avoid the temptation to adduce France's apparent singularity simply and circularly to French *classicism* and the critical rationality with which French classicism is confederate. According to this view, the bane of the baroque in France is the collective historical personage whose triumph is said to coincide with the advent of the modern subject in the philosophy of Descartes.[9] Demanding the critical 'clarity' and 'distinctness' that define the Cartesian ego as the authoritative type of modern selfhood, French culture deliberately eschews the high-minded enthusiasms and spectacular bipolar excesses endemic to baroque style. As Deleuze remarks in contrasting Leibnizian 'monadology' with the methodic 'essentialism' Descartes champions, the restless metamorphoses that characterize the baroque *conceit* yield to the luminous discipline of classical *concepts*. Where the baroque portrays thought and thing as mobile poles joined in an endless process of reciprocal transformation, classicism rigorously discriminates, fixing each term in its own distinct essence.[10] The result is classical *order*, the architectonic scheme of invariant identities that organizes experience to form the carefully sorted yet mutually reinforcing systems of nature, society, philosophy and art. By the end of the seventeenth century, France becomes the envy of the whole of 'cultured' Europe. Yet what makes it so is neither French military nor French mercantile might, both badly compromised by the self-lacerating futility of Louis XIV's Dutch Wars (1672-78) and the long economic decline they helped produce. The secret is French *taste*—the knowing rationality and decorous *savoir faire* distilled in the doctrine of 'honnêteté'.[11]

Over against this picture, I argue that the apparent absence of the baroque is an optical illusion produced by the special form it takes in French culture. The very classicism that persuades even the subtlest deconstructors of the *grand siècle*, Foucault, Marin or Deleuze, to regard it as a preeminently classical age shapes the characteristic French contribution to the baroque: the unique French sense of *texts* and the critical modes of *reading* it engenders. A paradigm is a passage from the preamble to Georges de Scudéry's nasty *Observations* (1637) on Corneille's *Le Cid*. Goaded in part by *Le Cid*'s unprecedented popular success, Scudéry launches an avalanche of furious accusations, alleging everything from incompetent plotting and the flouting of elementary rules of verisimilitude and decorum to depraved morals, hypocrisy, *lèse-majesté* and plagiarism—this last sustaining the charge that what few good things the play contains have been lifted verbatim from Corneille's model in Castro's *Mocedades del Cid*.[12] Scudéry nevertheless has a problem. If the play is so self-evidently bad, how do we explain what angers him, namely, its immense public appeal? His solution is to claim that the play's admirers are the victims of a collective hallucination:

> It is with certain Plays as with certain animals in Nature, that from afar seem Stars, but, close to [*de près*], are only tiny worms. All that glitters is not always precious, one sees beauties of illusion as well as genuine ones, and often the semblance of good passes for good itself. Nor am I surprised that the people, who carry judgment in their eyes, allow themselves to be duped by that one of all senses the easiest to deceive.[13]

While his motives are hardly of the purest, Scudéry mines the important distinction between how a play appears when encountered in the unreflecting immediacy of theatrical performance and what it is subsequently discovered to be when viewed 'close to', in a careful reading of its text. The distinction parallels the one Stanley Fish detects at the basis of the 'aesthetic of the good physician' in the moralist literature of seventeenth-century England, setting off the 'rhetorical' manipulation of sensual passion from the 'dialectical' stimulation of critical judgment and the habits of instructive self-scrutiny such judgment instils.[14] Scudéry's point is that the overwhelming illusions of dramatic action and delivery disable judgment by activating sensuous appetite and unreflecting identificatory response.[15] Reading, by contrast, engages active intelligence, sifting appearances to frame the careful discriminations alone capable of determining a work's true value. Where the play as scenic event dupes the beholder, the play as text invites an integrally rational assessment; and the harsh light of such assessment reveals *Le Cid* for the dramaturgically incompetent and morally bankrupt monstrosity it is.

Yet the crux is the contradiction Scudéry's strategy involves. The ideology asserted at his rival's expense is plainly classical: though Scudéry deploys high baroque conceits of his own, especially (and symptomatically) in comedy, Aristotle is the stick with which he beats Corneille.[16] But the trope that frames his Aristotelian critique is itself a prime example of high baroque perspectivism. The sudden shift of light and attitude that transforms Corneille's heroic illusion into a mass of pullulating worms exhibits the sort of anamorphic effect baroque scientists and philosophers as well as painters and poets exploited, now in fact, now as metaphor, through the 'curious perspective' of dioptric and catoptric lenses.[17] Still, as John Lyons's book on classical theory suggests, what occasions this anamorphic shift is not a special construction or lens, but a critical act of reading: 'If the dramatic theory of seventeenth-century France inaugurates a certain cultural modernity, it does so by disseminating the concepts of dramatic and literary criticism and by transferring authority from "authors" in the medieval sense to readers.'[18] The crucial thing is Scudéry's intense commitment to the text and the paradoxical routes by which the text exposes the illusions it perpetrates.

Deleuze treats this recursive quality, the backward turn of what he calls the 'pleat' or 'fold', as the central emblem of baroque culture; and it certainly shapes his reading of Leibnizian finalism. But it is remarkable how Deleuze *makes* the pleat in the very act of finding it, a reflex of the reading that ferrets it out. His account of Leibniz's notorious cosmological optimism, for instance, hinges on a chiastic inversion that sets the standard formula on its head: 'If this world exists, it is not because it is the best, but rather just the reverse; it is the best because it exists, because it is the world that is.'[19] Deleuze resorts to chiasmus again in order to plot the originality of Leibniz's version of the dualist picture of the relation of mind and body shared with Descartes. Thus Descartes presents mind as an ontologically distinct entity whose contingent (and therefore logically unnecessary) assignment to a body explains the impurities that 'obscure' the otherwise pellucid medium of 'mental' as opposed to carnal sight. For Leibniz, by contrast, the true relation is arrived at by the eminently Deleuzian route of a paradoxical reversal:

> I *must* have a body, this is a moral necessity, a 'demand'. And for start, I must have a body because there is obscurity in me [...] [Leibniz] does not say that the body explains what is obscure in the mind. On the contrary, the mind is obscure, the mind is at bottom dark, and it is this dark nature that explains and demands a body.[20]

As baroque as the twists and turns of Leibniz's finalist monadology is the pattern of Deleuzian hermeneutics: the orgy of critical ingenuity reproduces the phenomenon it fastens on. However, as important as the ingenuity is the *justice*. As I have explained elsewhere, Scudéry is in fact right about Corneille;[21] and Deleuze is right about Leibniz, too. The texts on which such readings focus their baroque acuity lay out the purchase points on which the readings fix their complicating folds.

Such is the moral of the texts explored here: the seventh of Cyrano de Bergerac's *Lettres diverses* (1654), 'Sur l'ombre que faisoient des arbres dans l'eau', and a fragment from Pascal's *Pensées*, 'Qu'est-ce que le moi?' The first thing to note is that both texts are readings. They not only allude to another text, in Cyrano's case Ovid's *Metamorphoses*, turned to demoralizing effect in the service of his underlying materialism; they actively *inhabit* another text in order to administer a characteristic twist or fold. And in each case the text in question is both famous and authoritative, one that owes its authority to the form it gives the modern subject: the text of Descartes. The point of each text is then how it reads Descartes, fastening on the telltales by which his writings occasion what we can only term the deconstruction Pascal and Cyrano effect. And not the least consequence of this deconstruction is to show that the ostensibly classical Descartes proves as baroque as the readers who cannibalize him.

The initial attack develops along a wide front, aimed less at specific passages than at the commanding presumption of Cartesian metaphysics as a whole: the dualist severance of mind and body presented as both a major finding and an enabling condition of rational reflection and the methodic 'search for the truth'.[22] For Cyrano and Pascal alike, the radical distinction of mind and body is not, as Descartes imagines, a pure deliverance of the special mode of philosophical experience formalized in the cogito; it is also the result of a project of self-fashioning. Dualism describes the form Descartes imposes on mind in virtue of what he takes knowledge to be: necessary and invariant as opposed to 'provisional', purely contingent insight of the ethical sort sketched out in the *morale provisoire*.[23] Descartes does in some sense *discover* disembodied mind as an implicate of the self-conscious testing of knowledge's sources and certainty. To this extent, mind is immanent to the self-correcting rational procedure that unearths it. But far from disclosing the essential nature of the mental substance whose existence it reveals, the discovery is circular in that it registers the modification mind has had to produce in its own structure to lend knowledge the shape it must assume to qualify *as* knowledge—as inner personal possession of the transcendental entity Descartes calls 'the truth'.

As a recent biographer reminds us, Cartesian epistemology and the metaphysics that buttress it are relatively late developments in Descartes's career.[24] Though the *Discours de la méthode* is the first published work, Descartes had already formulated the complete physical system mapped out in his treatises on the Universe and Man and further adumbrated in the three texts (on dioptrics, meteors and geometry) appended to the first edition of the *Discours* as 'trials' of the method. Descartes's epistemology is thus the fruit of meditations on a firmly-established enterprise that antedates it by more than a decade,[25] a work of explication that turns back on the scientific pursuits it prefaces in order to bring to light latent conditions already in force even if the scientist has remained indifferent to them. And what the epistemological turn discovers is dualism—but dualism conceived less as what categorically *is* the case of the mental activity it describes than as what would have hypothetically *to be* the case for something like knowledge as Descartes pictures it to occur.

The separation of mind and body walls off the rational search for truth from everything that distorts the operations of a well-regulated mind: our deceptive bodily senses and the 'humours' and 'passions' they express; and everything we inherit *along with* our passions, humours and sensory perceptions—the assumptions, customs, idioms and identities we acquire as historical inhabitants of a socially and culturally prefabricated world. This is indeed a major function of the process of hyperbolic doubt undertaken in the *Méditations métaphysiques*. In marshaling arguments designed to leave only those items that resist every attempt at sceptical reduction, Descartes tries to purge knowledge of undigested contents smuggled in from the realm of pre-philosophical experience. True, as attested by the extravagant hypothesis of an 'evil genius' credited with omnipotent powers of persuasive delusion, the lengths to which Descartes is prepared to go to eliminate such influences underscore their tenacity. Nor is it difficult to show how far Descartes remains a prisoner of contemporary ideology. Whence the cogency of Foucault's analysis of Descartes's dismissal of the ostensibly self-refuting postulate of madness in the first meditation (vol. 2, pp. 405-406). Descartes's conviction that the mere fact of questioning one's own sanity precludes the possibility it envisages reveals how deeply doubt is rooted in unquestioned canons of rational order for which madness proves unthinkably other.[26] The case Foucault makes regarding subjacent canons of reason can also be made concerning the acts of social identification to which Erica Harth, Michael Moriarty or Alain Faudemay draw attention. The search for infallible criteria enabling philosophers to distinguish true from false is ultimately complicitous with contemporary codes of taste and conduct designed to defend social discriminations blurred by the growing *embourgeoisement* of early modern French society. The question of the grounds on which right judgments of true and false, good and bad, tasteful and distasteful depend thus reinforce the class distinctions it is judgment's business to confer and certify.[27] But all of this suggests that dualism's meaning was from the start more practical than dogmatic: the doctrine

Descartes presents as supplying an unshakeable foundation for rational thought constitutes a *project* rather than a finding. To know, as Descartes conceives it, is to know unconditionally, converting the data of contingent, pre-scientific experience into items of permanent understanding. And this in turn demands divorcing not only the data, but the perceptions that deliver them from everything *in* experience that inevitably conditions them.

Such is the tenor of Descartes's own career as rehearsed in the autobiographical portions of the *Discours* and the first and second meditations. The problem of determining science's true ground reflects a prior commitment: it is a symptom of the degree to which the habits, prejudices, creeds, languages and traditions that define thought's human environment continue to shape our perspective on the world and the kind of place we take that world to be. The primary office of the procedure of hyperbolic doubt is in truth, as Husserl asserts, a sceptical 'suspension' of the 'natural attitude'. But if such a suspension seems necessary, it is just because there *is* a natural attitude and the preformed sense of nature it enfolds.[28] Dualism is the echo of a deed, something we do at once with and to mind in order to enable it to function independently of the embodied contexts that determine its sphere. The cogito enacts what it purports to discover, *bringing about* the desired detachment from bodily absorption in a naturalized social, cultural and psychological world that Descartes takes it to register.

In a passage late in the *Discours* already glanced at in chapter 1, Descartes outlines the content of the posthumous treatise on the World (1664), a testing of the waters motivated by the recent condemnation of Galileo that incidentally confirms the ineluctable situatedness dualism seeks to overcome:

> I planned to comprehend in it everything I thought I had learned, before writing it, touching on the nature of material things. But just as painters, being unable to represent equally on a flat canvas all the various faces of a solid body, choose one of the chief among them and, turning it alone toward the light source, leave the others in shadow, causing them to appear only so far as they can be seen while looking at the first; so I, fearing that I would be unable to put in my discourse everything I had in thought, undertook to expose fully only what I understood of light; then, on the occasion of light, to add something about the sun and the fixed stars, because it almost entirely proceeds from them; about the heavens, because they transmit it; about planets, comets and the earth, because they reflect it; and in particular about all the bodies that lie on the earth, because they are either coloured, or transparent, or luminous; and finally about man, because he is its spectator. (vol. 1, pp. 614-615)

The passage begins by addressing a problem of exposition. In keeping with the cogito's picture of human understanding as an act of mental vision divorced from all bodily admixture, and among them those attending human language and communication, Descartes's difficulty is to convey, in writing, 'everything I thought I had learned, *before* writing it, touching on the nature of material things'. The problem then is how to convey his physical system, *in* its entirety and *as* an entirety, to people who have not yet 'invented' or discovered it for themselves.[29] How does one communicate, in the inevitably flattening because sequential medium of discourse, what is by its very nature a volumetric whole, comprehensible only integrally, as a universal system? The solution flows from a strategic analogy. Just as painters are obliged to choose one face of a given object, making others appear 'only so far as they can be seen while looking at the first', so Descartes chooses to begin with light, proceeding from there, by a chain of pseudo-causal inferences, to discuss the sun and stars because they produce it; the heavens because they transmit it; planets, comets and the earth because they reflect it; then the various bodies found on the earth forasmuch as light illumines them; and so on down to Man 'because he is its spectator'.

Yet it is striking that, arising at the point where the exposition reaches its at once logical and causal culmination, the figure of Man as spectator turns out to have structured the entire development from the start. The passage on *Le Monde*, and by extension *Le Monde* itself, ends where it begins, with the transcendental figure of the Cartesian ego whose concerted act of vision converts light into the cosmic spectacle the text unfolds before our eyes. The structure of Cartesian science, in its character as an emergent rational whole, anticipates the movement of the metaphysics that supplies its theory. The progress of hyperbolic doubt concludes by hitting on the transcendental self whose thinking turns out to have been its condition of possibility all along. Just so, the exhibition of the universal system of nature folds back on the rational spectator whose activity *frames* the spectacle to which the system owes its self-ratifying authority.

The spectator thus makes a spectacle that reveals him as its source only because of the form he has given it by constructing himself as spectator. This in turn means that the spectator arises as a product of the picture he produces: his status as origin is implied not by the system of the world, but by the order of its representation.[30] The spectator is a correlate of the form to which Cartesian science reduces the world in order to shape it for the purposes of knowledge. The nature the cogito attributes the philosophical spectator as a bodiless 'thing that thinks' is an artifact of a methodical fiction—a necessary fiction perhaps, a sort of regulative idea directing the activity it makes possible, but a fiction nonetheless. If something like science proves possible, it must be on the basis of our rational power to divorce ourselves as minds from the spectacle of nature in order for there to be such a spectacle in the first place. If nature offers the purchase knowledge requires, it is because human beings are capable of adopting, as spectators, the attitude of detachment for which (in the passage) painters provide an analogy. Far from being the inalienable intellectual possession Descartes imagines, the knowledge science achieves is, at bottom, as provisional and strategic as the moral knowledge that enables us to negotiate a safe passage through the social contexts in which scientists live and work. It is something we create by striking a certain posture: a posture by which we modify our own natures in order to *become* minds divorced from bodies, or rather bodies whose new relation to the world is what Descartes construes as disembodied mind.

Consider in this context the mysterious matter of Descartes's dream. In the *Vie de M. Descartes* (1691), the philosopher's first biographer, Adrien Baillet, draws on a now-lost Latin manuscript, partially copied by Leibniz, that contained several unpublished writings composed in Descartes's youth: the 'Preambles' and 'Observations', recording some of his earliest surviving philosophical reflections, and the 'Olympica', recounting a dream experienced on the night immediately following the famous Illumination of 10 November 1619. Shut up alone in a heated room (the famous *poêle*) in an inn near Ulm in Germany, the young philosopher was granted a thrilling preview of what would become the Method. The preview's major theme was the literally cosmic scale of what its use would enable him to achieve: namely, science itself in the absolute, semi-mystical, Faustian sense still current in Descartes's day, before the diminution entailed by science's specialization as a particular professional discipline. Baillet relates how, in the state of nervous exhaustion the illumination brought on, the young philosopher had a brainstorm ('le feu lui prit au cerveau') during which 'he fell into a sort of enthusiasm that so disposed his already exhausted mind as to put it in a condition to receive the impressions of dreams and visions' (vol. 1, p. 53). The fruit of this at once eminently baroque and decidedly un-Cartesian state of mental excitement was a curious three-part dream.

The dream opens with a picture of the dreamer lost on an open road in the middle of the night, unable to stand upright owing to a heavy wind that blocks his forward progress, and terrified of falling (p. 53). As the dream continues, the wind abruptly reverses course. Having impeded the dreamer's advance, it now pushes him from behind the moment he seeks refuge from the nocturnal elements by directing his steps toward a building—the church attached to a school, clearly a memory of the Jesuit Collège de la Flèche, where Descartes received his formal education (p. 53). This initial phase gives way to the sudden terrified conviction that the preceding afternoon's vision had been a satanic delusion encouraged by some 'evil genius' intent on leading Descartes to madness and ruin (pp. 53-54). After urgent prayers to God pleading for forgiveness for his sins and for help in his terrible need, and a great clap of thunder followed by a burst of fiery light illumining the darkness (p. 54), the philosopher enters the third and final movement of the dream, where he encounters a series of writings. The first is a Dictionary that, though infusing the dreamer with 'the hope that it would be useful to him' (p. 55), turns out to be incomplete (p. 56). The second is a copy of the *Corpus poetarum*, a widely disseminated anthology of classical verse the dreamer opens to an idyll by Ausonius beginning *Quod vitae sectabor iter?* 'What road shall I follow in this life?' (p. 55) The third text, glossing the second, is a verse from another idyll by Ausonius, also contained in the *Corpus poetarum*, but presented to the dreamer by a stranger who suddenly appears with verses in his hand. The new idyll bears the Greek title *Nai kai ou Pythagorikou*, 'The Yes and No of Pythagoras' (p. 55).[31] The dream then concludes with a sustained act of interpretation begun while the philosopher is still immersed in the confused half-waking, half-sleeping state from which, 'doubting if he dreamt or if he meditated', the dreamer at last rouses himself (p. 57).[32]

The dream contains all of the ruling metaphors and many of the crucial episodes in Cartesian metaphysics. In the second part of the *Discours*, introducing the account of the method, Descartes describes the caution inspired by his disenchantment with the system of knowledge absorbed in school: 'But like a man who walks alone in darkness, I resolved to go so slowly and to employ so much circumspection in all things that, even if I made little progress, I would at least guard against falling.' (vol. 1, p. 584) This image of the method directly recalls the nocturnal wanderings that mark the first part of the dream. In addition to invoking the physical plan of the Collège de la Flèche, the church in which the dreamer seeks asylum prefigures the many architectural analogies ornamenting Descartes's writings. In particular, it anticipates the simile that introduces the discussion of the 'morale provisoire' in the third part of the *Discours*, where the philosopher admits that 'it is not enough', when setting about 'to rebuild the dwelling we live in', simply to 'demolish' the old one once we have secured designs and materials for its replacement; we must also supply ourselves 'with another, in which we may comfortably dwell while the new one is built' (vol. 1, p. 591). Similarly, the evil genius whose perfidious influence dominates the dream's opening sequence forecasts the *malin génie* whose apparition in the *Méditations* marks the climax of the procedure of hyperbolic doubt (vol. 2, p. 412). Descartes himself explicitly makes this connection. Thus, during the curious passage of self-diagnosis conducted at the boundary between waking and dream, he interprets the wind as 'nothing other than the evil Genius' who, having first impeded his advance, was then converted into a force for good 'that endeavoured to compel him to go where he intended to voluntarily' (vol. 1, p. 58). The burst of light that cleanses the dream of evil influences in its second phase looks toward the fiery principle that structures the exposition of the physical universe in *Le Monde*; and the Dictionary Descartes discovers in the third part of the dream is the exact equivalent of the 'great book of the world' for whose sake he abandoned the traditional learning imbibed in school (vol. 1, p. 577). As Descartes himself observes, the Dictionary is 'nothing other' than a compendium of 'all of the Sciences gathered together', thereby serving as a model for *Le Monde* itself (vol. 1, p. 56). Given the root of the word 'method' in the Greek *hodos* or 'road', the verse from Ausonius ('What road shall I follow in this life?') points squarely at the method (*meta-hodos*) whose invention provokes the dream. The dreamer himself interprets the Pythagorean title of Ausonius' second idyll as defining the central task philosophy undertakes—that of identifying 'truth and falsehood in human knowledge and the profane sciences' (vol. 1, p. 57). And overlapping the transition from half-sleep to full arousal, Descartes's attempts to interpret the dream stand at the frontier between dreaming and waking states that the first meditation cites as one of the more unanswerable reasons for doubting the veracity of our conscious thoughts (vol. 2, pp. 406-407).

The sheer number of points at which dream and philosophy meet underscores a further remarkable feature of the dream, namely, its absence from the official record of Descartes's life furnished in the *Discours*. As Baillet's transcription of the philosopher's own analysis of the dream makes clear (vol. 1, pp. 58-60), it is to the dream that Descartes expressly owes the testimony (defended on quite different grounds in the metaphysics) of God's assent to the truth of his philosophy. Nevertheless, the dream has been completely excised from the *Dis-*

cours's account of the memorable day. When it does finally surface in Descartes's writings, it is in disguise, as two of the monsters the knight errant of science must slay in the unfolding saga of hyperbolic doubt: in the form of dream itself, conceived as a deceiving simulacrum of reality, and in the figure of the evil genius, the very personification of falsehood and error, embodying the utmost extremity of anguished nescience and doubt.

So though unrecorded in the public text of Cartesian metaphysics, the dream leaves its traces everywhere. But what do these traces mean? Georges Poulet suggests that the dream springs directly from the terrible mutilation Descartes inflicts on his own personality in maintaining the attitude of dualist detachment required to reduce the world to perspicuous rational order.[33] In repressing the dream, he represses whole realms of experience intimately bound up with the *capacity* for dream: the sense of embodiment in a personal as against a purely intellectual history; the sense of unreasoning (rather than guardedly provisional) allegiance to a family, faith, people and way of life; perhaps above all, as symbolized by the appearance, in the courtyard of the school in which Descartes seeks refuge, of a man holding a melon brought from some foreign country (vol. 1, p.53), the sense of physical pleasures and appetites Descartes deigns to look at closely only in the late *Passions de l'âme* (1649), and even then solely with a view to breaking their scandalous grip on our powers of critical reflexion.[34] The dream marks the return of the repressed: the demonic underside of the hubris that, in insisting on its concealment, transforms it into a vengeful source of a bewilderment and terror.

But we can push the reading further, making the tale more tellingly personal than Poulet does. The complex tangle of substitutions, condensations and displacements legible in the dream enacts a fantasy one of whose referents is the baptismal name 'René' concealed beneath the obligatory patronym 'Descartes'. Whether in the form of the authorized legend recounting the methodized vision of Descartes's waking self or in that of the nocturnal fairytale of demonic possession and heavenly rescue played out in the dream, the hero undergoes an ordeal of death and resurrection, a dismembering descent into hell that gives way at last to a long, steep climb to wholeness and freedom. The metaphysician and natural scientist of the overt life and the scared somnambulist of the dream are alike *renés*, literally reborn. What is more, in engineering his rebirth as the dualist hero of a reformed science, Descartes simultaneously suppresses and transforms not merely his own body, the particular passionate, historically determinate, distressingly exigent machine he risks at every moment being mistaken for,[35] but as it were the body of embodiment itself.

The metaphors that structure the text of Cartesian metaphysics encode the multiform figure of the Mother lost and found. There is the biological mother from the prehistory of infancy. But there is also her symbolic twin, whose unacknowledged agency mediates the primal act of self-assertive intellect at the historic root of the dualist *res cogitans* that, in severing its links with the body, disowns embodying maternity as well. The Cartesian mother is thus twice lost: the first time as a matter of biography, Descartes's actual mother dying when he was one-year old; the second by way of metaphor, in Descartes's account of the sceptical crisis that overtook him as his formal schooling reached an end. Indeed, looked at closely, the passage in the first part of the *Discours* bearing on the philosopher's education describes a belated 'rapprochement', the moment when the developing child foresakes infantile engrossment in the nourishing maternal body in order to acquire independent personal identity through symbolic identification with the father. Having reached an age that 'permitted me to shake off obedience to my preceptors' (vol. 1, p. 576), Descartes (René) deserts the only mother he had known: the school (and faith) to which his father had sent him as an orphan to be 'nourished on letters since childhood' (vol. 1, p. 571). But the mother is also twice found. It is to her that he returns in the heated room in which he takes refuge during the picaresque travels through the Grimmelshausian Germany of the Thirty Years War to which his abandonment of the literary speculations of his schooldays led him. She accordingly provides, by symbolic association, the womblike asylum in which, floating in the amniotic medium of undistracted thought, the philosopher achieves his epoch-making breakthrough. And we meet her again in the dream: in the chapel to which, like a fearful infant first learning to walk, he turns for shelter from the night terrors of the dream's first movement; and then, when the dream achieves its climax with the divine imprimatur conveyed by the burst of illumining light and the coded messages delivered by an unknown hand, in the person of the Virgin Mary, to whom he vows a pilgrimage to secure her help in the great enterprise to which he henceforth consecrates his life (vol. 1, pp. 59-60). And in each case, having found her, he is at last set free, at once born again and as it were born for the first time as an autonomous, individuated being.

Each Descartes is thus René: the Cartesian text compulsively rehearses the story of a double birth. In the great paternity battle from which modern science emerges, the public persona (Descartes) obstinately insists that he has accomplished his own (re)birth by dint of sheer, self-originating intelligence and will, a Minerva sprung from the Jovian fecundity of his own brain. Yet the nocturnal René just as stubbornly invokes the secret ally without whom he could not succeed even though he can never confess so much as her existence: the mother (the body) he denies yet nonetheless ceaselessly reproduces as the silent partner to the primal act of science. The freestanding, autarchic Cartesian individual is not only double, but triangular. Just because it is portrayed as radically self-determined, the public role he resolves to play in the adult world of symbolic action demands that he represent in himself father, son and mother all at once.[36]

All of which lends a fresh resonance to Descartes's text. We have already noted in chapter 1 the sexual as well as intellectual hegemony informing the famous characterization of science as making us 'masters and possessors of nature' (vol. 1, p. 634). The same spirit infuses his insistence on the essential intimacy that identifies true acts of knowledge, as when he asserts that 'one can never conceive a thing so well, and make it one's own, when one learns it from another as when one discovers [*invente*] it for oneself' (vol. 1, p. 641). Beyond reinforcing the picture of scientific understanding as a vexatious seizure of the truths it conceives, the assertion enfolds the subtly gendered notion of conception itself. In this regard, the Œdipal triangle observed a moment ago stands out with special clarity. In the absence of other players in the primal drama, Descartes is obliged to double in himself as the mother of the truths he undertakes to sire. Whence the notorious doctrine of 'innate ideas' to which Locke so vigorously objects: 'seeds of truths that are naturally in our souls' (vol. 1, p. 636) prior to all experience whose job it is to reestablish the link with the world of physical embodiment that Cartesian science makes so difficult to explain.[37] Nor should we overlook Descartes's decision to commit not only the autobiographical *Discours*, but many of his scientific works, including the late *Passions de l'âme*, written largely at the instance of a woman, Elizabeth of Bohemia, Princess Palatine, to the mother tongue of his native French in preference to the paternal Latin of professional philosophy. Just because it is so signally absent, the dream becomes ubiquitous. Left officially unwritten, there is nothing for it but to *write*; and what it writes is nothing less than the text of its own deconstruction. The project of science assumes the character of an anagramme, a literary anamorphosis whose resolving perspective is the very thing it scrupulously elides. The cogito's picture of mental activity is incomplete, and distorted by its incompleteness. But it also contains, as indices or clues, the essential elements of what it misrepresents, legible to an eye adjusted to the light required to see them.

Such is the testimony of the Pascalian fragment, 'Qu'est-ce que le moi?' The projected *Apologie de la religion chrétienne* constantly targets Descartes as the very embodiment of both the intellectual pride the apology aims to humble and the idle curiosity in the natural world the apology portrays as an empty distraction from the care of the soul that ought to be a Christian's overriding concern.[38] What distinguishes the present fragment however is that, beyond citing Descartes's baleful influence, Pascal marshals the Cartesian text against itself, rewriting it, word for word, at his adversary's expense.

> *Qu'est-ce que le moi?* [What is self, or what am I, or, more literally, what is 'me'?]
>
> A man goes to the window to watch the passers-by; if I pass that way, can I say that he went there to see me? No; for he is not thinking of me in particular. But he who loves someone for his beauty, does he love him? No: for smallpox, which kills beauty without killing the person, will cause him to withdraw his love. And if someone loves me for my judgment, for my memory, does he love me? *me*? No, for I can lose those qualities without losing myself. Where then is this self if it is neither in the body nor in the soul? And how could one love the body or the soul if not for these qualities, which are in no way what make self, since they are perishable? For could one love the substance of a person's soul, abstractly, and whatever qualities it had? This cannot be, and would be wrong [*injuste*]. Thus one never loves anyone, but only qualities.
>
> Let us then no longer mock those who demand that we honour them for commissions and offices, for no one ever loves anyone except for borrowed qualities. (688/567)

The fragment has a precise location in Descartes's second meditation. The philosopher has just finished the famous example of verifying the identity of a malleable bit of wax over time to demonstrate that the mind grants the knowledge of physical objects we seem to derive from the senses.[39] He now encounters the problem of 'other minds' in the example of automata constructed to look and act in every way like real human beings. Descartes explains how part of the problem of determining the true source of our knowledge of the ongoing identity of the bit of wax stems from habits of speech. Though it is the mind alone that judges that the mutable and contradictory information the senses supply refers to one and the same object, still,

> we say that we see the same bit of wax when one presents it to us, and not that we judge that it is the same because it has the same colour and figure; whence I would almost conclude that we know the bit of wax by the sight of our eyes and not solely through mental inspection, were it not that, by chance, I look from a window at some men passing in the street, at sight of whom I do not fail to say that I see men, just as I say that I see a bit of wax; and yet what do I see from this window if not hats and coats that may cover spectres or feigned men moved by hidden springs [*sub quibus latere possent automata*]? But I judge that these are true men, and thus do I understand solely through the power of judgment that resides in my mind what I thought I saw with my eyes. (vol. 2, pp. 426-27)

The problem is that, from the standpoint of the senses, there is in principle nothing to distinguish a true human being from a diabolically clever replica capable of simulating the appearances and behaviours we associate with the genuine article. Unlike Alan Turing and his progeny among exponents of what John Searle calls 'strong Artificial Intelligence',[40] Descartes assumes that we do in fact make the distinction—primarily (though he does not say so here) on the basis of language and the general range of intelligent activities of which language, and especially the critically self-conscious language of rational reflexion, constitutes the canonic token.[41] An automaton may act all of the physical parts of a human being, but it cannot talk—or at least, in talking, cannot exhibit the self-determined rational spontaneity on whose grounds I judge that other minds (as distinct from bodies) exist.

But this offers Pascal his opening, the point at which he enters the text in order to rewrite it. In an extraordinary anticipation of the Turing Test, Pascal realizes that, for all language may be a rational behaviour, it remains *behaviour*, and thus a constituent of the physical world from which Descartes distinguishes mind.[42] Moreover, insofar as behaviour is an entirely physical event, it can be imitated. There is then in principle, at least on the grounds Descartes claims, no way to distinguish mind from non-mind since there is no way to distinguish behaviour from behaviour. Even Descartes must acknowledge that other minds cannot in fact distinguish themselves on the basis of behaviour since it requires a separate act of judgment to assert a behavioural distinction I discover (or 'invent') rather than strictly observe. And since the behaviour I judge to demonstrate the existence of another mind is as such susceptible to imitation, it follows that experience as Descartes defines it provides no means of making the distinction even when adjusted to allow for acts of mental inspection independent of the mere mechanical work of the senses.

Yet Pascal aims not simply to rebut Descartes's proof of other minds; he means to defeat Cartesian mind itself, and by specifically Cartesian means. To this end, the fragment not only critiques, but radicalizes the cogito. Where Descartes pursues the subtractive process of hyperbolic doubt until he reaches the unshakeable certainty of his own conscious ego, whereupon he comes to a prudent halt, Pascal sees no reason to stop at consciousness, but pushes on until even that evaporates.[43]

The first step is a shift of perspective. In Descartes, the problem of other minds arises in the context of a supplementary argument on dualism's behalf. By showing how the knowledge of other minds belongs to the mind alone, a product of the judgments it forms on the basis and yet, in the final analysis, independently of information derived from the senses, Descartes reinforces the distinction between mind and body the cogito enshrines. And this in turn enables him to say again, 'Je suis, j'existe'. However, where Descartes is content simply to repeat 'I am, I exist', Pascal now asks, what *is* this thing, this 'I' or (more pointedly) this 'me' (*moi*) whose existence I assert? 'Qu'est-ce que le moi?' 'Mind', Descartes circularly replies. But Pascal sees the circle, and jumps at it.

It is important that the mere fact of explicitly asking the question that Descartes elides by presenting it as its own circular answer also changes that question. The change is moreover implicit in the grammar involved. For the question entails a case shift, replacing the nominative 'I' (*je*) of the cogito with the objective 'me' (*moi*) on which the question turns. French could of course, like English, frame the question in the nominative, asking 'Qu'est-ce que je suis?' 'What am I?' The form Pascal chooses is nonetheless more natural at least to the extent of being more idiomatic. To ask, in French, what I am (as opposed, for instance, to what I do or say or think) spontaneously (idiomatically) demands the objective form of the pronoun, turning the 'je' of subjective agency into the passive 'moi'. Further, in French and English alike, the objective form of the pronoun is more fundamental in that it is the one to which we naturally resort for emphasis or to mark the urgency of self-reference: 'What about me?' 'Me, too'. 'Et moi alors?' 'Moi, je'. The point is that, once attention turns from self as transitive agent to self as phenomenon, the ontological ground of action or thought, both tongues prescribe the objective form—in French, by shifting from 'je' to 'moi', in English from 'I' to 'me' or, more strikingly still, from 'I' to the third-person 'self'. Thus the very form of the question Pascal puts concerning the nature of the Cartesian thing-that-thinks, a form grammar dictates as a function of what ordinary language tacitly takes self to be, enjoins a change of case. And this in turn demands a displacement in whose light Descartes's stress on the 'I' of autonomous agency is shown to be both inadequate and misleading.

This leads to the second step, which takes the form of a reversal. Pascal turns Descartes's example against itself by placing himself, as 'moi', not where Descartes does—namely, at the spectator's vantage point, the convenient window from which the Cartesian ego watches the passers-by—but rather outside in the street, among the passers-by themselves. The problem accordingly ceases to be one of determining how I verify that other minds exist; it becomes rather one of knowing how other minds verify mine. What am I—what, if you like, is *in* my mind—that others know I exist? How moreover do they determine that I even have a mind and, along with it, the sort of identity Descartes claims I would discover for myself were I, 'once in my life' (vol. 2, p. 404), to follow him down the road of doubt toward truth?

So having first changed Descartes's question by asking it, Pascal now reformulates its premises by shifting ground: 'A man goes to the window to watch the passers-by; if I pass that way, can I say he went there to see me?' The answer, clearly, is no. What the Cartesian onlooker goes to the window to see is not me, but 'passers-by', among whom I happen to be numbered. Assuming he does see me as opposed to someone else, it is an accident. But in seeing me by accident, an anonymous pedestrian the onlooker neither sets out to see nor recognizes, does he in fact see *me*? In one obvious sense, he does not: to see me demands not only observing a hat and cloak go by as cover for a passing humanoid shape, but acknowledging that it is just *me* who passes rather than someone else. Still, even if we concede the point, a further question arises. Supposing that the onlooker does in fact see me, just what is it he sees? If indeed, following Descartes's argument more closely, he sees me less than he *judges* that he sees me, in what do I consist?

At this point Pascal ups the ante by suggesting not only how aleatory my existence becomes when seen to be located in someone's mere judgment that I exist, but something of why it should matter that another mind—that, for example, of a man at his window, watching the passers-by—accredit it. And this too is implicit in the grammar involved, turning the cogito's 'I' into the objective yet exigent 'me' ('et moi alors?') with which Pascal replaces it. The question the fragment now poses is not merely academic; it points to something like the grounds of human happiness. I want others not just to judge that I exist, but to look out for me in hopeful expectation: I want them not merely to know I am there, but to *love* me. I want, further, to be loved in and for myself, as *me*. This admission changes the original equation by revealing something it overlooks and even conceals. For all philosophy may be content to establish my existence on purely rational grounds, as a proposition to which it is prepared to assent, that for the sake of which I exist has nothing rational about it. Further, it contains a sense of others—indeed, a *need* for others—far more passionate and powerful than mere reason can accommodate.

I want to be seen by the looker at the window because I want to be loved. Let us assume for a moment that, despite going to the window for other purposes, the Cartesian spectator does see me, and even loves me. What is there to love? Since what is visible from the window is in the first instance my body, let us suppose he loves just that—for its beauty, for example. But is it yet me he loves in loving my beauty: 'But he who loves someone for his beauty, does he love him?' Again, the answer is no: 'for smallpox, which kills beauty without killing the person, will cause him to withdraw his love'. If the other genuinely loves me, it cannot be my beauty he loves, for I can lose that beauty and still be me. So if it is in fact *me* he loves rather than the vulnerable gift of good looks, he must logically go on loving me despite the loss.

But this merely deepens the mystery. For what am I that the other should at least logically go on loving me even after the loss of beauty? In this new context, Pascal makes a concession, but one that gives a turn or twist, a Deleuzian fold, to what it concedes. He will now allow the dualist hypothesis, the radical distinction between mind and body that identifies self with the one as against the other. He allows it, however, only against the background of a certain pathos: that of a chance passer-by who wants to be loved and now finds himself driven by the loss of beauty to seek refuge in what that loss leaves intact. Since it is not in the end my body the other loves in loving me, it must then be my *mind*. Yet what is mind that someone could be said to love it? Presumably mind is its faculties—judgment or memory.[44] 'And if one loves me for my judgment, for my memory, does he love me? *me*?' Once again the answer is no. As soon as mind gets defined as something more than Descartes's at once fuzzy and tautological 'thing that thinks', as soon as we try to pin down the actual properties of this extensionless being Descartes arrives at by a process of pure subtraction as what is left over once we have eliminated everything about which it is said in a remarkably undifferentiated way to 'think', it falls under the same reduction as the body. For I can have a stroke, for instance, and lose those faculties of judgment or memory that assure both me and others (if anything does) that I have a mind, and yet the central problem remains. 'I can lose these qualities without losing myself'; I can lose these qualities and still retain something I call 'me'.

If the other genuinely loves me—loves *me*, mind, rather than the subtractable qualities I must nevertheless possess to make it possible to say that it is in fact me he loves rather than someone else—he could and indeed must in principle go on loving me even if to the loss of beauty I add the loss of the only things that entitle me to claim to have a mind. But here the question reaches its crisis. And it is here too that we grasp the full force of Pascal's move in shifting ground from the philosophy of mind to the realm of human emotion—the realm of 'passions' that Descartes does not fully address until the *Passions de l'âme*, and only then as a means of explaining (and thus disciplining) the unfortunate disorders to which the soul's contingent habitation of a body exposes it.[45] The question of what it is the other loves in loving me enables Pascal to push the problem of doubt beyond the stage at which Descartes stops it. The need for love motivates a radicalization of dualism that sacrifices not only body to mind, but mind to a sense of self that wants to be loved *even in the absence of mind*—a sense of self that stubbornly insists on its enduring existence and need even when there remains nothing in body or mind alike that some other could conceivably care for.

'But where then', Pascal asks, 'is this self if it is neither in the body nor in the soul?' More to the point, 'how could one love the body or the soul if not for these qualities, which are in no way what make the self, since they are perishable?' Is there, for example, to speak in Aristotelian terms, some sort of quiddity or substance, a 'me-ness' independent of the perishable accidents with which it happens to be associated and by which it makes itself known? And what if there were? Could anyone actually love it in the deep and unconditional way Pascal's excavation of the human need for love demands? 'Would one love the substance of a person's soul, abstractly, and whatever qualities it had?' The answer is yet again no. 'Cela ne se peut'—it cannot be done. Nor would it be merely impossible; it would be *wrong* ('injuste'), and wrong not only because there is nothing in my self for anyone to love, but because in the last analysis (and the fragment is nothing if not a ruthless analysis, an infinite breakdown paralleling the terrifying spectacle of the 'infinitely small' in the fragment on the 'two infinities') there is nothing to self at all. It is not, in other words, simply that, when all appearances are stripped away, the 'moi' proves too subtle or elusive to detect; it is itself pure appearance, a baroque trick of the light, a trompe-l'œil that falls apart as soon as we look too closely. 'Let us then no longer mock those who demand that we honour them for commissions and offices, for no one ever loves anyone except for borrowed qualities.'

By the fragment's close, the Cartesian ego is not merely refuted, but destroyed; and it is destroyed by the very probing of the grounds of human identity of which the cogito is presented as the terminus and fruit. Yet devastating as Pascal's critique may be, it shares its target's fundamental attitude: despite invoking, in the subject's ceaseless search for love, those others in whom alone such love could reside, the Pascalian *moi* remains in the finally asocial and atemporal space of private meditation Descartes's ego occupies. It is therefore up to Cyrano to launch the full-scale assault only latent in Pascal.

Like the *Discours*'s account of *Le Monde*, Cyrano's Letter VII, 'on the shadow cast by trees in water', begins by defining a perspective; and this perspective frames a peculiar verbal spectacle that folds back on itself to interrogate its source in the ego from whose position it springs. But Cyrano's intent is *parodic*, conducting (in accordance with its mirror motif) a reversal or inversion consummated in the pyrotechnical display of radical antitheses with which the letter closes. Descartes abstracts the subject from the world, placing it in the dualist posture of corporeal divorce. By contrast, Cyrano plunges it headfirst into the very midst of its physical environment, a contingent participant in the equally contingent flux of the natural scene:

Le ventre couché sur le gason d'une riviere, et le dos estendu sous les branches d'un saule qui se mire dedans, je voy renouveller aux arbres l'histoire de Narcisse; cent peupliers precipitent dans l'onde cent autres peupliers, et ces aquatiques ont esté tellement épouventez de leur cheute, qu'ils tremblent encores tous les jours au vent qui ne les touche pas; je m'imagine que la nuict ayant noircy toutes choses, le Soleil les plonge dans l'eau pour les laver.[46]

[Lying on my stomach on the grass beside a river, and my back stretched out beneath the branches of a willow reflected in it, I watch the trees renew the history of Narcissus. A hundred poplars cast a hundred other poplars in the stream, and these aquatic creatures are so frightened by their fall that they continuously tremble at a wind that does not touch them. I imagine to myself that, because night has blackened all things, the Sun plunges them in the water to wash them.]

What Cyrano 'imagines' in the river unfolds from the outset under the sign of chance. The letter describes what happens to be visible to someone adopting the curiously undignified posture of an idler stretched out on his stomach on a riverbank, peering into the simultaneously reflecting and transparent medium of passing water. The effect not only differs from, but directly counters the attitude the Cartesian ego strikes. Cyrano as it were kicks the feet out from under Cartesian method in order to help us see things method systematically overlooks.

The work of imagination this occasions is inherently suspect. In Montaigne's authoritative reflections on the subject, imagination typifies the treacherous powers of self-mystification that infect 'l'humaine capacité', the scope, but also, by the same token, the limits of humanity's grip on reality.[47] As such, it systematically opposes not only reason, the faculty of judgment charged with unmasking imagination's self-deceiving fantasies, but even human will. Montaigne develops this point when, discussing the persuasive force of sexual dreams, he wryly comments on the male organ's lamentable 'indocility':

> One is right to remark on the indocile freedom of this member, intruding itself so importunately when we have nothing to do with it, and failing so importunately when we have the most to do with it, and thereby imperiously challenging the authority of our will, rejecting with such pride and obstinacy both our mental and our manual solicitations.[48]

Imagination is also one of the monsters Descartes sets out to slay on the road of methodic doubt, encountered both in dream and in the delusions of the insane, unhappy creatures

> whose brains are so disturbed and clouded by the black vapours of bile that they constantly assure us that they are kings when they are very poor, that they are clothed in gold and purple when they are quite naked, or imagine themselves to be water jugs or to have bodies made of glass. (vol. 2, p. 406)

Finally, it is to the bewitching influence of imagination, 'that haughty power inimical to reason', that Pascal turns to explain humanity's incapacity to look its true condition in the face:

> Imagination.
> It is the dominant part of man, the mistress of error and falsehood, and all the more perfidious in that she is not always so; for she would be an infallible measure of truth were she an infallible rule of lies. (44/78)

Still, as indicated by Pascal's concession that the imagination's workings are never in fact unadulterated falsehood, the suspicion in which the faculty is held is far from uniform or unambiguous.[49] In confessing that he merely imagines the startling visions the letter reports, Cyrano claims an indulgence commensurate with the playful lack of moral and philosophical *sérieux* their fancifulness implies. But the visions' unreality does not make them pointless. For one thing, Cyrano's play is carefully structured by readings, and in particular, as the letter continues, in the Ovid of *Metamorphoses* 1.452-567, recounting the Rape of Daphne:

> mais que diray-je de ce miroir fluide, de ce petit monde renversé, qui place les chesnes au dessous de la mousse, et le Ciel plus bas que les chesnes? Ne sont-ce point de ces Vierges de jadis metamorphosées en arbres, qui desesperées de sentir encore violer leur pudeur par les baisers d'Apollon, se precipitent dans ce fleuve la teste en bas? ou n'est-ce point qu'Apollon luy-mesme offensé qu'elles ayent osé proteger contre luy la fraischeur, les ait ainsi penduës par les pieds? (ll. 12-21)

> [but what shall I say of this fluid mirror, of this little upside down world, that sets oaks below moss, and Heaven lower than oaks? Are these not some of those Virgins of yore metamorphosed into trees, who, in despair at feeling Apollo's kisses still violating their modesty, cast themselves headlong into this river? Or is it not rather that Apollo himself, offended that they should dare to shield their freshness from him, has hanged them thus by their feet?]

At one level, the allusion to Ovid underscores the mythological extravagance and thus the vanity of Cyrano's fancies. Though the letter begins in the world of common experience, it quickly leaves it for the feral realm of poetic fiction epitomized by the bewitching erotic daydreams of Ovidian verse. But, at another level, the allusion urges two points in imagination's defence. The first is that, insubstantial and, as Montaigne, Descartes and Pascal all observe, even lawless and depraved as the faculty may be, imagination is the fount of poetry and therefore, by extension, of human creativity itself. The implicit argument about imagination is then more deeply an argument about the free creative power of the human mind: the very power in whose name critics like Bellori or Roger de Piles assail the deplorable ordinariness of Caravaggio and Rembrandt, and on whose authority Aristotle (*Poetics* 1451a-b) classically asserts that poetry 'is a more philosophical and a higher thing' than mere fact-based history.[50] The capacity to make us see what literally is not there is not merely a testament to human weakness, folly, corruption and error; it also bears witness to the uplifting faculty of invention demanded of great artists and the central moral mission with which the culture charges them. The idea will not become explicit until the letter's peroration (ll. 63-74), where Cyrano defines his visions as the outpourings of inspired 'enthusiasm'. Nonetheless, he implicitly (if mockingly) appeals to the neo-Platonic idealism so central to high aesthetic doctrine and to the quasivatic powers of visionary inspiration that doctrine claims.

However, author of *L'Autre monde* (1655), a science fiction whose fanciful picture of the 'states and empires of the Moon and Sun' is balanced by the well-informed if playful eye it keeps on the laws of physics as then understood,[51] Cyrano further appeals to the imaginative energies that empower science as well as art. Consider the continuation of the passage in the *Discours* devoted to *Le Monde*. With the still recent example of Galileo's recantation before his eyes, Descartes prudently distances himself from the great controversies dominating the contemporary scientific scene. He accordingly presents the more detailed account of the book's cosmic panorama as a thought experiment designed to sidestep direct confrontation with the Aristotelian establishment in order to avoid getting entangled in the dangerous polemics surrounding the discussion of physical and astronomical matters during the 1630s:

> Indeed, in order to adumbrate these things somewhat so as to be able to say more freely what judgments I had formed about them without being obliged either to endorse or to refute the opinions currently received among the learned, I resolved to leave this world [i.e., the real one] to their disputes and to speak only of what would happen in a new world were God now to create somewhere in imaginary spaces enough matter to compose one, and supposing that He were to agitate the various parts of this matter diversely and without order so as to compose a chaos as confused as any poets might fancy, and also supposing that, afterward, He did no more than lend nature His ordinary assistance and left her to act according to the laws He has established. (vol. 1, p. 615)

The shift from 'this world here' to the 'imaginary spaces' of physical hypothesis already challenges the dualism whose application is supposed to sustain it. If Descartes abandons the world in which we actually live in favour of an entirely 'new one' of his own invention, it is precisely because he cannot in fact leave 'this world here' at all. On the contrary, every word he writes resonates against the ominous background of the theological suspicion his work will inevitably provoke and the powerful social institutions whose authority is invested in the physical science he intends to overturn. The 'new world' of Descartes's experiment is in this sense exactly comparable to the 'other world' of Cyrano's *L'Autre monde* in that both try to escape the overdetermining pressures of the social context in which they are conceived.[52] True, Cyrano's motives are more overtly moral and political, and the potential consequences of his book are correspondingly more radical. As Mary Campbell's analysis of early modern science fiction suggests, what she would call the 'alterity' of Descartes's hypothetical world is finally domesticated by a movement of mimetic return. Because *Le Monde*'s at least official aim is theoretical rather than social change, advancing the cause of knowledge as an end in itself, its value is measured by its success in replicating the world it ostensibly leaves behind. By contrast, what interests Cyrano in the counterfactual empires of the Moon and Sun is alterity embraced for its own sake. His goal indeed is to defeat the cosmological and therefore ideological certainties that uphold French society and the system of belief of which that society is the expression and guarantor.[53] Still, even as a physical scientist anxious to avoid the moral and political issues Cyrano engages, Descartes is just as vulnerable to the coercions that shape the social environment in which science perforce evolves. It is remarkable, for instance, that both books are posthumous: Cyrano's *L'Autre monde* remains unpublished until the bowdlerized edition his friend Lebret puts out in 1655; and *Le Monde* is not published until 1664, fourteen years after its author's death.[54] However narrowly Descartes may define its goals and implications, science remains an ineluctably social enterprise driven by the passions, biases, factional interests and ideological *partis pris* from which the dualist ego claims independence.[55]

But the shift from real to imaginary spaces also occasions a spectacular exhibition of the Faustian hubris fueling Cartesian science. *Le Monde* may well eschew the radical alterity at work in Cyrano, where anarchic fiction trumps the mimetic fidelity to which natural philosophy adheres. Yet the care with which Descartes isolates *Le Monde*'s experimental thought-world from the real one over which the learned violently argue not only betokens the risks science runs in challenging the views propounded in the Sorbonne; it betrays the exorbitant scale of Descartes's ambitions.

Descartes begins by identifying the basic properties of primordial matter in terms so lucid 'that it seems to me that there is nothing in the world more clear or more intelligible, except what was said earlier about God and the soul'. He then cautiously stipulates that this primordial matter contains none of the 'forms' and 'qualities' over which controversy rages in the Schools. Having got these self-protective preliminaries out of the way, he proceeds to specify the natural laws in accordance with which the elements of primordial matter will interact to produce the 'new world' of his experiment:

> and basing my laws [*raisons*] on no other principle than the infinite perfections of God, I tried to demonstrate all those about which there could be any doubt and to show that they are such that, even if God were to create several worlds, there could be none in which they failed to be observed. I then went on to show how the greater part of the matter of this chaos was obliged in accordance with these laws [*lois*] so to dispose and arrange itself as to make it resemble our heavens; how meanwhile some other of its parts had to compose an earth, and some planets and comets, and some others a sun and fixed stars. And here, expanding on the subject of light, I explained at length the kind of light that was to be found in the sun and stars, and how it traversed in an instant the immense spaces of the heavens, and how it came to be reflected from planets and comets toward the earth. I also added several things touching the substance, situation, movements and all the various qualities of these heavens and stars until I thought I had said enough to show that one could observe nothing in the heavens and stars of this world that must not or at least could not appear exactly the same as those of the world I was describing. (vol. 1, pp. 615-616)

What Descartes contrives to portray—indeed to create—in the imaginary spaces of physical hypothesis is exactly what the title of his book expressly indicates, the World itself. To be sure, the work of creation related here is purely theoretical: the experiment's success consists in replicating the God-made universe the natural scientist inhabits and labors to understand. But to the extent that, though confirmed by agreement with the world as given in empirical observation, the unfolding narrative depends on the discovery of material properties and natural laws that are *not* themselves given, the experiment demands a free creative act of imagination on the scientist's part. Small wonder then if, in the upshot, we sense a certain Promethean heat. With a rising roll of Biblical anaphorae, the passage sweeps to a triumphal close whose measure is the divine work of Genesis that supplies its latent paradigm:

> From there I went on to speak more particularly of the Earth: how, despite the fact that I had expressly supposed that God had given no weight to the matter of which it was composed, all of its parts nevertheless tended to move exactly toward its centre; how, there being water and air on its surface, the disposition of the heavens and the stars, and chiefly the Moon, had to cause in them an ebb and flow resembling in every circumstance those seen in our seas, as also a certain current in both the water and the air, running from east to west like the one also observed between the tropics; how mountains, seas, springs and rivers could naturally form, and how metals come to lie in the mines, and plants to grow in the fields, and generally how all bodies called mixed or composite are engendered. (vol. 1, pp. 616-617)

Descartes hedges the Promethean boast with prophylactic disclaimers. He insists, for example, that, despite the experiment's success in reproducing the world independently of all reference to its divine Creator, 'I did not want to infer from all of these things that this world was created in the way I proposed; for it is far more likely that God gave it from the beginning the form it was meant to have.' The fact remains that, 'without detracting from the miracle of creation', and provided only God were to confine himself to the means supplied by ordinary natural law, 'all things that are purely material could in time have taken the form in which we see them at present' (vol. 1, pp. 617-618). The miracle of Creation is a miracle no longer. Or rather Descartes has replaced it with a new one: the miracle of cosmic understanding within the reach of autonomous human thought. And yet the source of that miracle is less thought itself, the cold light of detached methodic reason Descartes explicitly champions, than the demiurgic power of imaginative invention the Cartesian rationalist shares with his Cyranian adversary. As extravagant as Cyrano himself may concede them to be, the unregulated enthusiasms his letter indulges ironically mirror the overreaching flights of imagination covertly sustaining the dualist rationality that scorns them. Descartes grounds the authority of his system, and thus his own authoritative identity as the autonomous mind or soul that frames that system, on its power to impose order on the chaos of mere sensory experience and on the restless energies of unchecked imagination exhibited in the repressed text of his dreams. In the development of his letter, Cyrano responds by parading imagination's demiurgic potential for all to see; and this world-making power arises less as a counter to than as a *version* of the poetic fictions Cartesian science enlists in the name of knowledge and the methodic pursuit of truth.

But the extravagant figures Cyrano derives from Ovid's *Metamorphoses* drive home a further point. Like the related French *esprit*, a word that disquietingly shuttles between playful 'wit' and contemplative 'mind', seat of the faculty of rational discrimination before whose sovereign tribunal wit's fancies are summoned in judgment, 'imagination' is a complex term. Its semantic range ambiguously extends from the poetic fictions Cyrano's demoralized Ovid typifies to the faculty of perception itself—the mental operation that converts the external world into the experimental 'images' or 'ideas' that form the raw material of poets and scientists alike. Cyrano's readings stand, here, over against another kind of reading, this too identified with modern science: the procedure Descartes's near contemporary Bacon lays at the very basis of the enterprise.

As we saw in chapter 1, Baconian science is not simply the experimental observation of nature by which scientists subject the vulgar pipedreams of human imagination to the manly discipline of empirical verification. It is more fundamentally what Bacon calls the 'interpretation' of nature: a hermeneutic activity aimed at unearthing, behind and beneath empirical appearances, the causal laws that engender them.[56] A key element in Baconian interpretation is the principle of reduction inscribed in the doctrine of 'qualities'—the very doctrine with which, in a chapter on 'the difference there is between our sensations and the things that produce them', Descartes opens his treatise on the World:

> Proposing to myself here to treat of light, the first thing I would like to draw your attention to is that there can be a difference between the sensation [*sentiment*] we have of it, that is, the idea that forms in our imagination by means [*par l'entremise*] of our eyes, and what is in the objects that produce this sensation in us, that is, what it is in the flame or in the Sun that we call by the name of Light. (vol. 1, p. 315)[57]

Early modern scientists unanimously distinguish between 'primary' qualities (solidity, extension, form or figure, motion and number) taken to be real in themselves as they arise in experience, and 'secondary' qualities like temperature, colour, smell or taste. As a class, secondary qualities are entirely unreal, mere epiphenomenal 'images', 'tokens', 'footprints' or 'signs' produced in our senses by primary forces too rapid, vast, powerful or minute to perceive directly.[58] Yet where secondary qualities refer to only one sense (smell, taste, touch, sight), the primary engage two, sight and touch, whose concerted action is all the more potent for combining the possessive control manual grasp implies with the physical and intellectual detachment vision demands. But this in turn exhibits the fundamental attitude of Cartesian science, the one embedded in the methodical self-discovery structuring *Le Monde*'s account of material nature. The dualist subject stands at the distance from experience implied by the need to see and manipulate appearances in order to reduce them to the underlying causal structure the play of primary qualities determines.

As a committed libertine and follower of the Epicurean Gassendi, Cyrano is a materialist, and one of his goals here is to make the *case* for materialism at Descartes's expense.[59] In this perspective, the letter anticipates the principle the sensualist Locke later advances, he too at Descartes's expense. Despite the testimony of his own dreams, Descartes conceives knowledge as an unconditional achievement of rational mind divorced from the senses. Against this view, Locke urges that the mind or (as he persists in calling it) 'the soul owes the perfection of rational thinking to the body'.[60] It is only through the senses and the information they supply that mind or soul, the reasoning part of the rational animal, has anything to work with; subtract the body and you extinguish the soul as well. Yet Locke, like Bacon and Descartes before him, retains the notion of soul itself, maintaining, if only terminologically, a distinction of kind thanks to which the order of knowledge, its form and necessity, remain purely and unassailably rational for all we owe the body in this respect. By contrast, the materialist Cyrano is entirely consequent. It is not just that, as the letter reminds us, human reason operates solely on the basis of concrete human habitation as a sensuous part of the world we hope to comprehend. We are the *product* of the senses and the material order they express.

Where then Descartes and, for all their empiricism, Bacon and Locke along with him deploy the methods of science in order to reduce the play of sensory perception, eliminating the illusions that seduce and deceive unalerted reason, Cyrano exploits it. The letter celebrates a systematically secondary reality, an ungraspable world of visual epiphenomena no less arresting for being illusion, a contingent trick of light and eye, angle and location, glancing reflection and unbridled fancy. Illusion is the reality he embraces, rescuing it from oblivion with the same hyperbolic energy that Descartes employs to stamp it out:

> Aujourd'huy le poisson se promene dans les bois: et des forests entieres sont au milieu des eaux sans se moüiller; un vieil orme entr'autres vous feroit rire, qui s'est quasi couché jusques dessus l'autre bord, afin que son image prenant la mesme posture, il fit de son corps et de son portrait un hameçon pour la pesche: l'onde n'est pas ingrate de la visite que ces saules luy rendent; elle a percé l'Univers à jour, de peur que le vase de son lict ne soüillat leurs rameaux, et non contente d'avoir formé du cristal de la bourbe, elle a vouté des Cieux et des Astres par dessous, afin qu'on ne pût dire que ceux qui l'estoient venus voir eussent perdu le jour qu'ils avoient quitté pour elle: maintenant nous pouvons baisser les yeux au Ciel, et par elle le Jour se peut vanter que tout foible qu'il est à quatre heures du matin, il a pourtant la force de precipiter le Ciel dans les abîmes: mais admirez l'Empire que la basse region de l'âme exerce sur la haute, apres avoir découvert que tout ce mirac(l)e n'est qu'une imposture des sens, je ne puis encore empescher ma veuë de prendre au moins ce Firmament imaginaire pour un grand lac sur qui la terre flote. (ll. 21-41)

> [Today the fish wanders in the woods, and whole forests stand among the waters without getting wet; among others, an old elm would make you laugh, which has almost lain down on the far bank, so that, his image assuming the same posture, he makes a fishhook of his body and portrait. The wave is not ungrateful for the visit the willows pay her; she has pierced the Universe to let the daylight through, for fear that the mud of her bed might sully their branches; and not content with having formed crystal of mud, she has vaulted the Heavens and the Stars from beneath so that no one may say that those who have come to see her have lost the light of day they left for her. Now we can lower our eyes to Heaven, and by her means the Day may boast that, weak as he may be at four in the morning, he has nevertheless strength enough to cast Heaven into the abyss. But admire the Empire that the lower region of the soul exerts over the higher; after having discovered that this whole miracle is nothing

more than an imposture of the senses, I still cannot prevent my vision from taking at least this imaginary Firmament for a great lake on which the earth floats.]

As an organ of free imaginative invention, Cyrano's letter portrays a world of irreducible appearance. The letter literalizes the figments of Cyranian imagination, producing birds that fly in water and fish that swim among trees while willows dip their heads in rivers and drown. The magic metamorphoses of Ovidian verse thereby acquire a tangible vitality denied the cool asperities of rational cognition. Narcissus died for love of what Jacques Lacan rightly styles an inanity,[61] a chance image formed on a mindless reflecting plane. But, like Lacan, Cyrano 'renews' the inanity in tribute to the fascinating hold it maintains on our perceptions and identities even when we see through it to the motionless ground beneath.

Among the many consequences of this renewal, I retain the two most salient. The first is the way in which the personified *onde* or wave 'form[s] crystal out of mud' and 'vault[s] the Heavens and Stars from beneath'. The passage deploys a Protagorian allegory of a thoroughgoing materialist philosophy of mind. In Descartes's summary of *Le Monde*, the pellucid medium of sight turns out to have conditioned the world's form as natural spectacle from the start. Cyrano, by contrast, inverts the poles of the relation by showing how the flux of uncontrolled appearances moulds the transparent 'crystal' of rational intelligence out of the 'mud' of bodily experience. Far from imposing perspicuous order on the fluent chaos of primordial matter, mind is a mere local determination of the elemental forces it tries to master: what looks like the rational structure our mental powers *give* the world is in fact the shape they take *from* it, a product of our status as participants in rather than remote beholders of physical nature. Nor is the conception of physical nature left intact. In claiming that the flux of natural phenomena not only reverses the relation between mind and body, but 'vault[s] the Heavens and Stars from beneath', Cyrano denies a central axiom of Aristotelian cosmology, challenged yet not defeated by Galileo and Descartes: the radical ontological distinction between the presumed perfection characterizing the 'fixed stars' and the 'crystalline spheres' that guide their unerring celestial motions and the messy contingency of 'sublunary' life. The invitation to reimagine heaven 'from beneath' anticipates the properly *universal* laws of motion Newton's *Principia* (1687) expounds.

But Cyrano goes on to develop the still deeper materialist insight announced in the call to 'admire the Empire that the lower region of the soul exerts over the higher'. The insight initially arises as an act of homage extorted by the admission that, even though 'this whole miracle is nothing but an imposture of the senses', he cannot prevent himself from taking it for real. However, in revealing the 'Empire that the lower region of the soul exerts over the higher', the letter unmasks the inferior spring of Empire itself. Cyrano picks his words carefully. The 'miracle' of the 'imposture of the senses' and the irresistible credence we lend it compel us to 'lower our eyes to Heaven' and confess the feeble Daylight's power 'to cast Heaven into the abyss'. This material miracle has cosmic consequence, deforming the metaphysics of orthodox faith. Descartes protests his innocence of any intent to detract from the miracle of creation as handed down by the ecclesiastical tradition to which he claims to remain loyal. Indeed, belief in God holds open the symbolic place the Cartesian demiurge arrogates as his own. But if mind is a determination of matter, so are its contents: the God in whom we believe is as great a trompe-l'œil as the illusion that throws his mythical dwelling beneath our feet. Nor should the political stakes escape us. In the development, an insolent Lark invades the watery kingdom of the Pike, taunting 'ce tyran des Rivieres' (ll. 57-58) with his elusive wit, impertinently darting from place to place without ever being quite anywhere at all. The challenge to both science and theology implicit in the disorienting imagery of the 'fluid mirror', a mirror that projects our material natures back to us in part just by virtue of its giddy fluency, authorizes an assault on the entire social order science and theology conspire to edify.

And here we note a curious turn in midstream. The letter begins by affirming the reality of appearance; with the image of the pike vainly trying to destroy the infuriating lark, it shifts to an attack on social reality *as* appearance. If even Cartesian mind, the mask of good or common sense worn by the persona of rational judgment, can be so easily dismantled, what becomes of other spectacles? In particular, what becomes of the collusive ceremonials of state and cosmos, of monarchy and what Pascal calls the physical 'machine' of the universe, whose apparent permanence and regularity are so confidently cited as proof of the providential nature of natural and social worlds alike? If mere appearance is real, then reality is appearance. But if reality is appearance, then *nothing* is real, including and especially the existing social system. The monarch is dethroned, reduced to the comic spectacle of Cyrano's stupid, impotent fish furiously dueling with shadows. And once the monarch has been deposed, so too has the moral order that sustains him on condition that he defend it. In the realm of pure sense, rescued from rational reduction, high and low change places. Just as sense overcomes judgment, so the lark baffles the pike, and the wily libertine the ponderous prince who censures him. But then, as Pascal urges in a fragment on the imaginary authority of ceremonies of state, the king is no more real than the rest:

> The habit of seeing kings accompanied by guards, drums, officers and all of the things that bend the machine towards respect and terror brings it about that their face, when sometimes seen on its own, deprived of its accompaniment, imprints in their subjects respect and terror because we fail to separate the thought of their person from the entourage with which it is ordinarily joined. And the world, which does not understand that this effect is a product of habit, believes that it stems from a natural force. Whence these words: the character of divinity is imprinted on his face, etc. (25/59)

The reality of the sovereign, what indeed *makes* him the sovereign, entirely consists in the awful yet deluded appearances with which overawed belief invests him.

In *The Origin of German Tragic Drama*, Benjamin asserts that allegories, the radiant guarantors of cosmic order and meaning, are in fact mere ruins: 'Allegories are, in the realm of thoughts, what ruins are in the realm of things.'[62] In the time of theatrical appearance, the stunning scenic present of the Jonsonian masque or Rubens's portrayals of the True Faith or the absolutist State, this is a mistake. As we noted in the introduction, Benjamin's sense of baroque culture is overdetermined by a donnish predilection for emblem books that leads him to read baroque allegories as though they were a subspecies of the *vanitas* images to which his saturnine temperament drew him.[63] But however wrong Benjamin may be concerning the immediate impact allegories had on contemporary readers and beholders, he is right about the mental and social realities that, in the subsequent course of historical events, inevitably expose and deface such performances. Cyrano's river, the Protagorian medium of perpetual flux and change, is the allegory of allegory's ruin—of *history* conceived as the ineluctable advance of unfolding ruin itself.

And what in all this of self? By its close, Cyrano's letter gathers a momentum that mimics the one with which the imaginary world of Cartesian hypothesis turns out to reproduce the world we live in. Yet in Descartes, the spectacle of creation ultimately promotes a Promethean agency revealed with the climactic discovery of the 'spectator' whose originary presence calls the world into being from the first. In Cyrano, by contrast, the spectacle overwhelms the beholder. Conjuring up a world of random appearance from which there is no escape precisely because it is a creature of our own minds, the work of sensuous imagination destroys the fantasies that set it in train. The result is a movement of pure panic in which the narrator recoils from the picture he has just drawn. 'Moymesme', he writes in a present tense that underscores his inextricable engagement not only as the scene's protagonist, but as its *author*, spring of the uncanny mirror-world whose hallucinatory hold he now anxiously tries to break, 'moymesme j'en demeure tellement consterné que je suis contraint de quitter ce tableau' [I myself am left so dumbstruck that I am compelled to quit the picture] (ll. 61-63). The letter opens by planting Descartes's transcendental spectator in the natural world he imagines he dominates as a distant spectacle. It now ends by staging the spectator's utter overthrow, driving him from the text on pain of undoing him altogether. Put in context with Descartes's identification of the human spectator with the principle of light he posits as the metaphysical *end* toward which created nature turns as to its source, this yields a final twist that reduces the writer's light-engendered self to 'nothing' at all:

Je vous prie de suspendre [la] condamnation [de ce tableau], puis qu'il est malaisé de juger d'une ombre: car quand mes antousiasmes auroient la reputation d'estre fort éclairez, il n'est pas impossible que la lumiere de celuy-ci soit petite, ayant esté prise à l'ombre: et puis, quelle autre chose pourrois-je ajouter à la description de cette Image enluminée, sinon que c'est un rien visible, un cameleon spirituel, une nuit, que la nuit fait mourir; un procez des yeux et de la raison, une privation de clarté que la clarté met au jour; enfin que c'est un esclave qui ne manque non plus à la matiere, qu'à la fin de de mes lettres. (ll. 63-73)

[I pray you to suspend condemnation [of this picture], since it is difficult to judge of a shadow: for even if my brainstorms [*antousiasmes*] had the reputation of being highly enlightened, it is not impossible that the light shed by this one should prove slight, having been drawn from shade; and then, what more could I add to the description of this illuminated Image, except that it is a visible nothing, a spiritual [or mental, or witty] chameleon, a night that the night causes to die; a trial of eyes and reason, a privation of clarity that clarity brings to light; in sum, that it is a slave as bound to the matter as to the end of my letters.]

The light that, in Descartes, invades the maternal night of primal chaos in order to engender an imagined world designed to dispel the darkness that shrouds the real one is now portrayed as merest shadow. Indeed, in Cyrano's version of Cartesian genesis, the light is itself mere 'night', the fruit of 'brainstorms' of the sort Descartes represses with his dream—an 'illuminated Image' in whose afterglow the letter invites us to reimagine the world and our place in it as the 'visible nothing' they are. The very intensity with which the letter makes us see what is not there underscores the hallucinatory vividness to which all perception is subject. Just because we perceive Cyrano's nothing so clearly, vision becomes a 'privation of clarity that clarity brings to light', as empty yet weirdly compelling as the optical illusions that eye and light manufacture at the triangulated surface of a stream. Worse still, a 'trial of eyes and reason' that reveals how far these symbols of enlightenment are at the mercy of the physical laws that command natural embodiment, the image with which the letter fills our minds convicts the mind itself of falsehood. A 'chameleon' that borrows such colour as it owns from its physical environment, the image is nonetheless not just carnal illusion. On the contrary, Cyrano calls it 'spiritual', an adjective whose ambiguity we have already compared to that assigned the faculty of imagination on which the letter spectacularly relies. For what in fact is 'spirit', Descartes's *esprit*? Is it rational *mind*, summoning the shifty deliverances of sensory appearance to judgment before its sovereign tribunal? Or is it mere fleeting, irresponsible *wit*, driven by enthusiastic fits whose persuasive power stems directly from their resistance to rational control? The text answers the question precisely by leaving it open, making it impossible to distinguish one sense of the word from the other. Mind or wit, spirit or fancy, Cyrano's 'spiritul chameleon' is in either case a 'slave' whose bondage to the letter's both scriptorial 'matter' and rhetorical 'end' indexes its deeper enslavement to the world to which letter and mind alike belong.

So where does all of this leave us? On the one hand, it gives us a sense of where the baroque is best looked for in French culture: in the twists and folds of the early modern text conceived as the dual site of writing and reading, of construction and critique. The critical dismantling of the authoritative self of Cartesian science inheres to the Cartesian text itself: Cyrano and Pascal invent it, but in the rhetorical sense of finding it ready to hand. However, this already suggests something else: the curious redundancy of the deconstructive habits of reading we bring to the classics of seventeenth-century France. What we imagine are problems *with* the authoritative texts of so-called French 'classicism' are in fact problems *for* them—so much so that the very gesture of presuming we have transcended them confirms our fascinated captivity. What is the French baroque? What Cioran once called a process of 'decomposition'[64] that defines the essential habitus of French intellectual culture to this day.

But what is true of the French baroque is true of the baroque in general. As we have seen by now in a variety of contexts, the monuments of baroque culture are a ceaseless prey to the kind of critical afterthoughts Cyrano and Pascal visit on the text of Descartes as a reflex of everything that text overlooks and yet indicts. True, like Descartes himself, many if not most baroque poets, artists and thinkers seem immune to the morals their own works point at their expense; the self-defeating ironies that 'Sur l'ombre que faisoient des arbres dans l'eau' or Pascal's fragment on self delight in exploiting lie dormant, lurking in the intimate darkness of the doubts, reveries and anxieties that shadow their overt persuasions. Yet Truth, we are told, is the daughter of Time; and so it is, especially in an era as sensitive as the baroque to the sudden shifts of light that risk at any moment exposing what we conspire to conceal. The dualist ego is a figment—but to that extent also a symptom—of the world whose historical metamorphosis it blindly advances just because it remains faithfully committed to the dated transcendental entity philosophical tradition calls 'the truth'.

And yet how can we portray this self-accusing historicalness when it is in its very nature to stalk us from behind, subverting the fictions we construct to screen it out? A measure of Descartes's failure is his historical incapacity even to imagine such a question—a failure one of whose sources is the fact that he confuses the imagination of a world *without* God, shaped by laws and forces immanent to its own design, with the world *as God sees it*, or rather as science sees it in his place. But a measure of Descartes's historic greatness is the room his writings leave for the time-borne ironies that ultimately overtake it. And what finally is this if not Descartes's true vocation as the self-doubled exponent of the sensibility, epoch and style we call baroque?

Notes

1 See Rorty, *Philosophy and the Mirror of Nature*, chap. 1, 'The Invention of the Mind', chap. 3, 'The Idea of a "Theory of Knowledge"', and chap. 4, 'Privileged Representations'.

2 Rousset's pioneering work in *La Littérature de l'âge baroque en France* has been extended ever since. For distinguished examples not mentioned below, see Lyons, *A Theatre of Disguise* (1978), Greenberg, *Detours of Desire* (1984), Buci-Glucksmann, *La raison baroque* (1984), Bernard Chedozeau, *Le Baroque* (Paris: Nathan, 1989), and Vuillemin, *Baroquisme et théâtralité* (1994). For a striking measure of just how difficult Rousset's effort remains, see Mitchell Greenberg's recent *Baroque Bodies: Psychoanalysis and the Culture of Absolutism* (Ithaca, NY: Cornell University Press, 2001), whose title indicates a desire to recover the French baroque side-

tracked by the author's ongoing obsession with the self-subjugating Œdipal discipline 'classical' absolutism is said to implant.

3   For a forceful indictment of the hypervaluation of the 'temps de Louis XIV', see the 'preamble' to Fumaroli, *Le Poète et le Roi*. Fumaroli argues that, if La Fontaine's stature as a poet has been obscured, the primary culprits are Louis himself, through the repression his administration exerted on literary taste and practice, and Voltaire, whose *Siècle de Louis XIV* (1751) set the tone for everything to follow. For Fumaroli's remarks on Voltaire in particular, with a discussion of the 'complementary' role played by Sainte-Beuve's *Port-Royal*, see pp. 17-22. See too Lyons, *Kingdom of Disorder*, which argues that the deepest lesson of French theories of tragic drama is what he calls 'the unity of peril' (chap. 4, esp. pp. 187ff.). Though designed to contain it, the classical stage is conceived as that place where anti-classical 'disorder' rules as a condition of tragedy as such.

4   On Corneille's education, see Fumaroli, *Héros et orateurs*, chap. 2, 'Corneille et la Société de Jésus', and chap. 4, 'Corneille et la rhétorique de l'humanisme chrétien'. For the curious way in which otherwise alert students of seventeenth-century French culture continue to regard Corneille as a classical poet, see Mitchell Greenberg, *Corneille, Classicism, and the Ruses of Symmetry* (Cambridge: Cambridge University Press, 1986) and *Subjectivity and Subjugation in Seventeenth-Century French Drama and Prose: The Family Romance of French Classicism* (Cambridge: Cambridge University Press, 1992), chap. 2, 'The grateful dead: Corneille's tragedy and the subject of history', and Dalia Judovitz, *The Culture of the Body: Genealogies of Modernity* (Ann Arbor, MI: University of Michigan Press, 2001), chap. 5, 'Incorporations: Royal Power, or the Social Body in Corneille's *The Cid*'. Greenberg and Judovitz's repressively 'classical' Corneille is an artifact of taking Cartesian rationalism to impose a normatively disembodied 'subject'—a thesis the present analysis challenges.

5   Victor-Lucien Tapié, *Baroque et classicisme* (Paris: Plon, 1957) and *Le baroque* (Paris: Presses universitaires de France, 1961); Charpentrat, *Le mirage baroque*; Buci-Glucksmann, *La folie du voir*; Jean-François Maillard, *Essai sur l'esprit du héros baroque (1580-1640): le même et l'autre* (Paris: Nizet, 1973); and Deleuze, *Le pli*. For Deleuze's remarks on Leibniz's 'German soul', endorsing Nietzsche's comparable portrait in *Beyond Good and Evil*, see p. 46.

6   Both the central symptom and chief instrument of the death of idealism is held to be the defeat of heroic individualism sealed with Louis XIV's seizure of power in 1661. For the classic statement, see Bénichou's *Morales du grand siècle*, emphasizing the role played by political and moral disenchantment in producing the high classicism of the later seventeenth century. Fumaroli urges a similar case in *Le Poète et le Roi* (pp. 25-42), underscoring the defeat of the Frondes and, with it, the demise of the freedom of thought and expression epitomized by Montaigne.

7   Pascal Dumont, 'Est-il pertinent de parler d'une philosophie baroque?' in *Le Baroque en question(s)*, ed. Didier Souiller, *Littératures classiques* 36 (Spring 1999), pp. 63-77. The baroque is not alone in being so marginalized. See, e.g., Joan DeJean, *Tender Geographies: Women and the Origins of the Novel in France* (New York: Columbia University Press, 1991), reasserting the centrality of the proto-feminist literature of romance associated with baroque *préciosité*, and the same author's later *Ancients against Moderns*, surveying the many casualties of the *querelle des anciens et des modernes* initiated by Boileau's contemptuous response to Charles Perrault's *Siècle de Louis le Grand* of 1687.

8 All of the major and most of the minor contemporary documents are collected in Armand Gasté (ed.), *La Querelle du Cid: Pièces et pamphlets* (Paris: H. Welter, 1899). For recent critical analyses focused on the socio-political juncture, see Christian Jouhaud, 'Power and Literature: The Terms of the Exchange, 1624-42', in Richard Burt (ed.), *The Administration of Aesthetics: Censorship, Political Criticism, and the Public Sphere* (Minneapolis, MN: University of Minnesota Press, 1994), pp. 34-82, and Hélène Merlin, *Littérature et public en France au XVIIe siècle* (Paris: Les Belles lettres, 1994), chap. 5, 'La querelle du *Cid*: de la république des lettres au *public*', and chap. 6, 'Public et publication: la querelle comme scène publique'.

9 The standard left-wing account is Foucault's, advanced in *Histoire de la folie* and *Les mots et les choses*. The general view Foucault promotes is notably enriched by Marin, *La critique du discours*, Greenberg, *Subjectivity and Subjugation* and (most recently) the misleadingly named *Baroque Bodies*, and Judovitz, *The Culture of the Body*. Note however that the basic assumptions concerning Descartes's contribution remain those informing Bénichou's *Morales du grand siècle* or Antoine Adam's *Histoire de la littérature française au XVIIe* (Paris: Del Duca, 1962) and *L'Age classique* (Paris: Arthaud, 1968-71).

10 On the distinction between 'concept' and 'conceit' and the related contrast between Leibniz and Descartes, see Deleuze, *Le pli*, pp. 55-56. See too the discussion of Leibniz's 'rupture avec la conception classique du concept comme être de raison', replacing the classical notion of the concept as crystallizing 'l'essence ou la possibilité logique de son objet' with the baroque idea that it comprises 'la réalité métaphysique du sujet correspondant' (pp. 73-78).

11 See Domna C. Stanton, *The Aristocrat as Art: A Study of the* Honnête Homme *and the Dandy in Seventeenth- and Nineteenth-Century France* (New York: Columbia University Press, 1980), Erica Harth, *Ideology and Culture in Seventeenth-Century France* (Ithaca, NY: Cornell University Press, 1982), and Michael Moriarty, *Taste and Ideology in Seventeenth-Century France* (Cambridge: Cambridge University Press, 1988).

12 Georges de Scudéry, *Observations sur Le Cid*, in Gasté, *La Querelle du Cid*, pp. 103-110. The same charge had earlier been leveled by Jean Mairet in a verse satire entitled 'L'Autheur du vray Cid Espagnol à son Traducteur François'. Gasté reprints Mairet's 'L'Autheur' (pp. 67-68).

13 Scudéry, *Observations*, in Gasté, *La Querelle du Cid*, p. 71.

14 For his introductory discussion of the distinction (chiefly drawn from Plato) between rhetoric and dialectic, see Fish, *Self-Consuming Artifacts*, pp. 1-2. Fish returns to a theme sounded in his earlier book on Milton, *Surprised by Sin: The Reader in Paradise Lost*, that of reading's place not only as a response to, but as an integral dimension of what we call 'the text'. This leads him to challenge a central tenet of New Criticism, the denunciation of the so-called Affective Fallacy by William K. Wimsatt and Monroe Beardsley in *The Verbal Icon: Studies in the Meaning of Poetry* (Lexington, KY: University of Kentucky Press, 1954); and the challenge leads in turn to the later, polemical *Is There a Text in This Class?* in which he moves from an interest in reading *in* to an insistence on reading *as* 'the text'. It is curious that the 'strong' reader-response views he has espoused since the mid-1970s begin as something rather different: an analysis of the rhetorical strategies by which texts inscribe their own readers in order to act on and transform them.

15 Ironic as it is for a playwright to talk this way, Scudéry echoes an ambivalence that has dogged Western theatre since early Christian times. His assault on Corneille an-

ticipates the critique to which the Jansenist Nicole's *Traité de la comédie* (first published in 1665; revised in 1666 and 1667) and the Gallican Bossuet's *Maximes et réflexions sur la comédie* (1694) subject theatre at large and Corneille in particular. For a general introduction to these problems, see Jonas A. Barish, *The Antitheatrical Prejudice* (Berkeley, CA: University of California Press, 1981). For a more focused account, see Marc Fumaroli, 'Sacerdos sive rhetor, orator sive historio: théologie et moralité du théâtre de Corneille à Molière', in *Héros et orateurs*, pp. 449-491.

16 For Scudéry's own baroquism, see his most famous play, the *Comédie des comédiens* of 1635. Meanwhile, Corneille's flaws from an Aristotelian viewpoint are a leitmotiv of the *Observations*: see, e.g., the savaging of Corneille's treatment of the 'rule of twenty-four hours' (Gasté, *La Querelle du Cid*, pp. 77-78). Scudéry's neoclassic Aristotle is accompanied by a moralizing Horace. During a remarkable diatribe directed at *Le Cid*'s Chimène, regarded as a monster of sexual deviance, filial disloyalty and bottomless dissembling, Scudéry reminds us 'que le Poeme de Theatre fut inventé, pour instruire en divertissant; et que c'est sous cet agreable habit, que se deguise la Philosophie, de peur de paroistre trop austere aux yeux du monde; et par luy (s'il faut ainsi dire) qu'elle semble dorer les pilulles, afin qu'on les prenne sans repugnance, et qu'on se trouve guary presque sans avoir connu le remede' (Gasté, *La Querelle du Cid*, pp. 79-80).

17 See Gilman, *The Curious Perspective*.
18 Lyons, *Kingdom of Disorder*, p. 203.
19 Deleuze, *Le pli*, p. 92
20 Ibid., p. 113.
21 See Christopher Braider, *Indiscernible Counterparts: The Invention of the Text in French Classical Drama* (Chapel Hill, NC: North Carolina Studies in the Romance Languages and Literatures, 2002), chap. 1, '*Cet hymen différé*: The Figuration of Authority in Corneille's *Le Cid*'.
22 For the unusual definite article ('*the* truth' rather than just 'truth'), see Bernard Williams's remarks in *Descartes: The Project of Pure Enquiry* (1978; Harmondsworth: Penguin Books, 1990), pp. 18-19, on the parallel need to translate Descartes's 'discours de la méthode' as 'discourse on *the* method' rather than the standard 'method'.
23 Although Descartes leaves open the possibility of returning to moral problems in order to reduce them to the methodic clarity already achieved in science and metaphysics, he never does so. The reason is that the dualist subject is unfit for actual moral agency. See Taylor's critique in *Sources of the Self*, chap. 8, 'Descartes's Disengaged Reason', where a reductively instrumental self-control entails a moral 'unbelief' that makes morality impossible. What we get instead is Cartesian *générosité*, a voluntarist self-overcoming whose ultimate fruit is Nietzschean and Heideggerian Will. See too the related critique in Williams, *Moral Luck*, chap. 7, 'Rawls and Pascal's Wager'. For Williams, the similarities between Rawls's attempt to frame a rational moral calculus and Pascal's 'wager' highlight a crucial difference: the fact that Pascal acknowledges morality's dependence on prior (rather than rationally posterior) moral beliefs. Thus Williams notes how Pascal's wager 'depended on certain assumptions. One was that there were two relevant alternatives: that the Christian God did not exist, or that he did exist, and that he sent believers to Heaven, and unbelievers to Hell. Next, Pascal assumed that there were certain actions which could lead to belief: if you started by insincerely acting as though God existed, you would end up sincerely acting so, i.e., believing in God' (p. 98). This illustrates two notions central to Williams's challenge to the idea of rationalizing morals: the notion of 'moral luck' (it *happens* that Pascal writes at a time when and in a culture where the

assumptions on which the wager hinges make sense) and the notion that moral concepts are 'thick', i.e., impenetrable to pure reason. What makes us assume or believe certain things, and the personal and emotional as well as moral consequences of so believing, are not only too dark and dense, but also lie too far back for us to detach ourselves from them in the way rational calculation demands.

24   Stephen Gaukroger, *Descartes: An Intellectual Biography* (Oxford: Clarendon Press, 1995), argues that Descartes's work as a philosopher has to be understood as a retrospective 'metaphysical legitimation' of his physical system rather than as articulating its prior mental and epistemological conditions. The legitimation is motivated by the condemnation of Galileo: Descartes turns to properly philosophical rather than physical matters in order to package his physics in a way the intellectual and political establishment will accept (see, e.g., pp. 11-12).

25   Descartes had composed the rather Scholastic *Regulae* as early as 1628; but while laying out the principles of the method, the *Regulae* offer no epistemology, omitting sustained discussion of the nature of the certainty the procedures of 'geometric' demonstration purport to give.

26   Foucault, *Histoire de la folie*, pp. 56-58; but see also Jacques Derrida's preening yet cogent critique of the reductiveness of Foucault's reading in 'Cogito et histoire de la folie', *L'écriture et la différence* (Paris: Seuil, 1967; 'Points' paper ed.), pp. 51-97.

27   For helpful discussions, see Harth, *Ideology and Culture*, Moriarty, *Taste and Ideology*, Viala, *Naissance de l'écrivain*, and Alain Faudemay, *La Distinction à l'âge classique: Emules et Enjeux* (Geneva: Droz, 1992). For comparable developments in England, see Steven Shapin, *A Social History of Truth: Civility and Science in Seventeenth-Century England* (Chicago: University of Chicago Press, 1994).

28   This is the topic of the first of Husserl's 'Cartesian meditations'. See Edmund Husserl, *Cartesian Meditations: An Introduction to Phenomenology*, trans. Dorion Cairns (The Hague: M. Nijhoff, 1960). See also Drew Leder's interpretation of dualism as a 'motivated misreading' in *The Absent Body* (Chicago: University of Chicago Press, 1990). Dualism is 'motivated' in that the discovery of somatic bases of error (e.g., in confused sense perception, the 'humoural' sources of madness or the blurred threshold between dreaming and waking) makes the body visible (Leder's 'dys-appearance': it appears when and because it malfunctions) as both an object of, and an obstacle to, consciousness or 'mind'. Descartes's mistake consists in hypostasizing a transient condition and the epistemic procedures needed to cope with it.

29   As Descartes explains in pt. 6 of the *Discours*, knowledge is by definition a private undertaking: 'on ne saurait si bien concevoir une chose et la rendre sienne, lorsqu'on l'apprend de quelque autre, que lorsqu'on l'invente soi-même' (vol. 1, p. 641). This essential privacy lies at the root of both the difficulty he encounters in communicating his discoveries and the rhetorical strategy he deploys to solve it.

30   See Dalia Judovitz, *Subjectivity and Representation in Descartes: The Origins of Modernity* (Cambridge: Cambridge University Press, 1988), esp. chap. 3, 'Theory of the subject as literary practice', which similarly presents the subject as an 'effect' of the representations it authors.

31   Needless to say, Ausonius' text recalls the Pythagorean Upsilon dividing the 'higher' road of philosophical Virtue from the 'lower' road of worldly Pleasure.

32   For the complete dream text, see Descartes, *Œuvres philosophiques*, vol 1, pp. 52-61. An English translation appears in W.T. Jones, 'Somnio Ergo Sum: Descartes's Three Dreams', *Philosophy and Literature* 4.2 (Fall, 1980), pp. 145-166.

33   Georges Poulet, 'Le songe de Descartes', *Etudes sur le temps humain* I (Paris: Plon, 1952; Editions du Rocher paper ed.), pp. 63-96. This reading should be supple-

mented by Jones's, which attempts (with the help of Descartes's enigmatic reference in the 'Préambules' to the 'celeberrimis in G. F. R. C.', decoded as the 'most illustrious German Brotherhood of Rosicrucians') (Œuvres philosophiques, vol. 1, p. 46, where Alquié arrives at the same decrypt) to relate it to youthful dabblings in the Black Arts. (But see Gaukroger, Descartes, pp. 102-103, who summarily dismisses the idea that Rosicrucianism could have 'influenced [Descartes's] thoughts in any significant way'.) Even if we accept Jones's and Alquié's conjecture, the frightening, satanic moment in the dream is more economically explained by what I have characterized as the Faustian hubris informing the whole Cartesian enterprise.

34 The melon's symbolism can be deepened further. As we will recall again shortly, a major intellectual condition of early modern science is the doctrine of 'qualities', which draws a sharp distinction between 'primary' qualities deemed real in themselves as they appear in experience and 'secondary' qualities (temperature, colour, smell, taste) seen as mere epiphenomenal 'images', 'traces' or 'signs' produced in our senses by otherwise occult primary forces. Crucial as the distinction of qualities was in enabling science to formulate the principle of reduction at the base of modern causal and mechanical explanation, it was (and still is) experienced, in its reductiveness, as alienating. This is where the melon comes in—a feast of colour, texture, taste and smell that restores the fundamental *feel* that gives the world meaning.

35 This lends a new resonance to the passage in the second meditation where Descartes notes how mere outward appearance provides no basis for telling whether men seen passing in the street are in fact men rather than automata designed to look like men (vol. 2, pp. 426-427; Latin, vol. 2, pp. 188-189). For what is true of other men is true of Descartes. Indeed, as we will see shortly, Pascal exploits the fact of being one's own mechanical double to devastating effect in the ironically radicalized version of the cogito offered in 'Qu'est-ce que le moi?' For commentaries on the anxieties that Descartes's automata index, see Judovitz, *The Culture of the Body*, chap. 3, 'The Automaton as Virtual Model', and Campbell, *Wonder & Science*, pp. 101-109.

36 A survivor of the Illumination is the *Praeambulae* prefacing the now-lost manuscript account of the dream. Under the puzzling title, 'Préambules. La crainte de Dieu est le commencement de la sagesse', Descartes writes: 'Les comédiens, appelés sur la scène, pour ne pas laisser voir la rougeur sur leur front, mettent un masque. Comme eux, au moment de monter sur ce théâtre du monde où, jusqu'ici, je n'ai été que spectateur, je m'avance masqué' (vol. 1, p. 45). Two points arise: the powerful sense of Descartes's coming out as a fully autonomous agent destined to play a part on the great stage of the world; and the way the assumption of adult selfhood gets bound up with the idea of wearing a mask—but a mask designed less to conceal its wearer's face than to *give* him the face he needs to play a part at all. For what role does Descartes mean to play if not the most symbolically complex of all: that of *being his own man*? For analyses of the Cartesian subject's status as a persona indexed to a mask, see Jean-Luc Nancy, *Ego Sum* (Paris: Flammarion, 1979), esp. the section entitled 'Larvatus pro Deo' (pp. 61-94), and Judovitz, *Subjectivity and Representation*, pp. 32-38.

37 Locke devotes the *Essay*'s entire first book to refuting Descartes's theory of innate ideas. The chain of arguments runs as follows: there are in fact only two bases of knowledge, experience and reflection; reflection cannot operate in the absence of experience; experience cannot occur except by means of sensory impressions; 'the soul' therefore 'owes the perfection of rational thinking to the body'.

38 For explicit references to Descartes, see Lafuma 84, 553, 887, 1001, 1005, 1008; Sellier 118, 462, 445. Sellier does not include Lafuma's last three fragments, which are items of Pascalian tabletalk preserved by the Périer family.
39 For a stimulating discussion of both the 'bit of wax' and the 'intertextual labyrinth' drawn from the philosophical tradition from Aristotle's *De anima* through Ovid and Plotinus to Thomas Aquinas, see Lezra, *Unspeakable Subjects*, pp. 103-114.
40 For a concise sample of the author's quarrel with 'strong AI', see John Searle, *The Rediscovery of the Mind* (Cambridge, Mass.: MIT Press, 1992), pp. 43-45.
41 See, e.g., *Discours*, pt. 5, *Œuvres philosophiques*, vol. 1, pp. 628-631, where Descartes discusses the issue at length in relation not only to the distinction between humans and animals (and notably the case of parrots to which Locke later turns), but also to the problem of automata.
42 It is tempting to speculate on the role Pascal's invention of a primitive computer (the *pascaline*) played in enabling him to anticipate the Turing Test. Constructing such a machine demands grasping the formalizable because fundamentally *rote* nature of acts of calculation we normally conceive as distinctively 'mental'.
43 However, while Pascal wholly dissolves consciousness in *this* fragment, others (e.g., 113/145 or 200/231) point in the opposite direction. This reminds us of two features of the *Pensées*. (a) Insofar as the *Pensées*'s unfinished status enables us to draw any inferences at all, Pascal's method is invariably *chiastic*, veering back and forth between incompatible extremes. (b) As fragmentary notes toward a book Pascal never wrote, it is dangerous to identify his intentions with any one passage if only because it is often impossible to know to which of the voices in the *Apologie*'s projected dialogues a given fragment was to be assigned. In the present instance, the evaporation of Cartesian consciousness may be seen either as a tactical assault on Cartesian hubris intended to give way at another stage to praise of the human soul of the sort the 'roseau pensant' fragments give or (though this, I admit, doubtfully) as voicing the despair to which a Cyranian materialist might be brought by thoroughly consequent reflection on the soul's Epicurean mortality.
44 In light of Lezra's analysis of the repression of memory in Descartes's *Meditations* (*Unspeakable Subjects*, chap. 2, 'The Ontology of the Letter in Descartes's Second Meditation'), it is interesting that an essential step in Pascal's revision of Descartes is the excavation of memory's contribution to the Cartesian self's identity.
45 Descartes opens *Les Passions de l'âme* by discussing the passions' essentially passive character as contrasted with the various external and internal 'actions' that cause them. See art. 1, 'Que ce qui est passion au regard d'un sujet est toujours action à quelque autre égard', *Œuvres philosophiques*, vol. 3, pp. 951-952. This distinction is crucial to Descartes's theory as a whole, especially in pts. 1 and 2, expounding the physiological basis of the passions and the contrast between what we are made to feel by forces operating from 'without' and the actions to which we determine ourselves from 'within' by an effort of rational will.
46 For the full text, see Cyrano de Bergerac, *Lettres*, ed. Luciano Erba (Milan: Vanni Scheiweller, 1965), pp. 37-39; for the passage, p. 37, lines 5-12. Subsequent references appear by line in the text. I quote the French owing to its dense verbal and figurative texture, and because, unlike *L'Autre monde*, the Letters remain little read. Indeed, the only analysis of 'Sur l'ombre' I know is Ross Chambers's ' "Que diray-je de ce miroir fluide?": Text and Its Double in a Letter by Cyrano', *Australian Journal of French Studies* 14 (1977), pp. 121-140. Still, Chambers's brilliant reading focuses exclusively on narratological rather than intellectual or cultural issues.

47 See Montaigne, 'De la force de l'imagination', *Essais* 1: 21. But imagination is a constant in the *Essais*, illustrating humanity's limitless capacity for self-deception.
48 Montaigne, *Essais* 1: 21, pp. 147-148.
49 See Pascal's paradoxes on 'justice' and 'force' (*Pensées* 81/116). Pascal argues both sides against the middle: the basis of political order is imaginary, yet, in view of human depravity, it is both just and necessary that this be so.
50 Aristotle, *Poetics*, p. 54.
51 Though direct application of physical law is episodic in Cyrano, it is nonetheless a theme. See, e.g., *L'Autre monde*, ed. Henri Weber (Paris: Editions sociales, 1975), p. 46 (invoking the example of relative motion in defence of scientific hypotheses that contravene the evidence of uninformed sense), pp. 52-53 (a pre-Newtonian intuition of the proportional relation of mass and distance as encountered during the fictional Cyrano's voyage to the Moon) and p. 59 (ironically deploying the ascensional force of hot air to explain the otherwise miraculous apotheosis of the prophet Enoch).
52 Both authors join More, Bacon, Kepler and Campanella in the mainstream of the tradition of early modern Utopias. The move to another, largely better world than the one we inhabit implicitly criticizes current social arrangements by suggesting the possibility of improving them, yet in a form whose transparent fictiveness avoids direct confrontation with the prevailing order. While it cannot by itself protect writers from censorship, utopian equivocation creates defensive distancing effects and camouflaging ambiguities—especially when, as Annabel Patterson suggests in a passing reference to More, we add the estranging medium of Latin to distance and fictionality. See *Censorship and Interpretation: The Conditions of Writing and Reading in Early Modern England* (Madison, WI: University of Wisconsin Press, 1984), p. 183.
53 See Campbell, *Wonder & Science*, pp. 171-180. Campbell does not compare Cyrano with Descartes, but with Francis Godwin; and the point of the comparison with Godwin is limited to showing that, where Godwin uses the narrative of a voyage to the moon for escapist wishfulfilment, Cyrano turns it into a weapon of radical critique. Yet a passing remark on the explicit fictiveness of Cyrano's *Autre monde* suggests an analysis akin to the one proposed here. Campbell writes that, unlike the tamer Godwin, Cyrano 'is for fiction, at least in *L'autre monde*, as a concept acidly destructive of scientific (perhaps more specifically Cartesian) certainty' (p. 171).
54 On the first edition, suggestively entitled 'Le Monde de M. Descartes', see *Œuvres philosophiques*, vol. 1, pp. 307-308. For Cyrano's *L'Autre monde*, see Erica Harth, *Cyrano de Bergerac and the Polemics of Modernity* (New York: Columbia University Press, 1970), pp. 51-52.
55 Descartes's case underscores the general justice of the critical viewpoint adopted by recent sociology of science, especially in Latour. See, e.g., Bruno Latour and Steven Woolgar, *Laboratory Life: The Social Construction of Scientific Facts* (Beverly Hills, CA: Sage Publications, 1979), an 'ethnography' of scientific activity that popularized the paradoxical notion that the 'facts' on which science claims to rest are 'constructed' by the actions scientists perform. See too Latour's *Science in Action: How to Follow Scientists and Engineers through Society* (Cambridge, MA: Harvard University Press, 1987), a 'sociology' that exposes the 'Janus-headed' nature of science (one face presents the monument of scientific knowledge, the other the messy nescience of science as social practice), and *Nous n'avons jamais été modernes: essai d'anthropologie symétrique* (Paris: Editions de La Découverte, 1991), challenging the presumed 'modernity' and thus epistemological autonomy of both science and the philosophical tradition confederate with it. (Here the leading idea is that, if the science of anthropology is correct, then the relativist lessons it

teaches concerning non- or pre-scientific cultures symmetrically apply to anthropology itself and the other so-called 'modern' sciences along with it.) Though this is not the place to quarrel with Latour, I cannot resist making two comments. First, even as it lends colour to Latour's relativistic interpretation of science as social 'action', Descartes's case also illustrates the self-correcting features of the particular *kind* of action science is: while Cartesian *metaphysics* may be incorrigible, Cartesian *science* is not. Second, the distinction between science as the epistemic edifice mainly presented in schools and to the general public and science as the inherently social activity observed behind the scenes in the 'laboratory' has never been as hermetic as Latour's relativism demands. Such is moreover the testimony of much of Latour's own evidence. In the introduction to *Science in Action*, e.g., he presents two case histories (Watson and Crick's discovery of the double helical structure of the DNA molecule; the invention of the high-speed personal computer) intended to illustrate the radical divorce between science as monument and science as practice: a divorce so complete as to require a revolution in perspective—the opening, as Latour puts it, of nothing less than 'Pandora's box'. Yet it is striking that the documents Latour draws on are not (as his rhetoric suggests) neglected archival materials, lab books, correspondence or even professional papers, but popular bestsellers: James Watson's *The Double Helix* (1968) and Tracy Kidder's *The Soul of a New Machine* (1981).

56 See Bacon, *The New Organon*, p. 130.
57 Note that the fundamental antagonist encountered at the very threshold of positive science is none other than *imagination* in the ambiguous role recalled earlier: that of being the source of the 'ideas', 'sensations' or perceptions on which we work, but from which we must also distinguish the true nature of things, available only in supersensory acts of 'intuition'. For a helpful account of Cartesian intuition, see Judovitz, *Subjectivity and Representation*, pp. 60-65 and pp. 70-73.
58 For a classic formulation, see Locke, *Essay*, bk. 2, chap. 8, sections 7-10.
59 For a helpful introduction to Cyrano's materialism, see Harth, *Cyrano de Bergerac*. Of special interest, given our focus on one of the *lettres diverses* devoted to what Cyrano ironically calls 'miracles de rivières', are chaps. 1 and 2, describing Cyrano's efforts to explain away supposed miracles by assigning them a reductive material basis directly accessible to unaided (and thus unblinkered) human reason.
60 Locke, *Essay*, bk. 2, chap. 1, section 16.
61 See Jacques Lacan, 'Le stade du miroir comme formateur de la fonction du Je telle qu'elle nous est révélée dans l'expérience psychanalytique', in *Ecrits* I (Paris: Seuil, 1966), p. 89, contrasting the human experience of the mirror image with 'le contrôle de l'inanité de l'image' observed among monkeys and chimpanzees.
62 Benjamin, *The Origin of German Tragic Drama*, p. 178.
63 Benjamin's one-sided view of the bipolar character of baroque culture stems from a sense of allegory determined by the black-and-white woodcuts and engravings of emblem books rather than the multi-coloured incitements of painting. In the run-up, e.g., to the characterization of allegory cited above, the claim that 'in allegory the observer is confronted with the *facies hippocratica* of history as a petrified, primordial landscape' (*Origin of German Tragic Drama*, p. 166) follows a discussion of baroque Melancholy for which Dürer's *Melencolia I* (pp. 149-151) sets the tone.
64 See E.M. Cioran, *Précis de décomposition* (Paris: Gallimard, 1949), a primer in the art of recursive suspicion that recalls the Tacitean 'sententiousness' of La Rochefoucauld, Gracián and Pascal.

Bibliography

Adam, Antoine. *Histoire de la littérature française au XVIIe* (Paris: Del Duca, 1962)
Adam, Antoine. *L'Age classique* (Paris: Arthaud, 1968-71)
Aers, David. 'A Whisper in the Ear of Early Modernists; or, Reflections on Literary Critics Writing the "History of the Subject"', in David Aers (ed.), *Culture and History, 1350-1600: Essays on English Communities, Identities, and Writing* (Detroit, MI: Wayne State University Press, 1992), pp. 177-202
Agamben, Giorgio. 'The Prince and the Frog: The Question of Method in Adorno and Benjamin', in *Infancy and History: Essays on the Destruction of Experience*, trans. Liz Heron (London: Verso, 1993), pp. 107-24
Alberti, Leon Battista. *On Painting*, ed. and parallel trans. Cecil Grayson (London: Phaidon, 1972)
Alpers, Svetlana. 'Describe or Narrate?: A Problem in Realistic Representation', *New Literary History* 8 (1976-77), pp. 15-41
Alpers, Svetlana. *The Art of Describing: Dutch Art in the Seventeenth Century* (Chicago: University of Chicago Press, 1983)
Alpers, Svetlana. *Rembrandt's Enterprise: The Studio and the Market* (Chicago: University of Chicago Press, 1988)
Althusser, Louis, and Balibar, Etienne. *Reading Capital*, trans. Ben Brewster (New York: Pantheon, 1970)
Argan, Giulio Carlo. *The Baroque Age* (1964; 1st paper ed. Geneva: Skira; New York: Rizzoli, 1989)
Aristotle. *Poetics*, trans. James Hutton (New York: Norton, 1982)
Ascoli, Albert Russell, and Kahn, Victoria (eds), *Machiavelli and the Discourse of Literature* (Ithaca, NY: Cornell University Press, 1993)
Austin, J.L. *Philosophical Papers*, 2nd ed., ed. J.O. Urmson and G.J. Warnock (Oxford: Oxford University Press, 1970)
Austin, J.L. *How to Do Things with Words*, 2nd ed. J.O. Urmson and Marina Sbisà (Cambridge, MA: Harvard University Press, 1975)
Bacon, Sir Francis. *The Essays, or Counsels Civil and Moral*, ed. Brian Vickers (Oxford: Oxford University Press, 1999)
Bacon, Sir Francis. *The New Organon and Related Writings*, ed. Fulton H. Anderson (Indianapolis, IN: Bobbs-Merrill, 1960)
Bal, Mieke. *Reading Rembrandt: Beyond the Word-Image Opposition* (Cambridge: Cambridge University Press, 1991)
Bal, Mieke. *Quoting Caravaggio: Contemporary Art, Preposterous History* (Chicago: University of Chicago Press, 1999)
Baldini, Nicoletta. *Niccolò Soggi* (Florence: EDIFIR, 1997)
Baltrusaitis, Jurgis. *Anamorphoses ou perspectives curieuses* (Paris: O. Perrin, 1955)
Baltrusaitis, Jurgis. *Anamorphoses ou magie artificielle* (Paris: O. Perrin, 1969)
Baltrusaitis, Jurgis. *Anamorphoses ou Thaumaturgus opticus* (Paris: Flammarion, 1984)
Barish, Jonas A. *The Antitheatrical Prejudice* (Berkeley, CA: University of California Press, 1981)

Baxandall, Michael. *Giotto and the Orators: Humanist Observers of Painting in Italy and the Discovery of Pictorial Composition, 1350-1450* (Oxford: Clarendon Press, 1971)
Baxandall, Michael. *Patterns of Intention: On the Historical Explanation of Pictures* (New Haven: Yale University Press, 1985)
Baxandall, Michael. *Painting and Experience in Fifteenth-Century Italy: A Primer in the Social History of Pictorial Style*, 2nd ed. (Oxford: Oxford University Press, 1988)
Bazin, Germain. *The Baroque: Principles, Styles, Modes, Themes* (Greenwich, CT: New York Graphic Society, 1968)
Bellori, Giovanni Pietro. *The Lives of Annibale and Agostino Carracci*, trans. Catherine Enggass (University Park, PA: Pennsylvania State University Press, 1968)
Bellori, Giovanni Pietro. *Le vite de' pittori, scultori e architetti moderni*, ed. Evelina Borea (Turin: G. Einaudi, 1976)
Bénichou, Paul. *Morales du grand siècle* (Paris: Gallimard, 1948)
Benjamin, Walter. *Illuminations*, ed. Hannah Arendt, trans. Harry Zohn (New York: Schocken, 1968)
Benjamin, Walter. *Reflections: Essays, Aphorisms, Autobiographical Writings*, ed. Hannah Arendt, trans. Edmund Jephcott (New York: Schocken, 1978)
Benjamin, Walter. *The Origin of German Tragic Drama*, trans. John Osborne (London: New Left Books, 1978)
Benjamin, Walter. *The Arcades Project*, trans. Howard Eiland and Kevin McLaughlin (Cambridge, MA: Harvard University Press, 1999)
Berger, Harry, Jr. *Imaginary Audition: Shakespeare on Page and Stage* (Berkeley, CA: University of California Press, 1989)
Berger, Harry, Jr. *Fictions of the Pose: Rembrandt against the Italian Renaissance* (Stanford, CA: Stanford University Press, 2000)
Bernstein, Michael André. *Five Portraits: Modernity and the Imagination in Twentieth-Century German Writing* (Evanston, IL: Northwestern University Press, 2000)
Bidermann, Jacob. *Cenodoxus*, ed. D.G. Dyer with parallel trans. by D.G. Dyer and Cecily Longrigg (Austin, TX: University of Texas Press, 1974)
Blumenberg, Hans. *The Legitimacy of the Modern Age*, trans. Robert M. Wallace (Cambridge, MA: MIT Press, 1983)
Blunt, Anthony. *Nicolas Poussin* (New York: Bollingen, 1967)
Bonafoux, Pascal. *Portraits of the Artist: The Self-Portrait in Painting* (New York: Skira/Rizzoli, 1985)
Bourdieu, Pierre. *La distinction: critique sociale du jugement* (Paris: Minuit, 1979)
Bourdieu, Pierre. *Méditations pascaliennes* (Paris: Seuil, 1997)
Braider, Christopher. *Refiguring the Real: Picture and Modernity in Word and Image, 1400-1700* (Princeton, NJ: Princeton University Press, 1993)
Braider, Christopher. 'The Paradoxical Sisterhood: *Ut Pictura Poesis*', in *Cambridge History of Literary Criticism* (Cambridge: Cambridge University Press, 1999), vol. III, *The Renaissance*, ed. Glyn P. Norton, pp. 168-175
Braider, Christopher. *Indiscernible Counterparts: The Invention of the Text in French Classical Drama* (Chapel Hill, NC: North Carolina Studies in the Romance Languages and Literatures, 2002)
Braudel, Fernand. *Civilisation matérielle, Economie et Capitalisme, XVe-XVIIIe siècle*, vol. III, *Le Temps du Monde* (Paris: Armand Colin, 1979)
Brown, Jonathan. *Velázquez: Painter and Courtier* (New Haven, CT: Yale University Press, 1986)
Broude, Norma, and Garrard, Mary D., (eds), *Feminism and Art History: Questioning the Litany* (New York: Harper and Row, 1982)

Bruneau, Marie-Florine. *Racine: Le jansénisme et la modernité* (Paris: Corti, 1986)
Bryson, Norman. *Word and Image: French Painting of the Ancien Régime* (Cambridge: Cambridge University Press, 1981)
Bryson, Norman. *Vision and Painting: The Logic of the Gaze* (New Haven, CT: Yale University Press, 1983)
Bryson, Norman. 'Two Narratives of Rape in the Visual Arts: Lucretia and the Sabine Women', in Sylvana Tomaselli and Roy Porters (eds), *Rape: An Historical and Cultural Enquiry* (Oxford: Blackwell, 1986), pp. 152-173
Buci-Glucksmann, Christine. *La raison baroque: de Baudelaire à Benjamin* (Paris: Galilée, 1984)
Buci-Glucksmann, Christine. *La folie du voir: de l'esthétique baroque* (Paris: Galilée, 1986)
Burckhardt, Jacob. *The Civilization of the Renaissance in Italy*, trans. S.G.C. Middlemore, 3rd ed. (London: Phaidon, 1950)
Calabrese, Omar. *Neo-Baroque: A Sign of the Times*, trans. Charles Lambert (Princeton, NJ: Princeton University Press, 1992)
Campbell, Mary Baine. *The Witness and the Other World: European Travel Writing, 400-1600* (Ithaca, NY: Cornell University Press, 1988)
Campbell, Mary Baine. *Wonder & Science: Imagining Worlds in Early Modern Europe* (Ithaca, NY: Cornell University Press, 1999)
Carroll, Margaret Deutsch. 'The Erotics of Absolutism: Rubens and the Mystification of Sexual Violence', *Representations* 25 (1989), pp. 3-30
Cascardi, Anthony J. *The Limits of Illusion: A Critical Study of Calderón* (Cambridge: Cambridge University Press, 1984)
Cascardi, Anthony J. *The Subject of Modernity* (Cambridge: Cambridge University Press, 1992)
Cascardi, Anthony J. *Ideologies of History in the Spanish Golden Age* (University Park, PA: Pennsylvania State University Press, 1997)
Cassirer, Ernst. *The Individual and the Cosmos in Renaissance Philosophy*, trans. Mario Domandi (New York: Barnes and Noble, 1963)
Chambers, Ross. ' "Que diray-je de ce miroir fluide?": Text and Its Double in a Letter by Cyrano', *Australian Journal of French Studies* 14 (1977), pp. 121-140
Chapman, H. Perry. *Rembrandt's Self-Portraits: A Study in Seventeenth-Century Identity* (Princeton, NJ: Princeton University Press, 1990)
Charpentrat, Pierre. *Le mirage baroque* (Paris: Minuit, 1967)
Chedozeau, Bernard. *Le Baroque* (Paris: Nathan, 1989)
Cioran, E.M. *Précis de décomposition* (Paris: Gallimard, 1949)
Clark, Sir Kenneth. *The Nude: A Study in Ideal Form* (1956; repr., Princeton, NJ: Princeton University Press, 1984)
Clark, Sir Kenneth. *Rembrandt and the Italian Renaissance* (New York: New York University Press, 1966)
Collingwood, R.G. *The Idea of History* (Oxford: Oxford University Press, 1946)
Coogan, Robert. *Erasmus, Lee and the Correction of the Vulgate: The Shaking of the Foundations* (Geneva: Droz, 1992)
Corneille, Pierre. *Œuvres complètes*, ed. Georges Couton (Paris: Gallimard, 1980-87)
Couton, Georges (ed.). *Théâtre du XVIIe siècle* (Paris: Gallimard, 1975-92)
Crary, Jonathan. *Techniques of the Observer: On Vision and Modernity in the Nineteenth Century* (Cambridge, MA.: MIT Press, 1990)
Cyrano de Bergerac, Savinien. *Lettres*, ed. Luciano Erba (Milan: Vanni Scheiweller, 1965)

Cyrano de Bergerac, Savinien. *L'Autre monde*, ed. Henri Weber (Paris: Editions sociales, 1975)
Daniell, David. *William Tyndale: A Biography* (New Haven, CT: Yale University Press, 1994)
Danto, Arthur. *Analytical Philosophy of History* (Cambridge: Cambridge University Press, 1965)
D'Aubignac, François Hédelin, abbé. *La Pratique du théâtre* (1657); facsimile of the Amsterdam edition of 1715 (Munich: Wilhelm Fink Verlag, 1971)
DeJean, Joan. *Tender Geographies: Women and the Origins of the Novel in France* (New York: Columbia University Press, 1991)
DeJean, Joan. *Ancients against Moderns: Culture Wars and the Making of a Fin de Siècle* (Chicago: University of Chicago Press, 1997)
De Lauretis, Teresa. *Alice Doesn't: Feminism, Semiotics, Cinema* (New York: Macmillan, 1983)
Deleuze, Gilles. *Le pli: Leibniz et le baroque* (Paris: Minuit, 1988)
Dempsey, Charles. *Annibale Carracci and the Beginnings of Baroque Style* (Glückstadt: J.J. Augustin Verlag, 1977)
Derrida, Jacques. 'Cogito et histoire de la folie', in *L'écriture et la différence* (Paris: Seuil, 1967; 'Points' paper ed.), pp. 51-97
Derrida, Jacques. 'Coming Into One's Own', trans. James Hulbert, in Geoffrey H. Hartman (ed.), *Psychoanalysis and the Question of the Text* (Baltimore: Johns Hopkins University Press, 1978), pp. 114-48
Descartes, René. *Méditations métaphysiques*, in *Œuvres philosophiques*, ed. Ferdinand Alquié (Paris: Garnier, 1988-92)
Dollimore, Jonathan. *Radical Tragedy: Religion, Ideology, and Power in the Drama of Shakespeare and His Contemporaries*, 2nd ed. (Durham, N.C.: Duke University Press, 1993)
Dumont, Pascal. 'Est-il pertinent de parler d'une philosophie baroque?' in Didier Soullier (ed.), *Le Baroque en question(s)*, Littératures classiques 36 (Spring 1999), pp. 63-77
Elkins, James. *What Painting Is: How to Think about Oil Painting, Using the Language of Alchemy* (New York: Routledge, 1999)
Evans, Richard J. *In Defense of History* (New York: Norton, 1999)
Faudemay, Alain. *La Distinction à l'âge classique: Emules et Enjeux* (Geneva: Droz, 1992)
Fielding, Henry. *Joseph Andrews*, ed. A.R. Humphreys (London: Everyman, 1973)
Fineman, Joel. *Shakespeare's Perjur'd Eye: The Invention of Poetic Subjectivity in the Sonnets* (Berkeley, CA: University of California Press, 1986)
Fish, Stanley E. *Surprised by Sin: The Reader in Paradise Lost* (Berkeley, CA: University of California Press, 1967)
Fish, Stanley E. *Self-Consuming Artifacts: The Experience of Seventeenth-Century Literature* (Berkeley, CA: University of California Press, 1972)
Fish, Stanley E. *Is There a Text in This Class? The Authority of Interpretive Communities* (Cambridge, MA: Harvard University Press, 1980)
Fish, Stanley E. *How Milton Works* (Cambridge, MA: Harvard University Press, 2001)
Forestier, Georges. *Le Théâtre dans le théâtre sur la scène française du XVIIe siècle*, 2nd ed. (Geneva: Droz, 1996)
Foucault, Michel. *L'Histoire de la folie à l'âge classique* (Paris: Plon, 1961; repr. Paris: Gallimard, 1972)
Foucault, Michel. *Les mots et les choses: une archéologie des sciences humaines* (Paris: Gallimard, 1966)

Foucault, Michel. *L'archéologie du savoir* (Paris: Gallimard, 1969)
Fox, Robin Lane. *Pagans and Christians* (New York: Knopf, 1987)
Freedberg, David. *The Power of Images: Studies in the History and Theory of Response* (Chicago: University of Chicago Press, 1989)
Fried, Michael. *Absorption and Theatricality: Painting and Beholder in the Age of Diderot* (Chicago: University of Chicago Press, 1980)
Fumaroli, Marc. *Héros et orateurs: Rhétorique et dramaturgie cornéliennes* (Geneva: Droz, 1990)
Fumaroli, Marc. *Le Poète et le Roi: Jean de La Fontaine en son siècle* (Paris: Fallois, 1997)
Garrard, Mary D. 'Artemesia and Susanna', in Norma Broude and Mary D. Garrard (eds), *Feminism and Art History: Questioning the Litany* (New York: Harper and Row, 1982), pp. 147-171
Garrard, Mary D. *Artemesia Gentileschi: The Image of the Female Hero in Italian Baroque Art* (Princeton, NJ: Princeton University Press, 1988)
Gasté, Armand, (ed.). *La Querelle du Cid: Pièces et pamphlets* (Paris: H. Welter, 1899)
Gaukroger, Stephen. *Descartes: An Intellectual Biography* (Oxford: Clarendon Press, 1995)
Gilman, Ernest B. *The Curious Perspective: Verbal and Pictorial Wit in Seventeenth-Century Literature* (New Haven, CT: Yale University Press, 1978)
Goffen, Rona. *Titian's Women* (New Haven, CT: Yale University Press, 1997)
Goffen, Rona (ed.). *Titian's Venus of Urbino* (Cambridge: Cambridge University Press, 1997)
Goldmann, Lucien. *Le Dieu caché: étude sur la vision tragique dans les Pensées de Pascal et dans le théâtre de Racine* (Paris: Gallimard, 1959)
Grafton, Anthony. *Commerce with the Classics: Ancient Books and Renaissance Readers* (Ann Arbor, MI: University of Michigan Press, 1997)
Grafton, Anthony, with April Shelford and Nancy Siraisi. *New Worlds, Ancient Texts: The Power of Tradition and the Shock of Discovery* (Cambridge, MA: Harvard University Press, 1992)
Greenberg, Mitchell. *Detours of Desire: Readings in the French Baroque* (Columbus, OH: Ohio State University Press, 1984)
Greenberg, Mitchell. *Corneille, Classicism, and the Ruses of Symmetry* (Cambridge: Cambridge University Press, 1986)
Greenberg, Mitchell. *Subjectivity and Subjugation in Seventeenth-Century French Drama and Prose: The Family Romance of French Classicism* (Cambridge: Cambridge University Press, 1992)
Greenberg, Mitchell. *Canonical States, Canonical Stages: Œdipus, Othering, and Seventeenth-Century Drama* (Minneapolis, MN: University of Minnesota Press, 1994)
Greenberg, Mitchell. *Baroque Bodies: Psychoanalysis and the Culture of Absolutism* (Ithaca, NY: Cornell University Press, 2001)
Greenblatt, Stephen. *Renaissance Self-Fashioning from More to Shakespeare* (Chicago: University of Chicago Press, 1980)
Greenblatt, Stephen. *Marvelous Possessions: The Wonder of the New World* (Chicago: University of Chicago Press, 1991)
Greene, Roland. *Unrequited Conquests: Love and Empire in the Colonial Americas* (Chicago: University of Chicago Press, 1998)
Greene, Thomas. *The Light in Troy: Imitation and Discovery in Renaissance Poetry* (New Haven, CT: Yale University Press, 1982)

Gryphius, Andreas. *Verliebtes Gespenst/Die geliebte Dornrose*, ed. Eberhard Mannack (Stuttgart: Reclam, 1985)
Guenée, Bernard. *Histoire et culture historique dans l'Occident médiéval* (Paris: Aubier Montaigne, 1980)
Hagstrum, Jeaan. *The Sister Arts: The Tradition of Literary Pictorialism and English Poetry from Dryden to Gray* (Chicago: University of Chicago Press, 1958)
Hampton, Timothy. *Writing from History: The Rhetoric of Exemplarity in Renaissance Literature* (Ithaca, NY: Cornell University Press, 1990)
Harth, Erica. *Cyrano de Bergerac and the Polemics of Modernity* (New York: Columbia University Press, 1970)
Harth, Erica. *Ideology and Culture in Seventeenth-Century France* (Ithaca, NY: Cornell University Press, 1982)
Harth, Erica. *Cartesian Women: Versions and Subversions of Rational Discourse in the Old Régime* (Ithaca, NY: Cornell University Press, 1992)
Hartnoll, Phyllis. *The Theatre: A Concise History*, rev. ed. (London: Thames and Hudson, 1985)
Haskell, Francis. *Patrons and Painters: A Study in the Relations between Italian Art and Society in the Age of the Baroque*, rev. and enl. ed. (New Haven: Yale University Press, 1980)
Hazard, Paul. *La Crise de la conscience européenne, 1680-1715* (Paris: Fayard, 1961)
Hegel, Georg Wilhelm Friedrich. *The Phenomenology of Mind*, trans. J.B. Baillie (rev. ed., 1931; repr. New York: Harper and Row, 1967)
Heidegger, Martin. *Poetry, Language, Thought*, trans. Albert Hofstadter (New York: Harper and Row, 1971)
Helgerson, Richard. *Adulterous Alliances: Home, State, and History in Early Modern European Drama and Painting* (Chicago: University of Chicago Press, 2000)
Hibbard, Howard. *Caravaggio* (New York: Harper and Row, 1983)
Hill, Christopher. *The World Turned Upside Down: Radical Ideas during the English Revolution* (London: Maurice Temple Smith, 1972)
Hill, Christopher. *The Experience of Defeat: Milton and Some Contemporaries* (New York: Viking Penguin, 1984)
Hobbes, Thomas. *Leviathan* (London: Everyman, 1965)
Holly, Michael Ann. *Panofsky and the Foundations of Art History* (Ithaca, NY: Cornell University Press, 1984)
Horkheimer, Max, and Adorno, Theodor. *The Dialectic of Enlightenment*, trans. John Cumming (New York: Continuum, 1990)
Hume, David. *Natural History of Religion*, ed. H.E. Root (Stanford, CA: Stanford University Press, 1957)
Hume, David. *A Treatise of Human Nature*, ed. Ernest C. Mossner (Harmondsworth: Penguin, 1969)
Hume, David. *Essays Moral, Political, and Literary*, rev. ed. Eugene F. Miller (Indianapolis, IN: Liberty Classics, 1987)
Hume, David. *Dialogues Concerning Natural Religion*, ed. Martin Bell (Harmondsworth: Penguin, 1990)
Husserl, Edmund. *Cartesian Meditations: An Introduction to Phenomenology*, tr. Dorion Cairns (The Hague: M. Nijhoff, 1960)
Jameson, Fredric. *The Political Unconscious: Narrative as a Socially Symbolic Act* (Ithaca, NY: Cornell University Press, 1981)
Jardine, Lisa. *Worldly Goods: A New History of the Renaissance* (New York: Doubleday, 1996)

Jay, Martin. *The Dialectical Imagination: A History of the Frankfurt School and the Institute for Social Research, 1923-1950* (Berkeley, CA: University of California Press, 1972; repr. 1996)

Jay, Martin. *Downcast Eyes: The Denigration of Vision in Twentieth-Century French Thought* (Berkeley, CA: University of California Press, 1993)

Jones, W.T. 'Somnio Ergo Sum: Descartes's Three Dreams', *Philosophy and Literature* 4.2 (Fall, 1980), pp. 145-166

Jouhaud, Christian. *La Main de Richelieu, ou le pouvoir cardinal* (Paris: Gallimard, 1990)

Jouhaud, Christian. 'Power and Literature: The Terms of the Exchange 1624-42', in Richard Burt (ed.), *The Administration of Aesthetics: Censorship, Political Criticism, and the Public Sphere* (Minneapolis, MN: University of Minnesota Press, 1994), pp. 34-82

Judovitz, Dalia. *Subjectivity and Representation in Descartes: The Origins of Modernity* (Cambridge: Cambridge University Press, 1988)

Judovitz, Dalia. *The Culture of the Body: Genealogies of Modernity* (Ann Arbor, MI: University of Michigan Press, 2001)

Justice, Steven. *Writing and Rebellion: England in 1381* (Berkeley, CA: University of California Press, 1994)

Kahn, Victoria. *Rhetoric, Prudence, and Skepticism in the Renaissance* (Ithaca, NY: Cornell University Press, 1985)

Kant, Immanuel. *Critique of Pure Reason*, trans. Norman Kemp Smith (London: Macmillan, 1929; repr. 1976)

Kant, Immanuel. *Observations on the Feeling of the Beautiful and Sublime*, trans. John T. Goldthwait (Berkeley, CA: University of California Press, 1960; repr. 1981)

Kant, Immanuel. *Prolegomena to Any Future Metaphysics*, trans. Paul Carus, rev. James W. Ellington (Indianapolis, IN: Hackett, 1977)

Kant, Immanuel. *Critique of Judgment*, ed. and trans. Werner S. Pluhar (Indianapolis, IN: Hackett, 1987)

Keller, Evelyn Fox. *Reflections on Gender and Science* (New Haven, CT: Yale University Press, 1985)

Kemp, Martin. *The Science of Art: Optical Themes in Western Art from Brunelleschi to Seurat* (New Haven, CT: Yale University Press, 1990)

Kuhn, Thomas S. *The Copernican Revolution: Planetary Astronomy in the Development of Western Thought* (Cambridge, MA: Harvard University Press, 1957)

Lacan, Jacques. 'Le stade du miroir comme formateur de la fonction du Je telle qu'elle nous est révélée dans l'expérience psychanalytique', in *Ecrits* I (Paris: Seuil, 1966; 'Points' paper ed.), pp. 89-97

Lacan, Jacques. *Les quatre concepts fondamentaux de la psychanalyse, Le séminaire de Jacques Lacan*, bk. 11, ed. Jacques-Alain Miller (Paris: Seuil, 1973; 'Points' paper ed.)

Lacan, Jacques. *Les écrits techniques de Freud, Le séminaire de Jacques Lacan*, bk. 1, ed. Jacques-Alain Miller (Paris: Seuil, 1975)

Langdon, Helen. *Caravaggio: A Life* (New York: Farrar, Straus and Giroux, 1998)

Latour, Bruno. *Science in Action: How to Follow Scientists and Engineers through Society* (Cambridge, MA: Harvard University Press, 1987)

Latour, Bruno. *Nous n'avons jamais été modernes: essai d'anthropologie symétrique* (Paris: Editions de La Découverte, 1991)

Latour, Bruno, and Woolgar, Steven. *Laboratory Life: The Social Construction of Scientific Facts* (Beverly Hills, CA: Sage Publications, 1979)

Leder, Drew. *The Absent Body* (Chicago: University of Chicago Press, 1990)
Lee, Rensselaer W. *Ut Pictura Poesis: The Humanistic Theory of Painting* (1940; repr. New York: Norton, 1967)
Lennon, Thomas M. *Reading Bayle* (Toronto: University of Toronto Press, 1999)
Leonardo da Vinci, *The Notebooks of Leonardo*, ed. and tr. Jean Paul Richter (1883; repr. New York: Dover, 1970)
Lessing, Gotthold Ephraim. *Laocoön: An Essay on the Limits of Painting and Poetry*, trans. Edward Allen McCormick (Indianapolis, IN: Bobbs-Merrill, 1962)
Lezra, Jacques. *Unspeakable Subjects: The Genealogy of the Event in Early Modern Europe* (Stanford, CA: Stanford University Press, 1997)
Lichtenstein, Jacqueline. *La Couleur éloquente: rhétorique et peinture à l'âge classique* (Paris: Flammarion, 1989)
Locke, John. *An Essay Concerning Human Understanding*, ed. Alexander Campbell Fraser (1894; repr., New York: Dover, 1959)
Lohenstein, Daniel Casper von. *Sophonisbe*, ed. Rolf Tarot (Stuttgart: Reclam, 1970)
Longino, Michèle. *Orientalism in French Classical Drama* (Cambridge: Cambridge University Press, 2002)
Lupton, Julia Reinhard, and Reinhard, Kenneth. *After Œdipus: Shakespeare in Psychoanalysis* (Ithaca, NY: Cornell University Press, 1993)
Lyons, John D. *A Theatre of Disguise: Studies in French Baroque Drama* (Columbia, SC: French Literature Publications, 1978)
Lyons, John D. *Exemplum: The Rhetoric of Example in Early Modern France and Italy* (Princeton, NJ: Princeton University Press, 1989)
Lyons, John D. *The Tragedy of Origins: Pierre Corneille and Historical Perspective* (Stanford, CA: Stanford University Press, 1996)
Lyons, John D. *Kingdom of Disorder: The Theory of Tragedy in Classical France* (West Lafayette, IN: Purdue University Press, 1999)
Mahon, Denis. *Studies in Seicento Art Theory* (London: The Warburg Institute, 1947; repr. Westport, CT: Greenwood Press, 1971)
Maillard, Jean-François. *Essai sur l'esprit du héros baroque (1580-1640): le même et l'autre* (Paris: Nizet, 1973)
Maravall, José. *The Culture of the Baroque: Analysis of a Historical Structure*, trans. Terry Cochran (Minneapolis, MN: University of Minnesota Press, 1986)
Margival, Henri. *Essai sur Richard Simon et la critique biblique au 17e siècle* (1900; repr. Geneva: Slatkine, 1970)
Margolis, Joseph. *Interpretation Radical But Not Unruly: The New Puzzle of the Arts and History* (Berkeley, CA: University of California Press, 1995)
Marin, Louis. *Etudes sémiologiques: Ecritures, peintures* (Paris: Klincksieck, 1971)
Marin, Louis. *La Critique du discours: sur la 'Logique de Port-Royal' et les 'Pensées' de Pascal* (Paris: Minuit, 1975)
Marin, Louis. *Détruire la peinture* (Paris: Galilée, 1977)
Marin, Louis. *Le portrait du roi* (Paris: Minuit, 1981)
Marin, Louis. *La parole mangée et autres essais théologico-politiques* (Paris: Klincksieck, 1986)
Marin, Louis. *Des pouvoirs de l'image: gloses* (Paris: Seuil, 1993)
Martin, John Rupert. *The Farnese Gallery* (Princeton, NJ: Princeton University Press, 1965)
Martin, John Rupert. *Baroque* (New York: Harper and Row, 1977)
Merleau-Ponty, Maurice. *Phénoménologie de la perception* (Paris: Gallimard, 1945)

Merleau-Ponty, Maurice. *Le Visible et l'invisible*, ed. Claude Lefort (Paris: Gallimard, 1964)
Merlin, Hélène. *Littérature et public en France au XVIIe siècle* (Paris: Les Belles lettres, 1994)
Miles, Margaret R. *Image as Insight: Visual Understanding in Western Christianity and Secular Culture* (Boston: Beacon Press, 1985)
Miles, Margaret R. *Carnal Knowledge: Female Nakedness and Religious Meaning in the Christian West* (Boston: Beacon Press, 1989)
Mitchell, W.J.T. *Iconology: Image, Text, Ideology* (Chicago: University of Chicago Press, 1986)
Montaigne, Michel de. *Essais* (Paris: Garnier-Flammarion, 1969)
Moriarty, Michael. *Taste and Ideology in Seventeenth-Century France* (Cambridge: Cambridge University Press, 1988)
Most, Glenn W., and Stowe, William W. (eds). *The Poetics of Murder: Detective Fiction and Literary Theory* (New York: Harcourt Brace Javonovich, 1983)
Mulvey, Laura. 'Visual Pleasure and Narrative Cinema', *Screen* 16.3 (1975), pp. 6-18
Nancy, Jean-Luc. *Ego Sum* (Paris: Flammarion, 1979)
Newman, Jane O. *The Intervention of Philology: Gender, Learning, and Power in Lohenstein's Roman Plays* (Chapel Hill, NC: University of North Carolina Studies in the Germanic Languages and Literatures, 2000)
Ockham, William of. *Philosophical Writings*, ed. and trans. Philotheus Boehner (New York: Nelson, 1957)
Oresme, Nicole. *De proportionibus, and Ad pauca respicientes*, ed. and trans. Edward Grant (Madison, WI: University of Wisconsin Press, 1966)
Orgel, Stephen. 'The Example of Hercules', in Walther Killy (ed.), *Mythographie der frühen Neuzeit: Ihre Anwendung in den Künsten* (Wiesbaden: Otto Harrassowitz, 1984), pp. 25-47
Panofsky, Erwin. *Perspective as a Symbolic Form*, trans. Christopher S. Wood (1927; New York: Zone Books, 1991)
Panofsky, Erwin. *Hercules am Scheidewege und andere antike Bildstoffe in der neueren Kunst* (Leipzig: B.G. Teubner, 1930; repr. Berlin: Edition Logos, Gebr. Mann Verlag, 1997)
Panofsky, Erwin. *Early Netherlandish Painting: Its Origins and Character* (1953; repr. New York: Harper and Row, 1971)
Panofsky, Erwin. 'Titian's *Allegory of Prudence*: A Postscript', *Meaning in the Visual Arts* (Chicago: University of Chicago Press, 1955; Phoenix paper ed.), pp. 146-168
Parker, Patricia. 'Preposterous Events', *Shakespeare Quarterly* 43.2 (1992), pp. 186-213
Pascal, Blaise. *Pensées*, ed. Louis Lafuma (Paris: Seuil, 1962)
Pascal, Blaise. *Pensées*, ed. Philippe Sellier (Paris: Classiques Garnier, 1991)
Passage, Charles E., and Mantinband, James H. *Amphitryon: The Legend and Three Plays (Plautus, Molière, Kleist)* (Chapel Hill, NC: University of North Carolina Press, 1974)
Patterson, Annabel. *Censorship and Interpretation: The Conditions of Writing and Reading in Early Modern England* (Madison, WI: University of Wisconsin Press, 1984)
Piles, Roger de. *Abrégé de la Vie des Peintres, Avec des reflexions sur leurs Ouvrages, Et un Traité du Peintre Parfait, de la connoissance des Desseins, et de l'utilité des Estampes* (Paris: François Muguet, 1699)
Pliny the Elder. *The Elder Pliny's Chapters on the History of Art*, ed. and parallel trans. K. Jex-Blake (1896; repr. Chicago: Argonaut, 1968)

Pollock, Griselda. *Vision and Difference: Femininity, Feminism, and the Histories of Art* (New York: Routledge, 1988)
Popkin, Richard H. *The History of Scepticism from Erasmus to Spinoza*, rev. ed. (Berkeley, CA: University of California Press, 1979)
Porter, Dennis. 'Backward Construction and the Art of Suspense', in Glenn W. Most and William W. Stowe (eds), *The Poetics of Murder: Detective Fiction and Literary Theory* (New York: Harcourt Brace Javonovich, 1983), pp. 327-340.
Posner, Donald. *Annibale Carracci: A Study in the Reform of Italian Painting around 1590* (London: Phaidon, 1971)
Poulet, Georges. 'Le songe de Descartes', *Etudes sur le temps humain* I (Paris: Plon, 1952; Editions du Rocher paper ed.), pp. 63-96
Praz, Mario. *The Flaming Heart: Essays on Crashaw, Machiavelli, and Other Studies in the Relations between Italian and English Literature from Chaucer to T.S. Eliot* (Garden City, NY: Doubleday, 1958)
Prendergast, Christopher. *The Triangle of Representation* (New York: Columbia University Press, 2000)
Quint, David. *Origin and Originality in Renaissance Literature: Versions of the Source* (New Haven, CT: Yale University Press, 1983)
Reiss, Timothy J. *The Discourse of Modernism* (Ithaca, NY: Cornell University Press, 1982)
Ripa, Cesare. *Iconologia*, repr. of the Roman edition of 1603 (Hildesheim: Georg Olms, 1970)
Ripa, Cesare. *Iconologia*, ed. Edward A. Maser, repr. of the Hertel edition of 1758-60 (New York: Dover, 1971)
Robb, Peter. *M* (Sydney: Duffy and Snellgrove, 1998)
Rodríguez García, José María. 'Solitude and Procreation in Francis Bacon's Scientific Writings—The Spanish Connection', *Comparative Literature Studies* 35.3 (1998), pp. 278-300
Rorty, Richard. *Philosophy and the Mirror of Nature* (Princeton, NJ: Princeton University Press, 1979)
Rousset, Jean. *La Littérature de l'âge baroque en France: Circe et le paon* (Paris: J. Corti, 1953)
Rousset, Jean. *Dernier regard sur le baroque* (Paris: J. Corti, 1998)
Sarpi, Paolo. *Storia del Concilio Tridentino*, ed. Giovanni Gambarin; repr. with intro. by Renzo Pecchioli (Florence: Sansoni, 1966)
Sawday, Jonathan. *The Body Emblazoned: Dissection and the Human Body in Renaissance Culture* (New York: Routledge, 1995)
Schama, Simon. *The Embarrassment of Riches: An Interpretation of Dutch Culture in the Golden Age* (New York: Knopf, 1987)
Schérer, Jacques. *La Dramaturgie classique en France* (1950; repr. Paris: Nizet, 1986)
Schwartz, Gary. *Rembrandt, His Life, His Paintings* (New York: Viking, 1985)
Searle, John. *The Rediscovery of the Mind* (Cambridge, MA: MIT Press, 1992)
Serres, Michel. *La Naissance de la physique dans le texte de Lucrèce* (Paris: Minuit, 1977)
Seward, Desmond. *Caravaggio: A Passionate Life* (New York: William Morrow, 1998)
Shakespeare, William. *The Merchant of Venice*, in *Complete Works*, ed. W.J. Craig (Oxford: Oxford University Press, 1905; repr. 1966)
Shakespeare, William. *Hamlet*, ed. John Dover Wilson (Cambridge: Cambridge University Press, 1936)

Shakespeare, William. *Richard II*, ed. John Dover Wilson (Cambridge: Cambridge University Press, 1939)
Shakespeare, William. *Twelfth Night, or What You Will*, ed. Sir Arthur Quiller-Couch and John Dover Wilson (Cambridge: Cambridge University Press, 1949)
Shapin, Steven. *A Social History of Truth: Civility and Science in Seventeenth-Century England* (Chicago: University of Chicago Press, 1994)
Sidney, Sir Phillip. *Apology for Poetry*, ed. Geoffrey Shepherd (New York: Barnes and Noble, 1973)
Silverman, Kaja. *The Acoustic Mirror: The Female Voice in Psychoanalysis and Cinema* (Bloomington: Indiana University Press, 1988)
Souiller, Didier (ed.). *Le Baroque en question(s)*, Littératures classiques 36 (Spring 1999)
Spinoza, Baruch. *Theological-Political Treatise*, trans. R.H.M. Elwes (1883; repr. New York: Dover, 1951)
Stafford, Barbara. *Body Criticism: Imaging the Unseen in Enlightenment Art and Medicine* (Cambridge, MA: MIT Press, 1991)
Stanton, Domna C. *The Aristocrat as Art: A Study of the Honnête Homme and the Dandy in Seventeenth- and Nineteenth-Century France* (New York: Columbia University Press, 1980)
Strauss, Leo. *Persecution and the Art of Writing* (Glencoe, IL: The Free Press, 1952)
Strauss, Leo. *Spinoza's Critique of Religion*, trans. E.M. Sinclair (New York: Schocken, 1965)
Summers, David. *Michelangelo and the Language of Art* (Princeton, NJ: Princeton University Press, 1981)
Summers, David. *The Judgment of Sense: Renaissance Naturalism and the Rise of Aesthetics* (Cambridge: Cambridge University Press, 1987)
Sypher, Wylie. *Four Stages of Renaissance Style: Transformations in Art and Literature, 1400-1700* (Garden City, NY: Doubleday, 1955)
Tapié, Victor-Lucien. *Baroque et classicisme* (Paris: Plon, 1957)
Tapié, Victor-Lucien. *Le baroque* (Paris: Presses universitaires de France, 1961)
Taylor, Charles. *Sources of the Self: The Making of Modern Identity* (Cambridge, MA: Harvard University Press, 1989)
Taylor, Ronald (ed.). *Aesthetics and Politics* (London: New Left Books, 1977)
Trevor-Roper, H.R. *The Crisis of the Seventeenth Century: Religion, the Reformation and Social Change* (New York: Harper and Row, 1968)
Valcanover, Francesco, et al. *Titian, Prince of Painters* (Munich: Prestel, 1990)
Valentin, Jean-Marie. *Theatrum catholicum: les Jésuites et la scène en Allemagne au XVIe et au XVIIe siècles* (Nancy: Presses universitaires de Nancy, 1990)
Viala, Alain. *Naissance de l'écrivain* (Paris: Minuit, 1985)
Vickers, Nancy J. ' "This Heraldry in Lucrece's Face" ', *Poetics Today* 6 (1985), pp. 171-184
Vuillemin, Jean-Claude. *Baroquisme et théâtralité: le théâtre de Jean Rotrou* (Paris: Papers on French Seventeenth-Century Literature, 1994)
Weber, Max. *The Protestant Ethic and the Spirit of Capitalism*, trans. Talcott Parsons (New York: Scribner, 1930)
Webster, John. *The White Devil* in Gamini Salgado (ed.), *Three Jacobean Tragedies* (Harmondsworth: Penguin, 1965)
Weizsäcker, Carl Friedrich von. *The Unity of Nature*, trans. Francis J. Zucker (New York: Farrar Straus Giroux, 1980)

Wellek, René. 'The Concept of the Baroque in Literary Scholarship', in *Concepts of Criticism*, ed. Stephen G. Nichols (New Haven, CT: Yale University Press, 1963), pp. 69-114
Whelan, Ruth. *The Anatomy of Superstition: A Study of the Historical Theory and Practice of Pierre Bayle* (Oxford: Voltaire Foundation, 1989)
White, Hayden. *Metahistory: The Historical Imagination in Nineteenth-Century Europe* (Baltimore, MD: The Johns Hopkins University Press, 1973)
White, Michael. *Isaac Newton: The Last Sorcerer* (Reading, MA: Addison-Wesley, 1997)
Williams, Bernard. *Descartes: The Project of Pure Enquiry* (1978; Harmondsworth: Penguin, 1990)
Williams, Bernard. *Moral Luck: Philosophical Papers 1973-1980* (Cambridge: Cambridge University Press, 1981)
Williams, Bernard. *Ethics and the Limits of Philosophy* (London: Fontana, 1985)
Wimsatt, William K., and Beardsley, Monroe. *The Verbal Icon: Studies in the Meaning of Poetry* (Lexington, KY: University of Kentucky Press, 1954)
Wittgenstein. Ludwig. *Philosophical Investigations*, 2nd ed., German text with parallel trans. by G.E.M Anscombe (New York: Macmillan, 1958)
Wölfflin, Heinrich. *Principles of Art History*, trans. M.D. Hottinger (London: G. Bell and Sons, 1932; repr. New York: Dover, 1950)
Wroe, Ann. *Pilate: The Biography of an Invented Man* (London: Jonathan Cape, 1999)
Yates, Frances A. *The Art of Memory* (Chicago: University of Chicago Press, 1966)
Zagorin, Perez. *Ways of Lying: Dissimulation, Persecution, and Conformity in Early Modern Europe* (Cambridge, MA: Harvard University Press, 1990)

Index

Adorno, T. 17-20, 27-29, 113
aemulatio 78-80, 103; *see also* imitation; ut pictura poesis
aesthetic, the 27-30, 42, 67-68, 78-79
aesthetics; *see* the aesthetic
Agucchi, G.B. 114
Alberti, L. B. 45, 79, 81, 89-92
allegory 8, 21-25, 131, 171
Alpers, S. 6, 45, 61, 96
Althusser, L. 16, 19
America, 'discovery' of 10-12
anamorphosis 8, 84-85, 147
anthropology 11, 42
Apelles 78, 80
apologetics 12-13, 156
Aristotle 9, 78, 80, 135, 144, 147, 160, 163
art
   and agency 114-115
   and the baroque 8, 111
   and history 4-5, 27-30
   and idealism 9, 81, 124-125
   and illusion 6, 8, 29-30, 42, 48, 62, 76-77
   and imposture 75
   language of 81, 127
   and ontology 111
   power of 55
   and science 146, 163-164
   and truth 4-5, 29-30, 76
   see also invention; painting; representation
Augustine of Hippo, St 43, 86, 102, 137
Ausonius 152-153
Austin, J.L. 2-4

Bacon, Sir F.
   gender 46-48, 67
   iconoclasm 61-63
   induction 45
   interpretation of nature 47-48, 167
   Magna instauratio 46-47, 63, 112

modern subject 113
New Organon 10, 61-63, 67
'Of Truth' 1-5
Baillet, A. 151-153
Bal, M. 5, 13, 15, 46, 51, 53, 56, 59-60, 66, 79
baroque, the
   and absolutism 9
   and allegory 21-22, 131, 171
   and aristocracy 6-7
   and art 8, 111
   and Carracci 115, 124
   and Catholicism 6-7
   and classicism 7, 126, 138-139, 146, 173
   and the Counter Reformation 5, 9
   definition of 5-13, 42
   and drama 132-139
   in England 5-7, 145
   in Flanders 6
   in France 5, 7, 144-148, 172-173
   in Germany 5, 16, 21-29, 138, 145
   and history 12-31, 132-139, 144, 171-173
   and idealism 9, 42, 124-125
   and imperialism 6
   in Italy 5-6, 9, 111
   and mannerism 5, 9
   and modernity 46, 111, 133-139
   and naturalism 9, 42, 124
   in the Netherlands 6-7
   and ontology 111, 127, 137-138
   and painting 75
   reception of 75
   and representation 42-46, 111
   and specularity 8
   and time 124-139, 144
   and vision 8, 42-44
   and visual culture 42-44
Baudelaire, C. 5, 16-20
Baxandall, M. 65-66, 78-79, 89
Bayle, P. 12
Bellori, G.P. 82, 114, 124, 163

Benjamin, W. 8, 30
  the baroque 16, 21-24, 27-29, 171
  Baudelaire 16-20, 27-28
  history 16-24, 27-28, 137-138
  modernity 17-21
  Origin of German Tragic Drama 5, 16, 19, 21-24, 137-138
  Passagen-Werk 16
  'The Storyteller' 20
  'Theses on the Philosophy of History' 17-21, 27
Berger, H., Jr. 23, 75-76, 78-79, 89, 98
Bergson, H. 19
Bernini, G.L. 126-128
Bidermann, J. 24
Blumenberg, H. 113
Boileau, N.D. 7
Bossuet, J.-B. 11, 145
Botticelli, S. 48-49, 80
Bourdieu, P. 16
Brant, S. 117
Bronzino, A. 82
Browne, Sir T. 14
Bruegel, P., the Elder 56-57
Bruno, G. 10-11
Bryson, N. 78-79, 90
Buci-Glucksmann, C. 5, 8, 42, 145
Bulwer, J. 43
Burckhardt, J. 113
Burton, R. 6

Calabrese, O. 5
Calderón de la Barca, P. 29, 59, 138
Campbell, M.B. 9, 11, 14, 43, 164
Caravaggio, M.M. da 9, 15, 28, 103, 124, 163
  Conversion of St Paul (Cerasi Chapel) 16, 81-82, 84-88, 99
  David and Goliath 87-88
  Death of the Virgin 82-83, 87
  and iconoclasm 81-82
  Judith and Holofernes 87
  Medusa (Uffizi) 88
  and painting 88
  reception of 82-84
  and self-portraiture 87-88
Carracci, A. 9
  Hercules at the Crossroads 16, 111-117, 124-129, 132-133, 137-139, 144

Cascardi, A.J. 5
Castro, G. de 146
Chardin, J.-B.-S. 64-66
Charles I 6
Charpentrat, P. 145
Christ 1, 3-4, 44, 90, 101-102, 125
Cicero 26-27, 80, 118, 133
Cioran, E.M. 173
Clark, Sir K. 49
classicism 7, 126, 138-139, 146, 173
Copernicus, N. 9-10
Corneille, P. 7, 25-26, 133, 145-148
cosmology 9-11; *see also* science
Cranach, L. the Elder 55, 119
Critical Theory 5, 9, 21, 27, 29
Cyrano de Bergerac, S.
  L'Autre monde 7, 11, 145, 163-165
  and Descartes 16, 161-173
  dualism 167-173
  history 171
  imagination 162-170
  materialism 167-170
  'Sur l'ombre que faisoient des arbres dans l'eau' 148, 161-173

Daniel 53-54, 61-63, 75
d'Aubignac, F. H. 134-135, 138
De Lauretis, T. 46
Deleuze, G. 5, 8, 145-148
Democritus 96
Dempsey, C. 115, 124
Descartes, R. 11, 15-16, 30, 97, 144
  and Cyrano 16, 161-173
  Discours de la méthode 45, 47, 98, 145, 149-151, 153, 155-156, 161, 164-167
  dream 151-156, 167
  dualism 147-161, 167-168, 171-173
  gender 46-48, 154-156
  imagination 162-168
  Meditations on First Philosophy 11, 29, 145, 153, 157-161
  metaphysics 16, 148-149, 152, 154
  method 152-153
  modern subect 113, 146
  Le Monde 45, 64, 66, 150-151, 153, 155-156, 161, 164-167
  nature 47-48
  'Olympica' 16
  painting 45-46, 150-151

Descartes (*cont.*)
    and Pascal 16, 148, 156-161, 172-173
    Passions de l'âme 154, 156, 160
    science 149-153, 156
    truth 149, 155-156, 173
di Benvenuto, G. 122-123
Diderot, D. 64
Dollimore, J. 6
Donne, H. 6
drama 119-124, 132-139, 144
dream 8, 29, 151-156, 167
dualism 8, 147-161, 167-173
Dumont, P. 145
Dürer, A. 119
d'Urfé, H. 145

Elizabeth of Bohemia 156
Elkins, J. 76
empiricism 2, 167-168
Enlightenment, the 5, 8-9, 14-15
Epicureanism 1, 9, 167
Epicureans; *see* Epicureanism
Erasmus, D. 10-11
example; *see* exemplarity
exemplarity 132-134, 139; *see also* history
exemplum; *see* exemplarity
Eyck, Jan van 90, 92-93

falsehood; *see* truth
Farnese, A. 112
Farnese, O. 112-113
Farnese Palace 112-113
Faudemay, A. 149
feminism 46, 51-53, 75, 79
Fielding, H. 14
Filidor, C.S. 21
Fineman, J. 95
Fish, S.E. 6, 8, 147
Forestier, G. 7
Foucault, M. 46, 75, 113, 115, 146, 149
Francis of Assisi, St 44
Freud, S. 22, 102
Fried, M. 64-65

Galileo Galilei 10-11, 150, 164, 169
Garnier, R. 133
Garrard, M.D. 79
Gassendi, P. 167

gender
    in Bacon 46-48, 67
    in Descartes 46-48, 154-156
    and nature 47-61, 111
    in painting 48-61
    and representation 46-61, 66-67, 111
    and science 46-48
    and truth 66-67, 75, 111
Gilman, E.B. 6
Giorgione da Castelfranco 49-51, 55
Giotto (Ambrogio di Bondone) 44, 80, 89
Godwin, F. 11
Goethe, J.W. von 19
Goffen, R. 48
Greenberg, M. 7
Greene, T. 78-79
Gryphius, A. 21, 24, 138
Guicciardini, F. 10
Halmann, J.C. 21, 138
Hals, F. 6
Hardy, A. 59-60
Harth, E. 149
Hegel, G.W.F. 13, 97-99, 119
Heidegger, M. 29, 91, 103
Helgerson, R. 6
Herakleitos 114
Herbert, G. 6
Hercules 15, 26-27
    and Christ 125
    and Christianity 117-118
    Crossroads legend 115
    dramatic interest of 119-124
    and modern subject 111-114, 132-139
    and philosophy 115, 117
    as political symbol 112-113
    and science 112
    and stoicism 115, 118
    and time 124-127, 132
Hibbard, H. 86
Hill, C. 27, 30
historiography 10, 17-19; *see also* history
history
    and the baroque 12-31, 132-139, 144, 171-173
    and exemplarity 132-134, 139
    and 'experience of defeat' 27, 30

and fable 123
and modern subject 114, 132-139
and nature 12, 14
and necessity 4, 31
philosophy of 13-14, 53
and the Real 30-31
and truth 3-5, 98, 136-137, 144, 173
see also immanence; materialism; modernity; ontology
Hobbes, T. 11-12, 81
Homer 78, 80
Hooke, R. 45
Horace 44, 78, 80
humanism 8, 10, 80, 91, 133-134, 145
Hume, D. 14-15
Husserl, E. 150

iconoclasm 2, 14, 42, 55, 60-63, 75, 81-82; *see also* idolatry
idealism 9, 42, 53, 80-84, 92, 103, 124-125, 163; *see also* imagination; imitation; invention
idolatry 2, 4, 14, 42, 53, 62-63, 75, 86; *see also* iconoclasm
idols; *see* idolatry
Ignatius of Loyola, St 76-77
illusion 6, 8, 29-30, 42, 48, 62, 76-78, 80, 90-92, 147, 167-168; *see also* trompe-l'œil; truth
imagination 14, 18, 76, 132, 136, 162-170; *see also* idealism; imitation; invention
imitation
  of antecedent models 78-81
  of Christ 44, 78
  definition of 78
  of nature 51, 78-81, 90-92, 103
  see also aemulatio; naturalism; painting; realism; representation; ut pictura poesis
immanence
  aesthetic principle of 15, 134-136, 144
  and history 21, 134-136
  metaphysics of 15, 81-82, 103, 170
  see also history; materialism; metaphysics; naturalism; ontology
invention
  and art 29, 163
  in Carracci 114, 125

and creative judgment 80
in Descartes 153, 164
double meaning of 30, 95
and drama 135
imaginative 166-169
of the mind 144
and rhetoric 30, 95
and self-invention 30
of subjectivity 95
and truth 29
see also art; idealism; imagination; imitation
Isis 67-68

Jameson, Fredric 31
Jansenism 7, 86, 137; *see also* Pascal
Jardine, Lisa 89
Jesuits; *see* Society of Jesus
Jodelle, E. 133
Jupiter 112-113, 155

Kahn, V. 131
Kant, I. 5, 28, 48, 67-68, 98
Keller, E.F. 46
Kepler, J. 11, 45
Klee, P. 20
Kyd, T. 133

Lacan, J. 5, 30-31, 43, 98, 169
Lafitau, J. 11
La Tour, G. de 127, 129
La Tour Landry, G. de 118
Le Brun, C. 114
Lee, R. 80
Leibniz, G.W. 5, 8, 145-148, 151
Leonardo da Vinci 114
lies; *see* truth
Livy 59
Locher, J. 117-118
Locke, J. 64, 66, 97, 167-168
Lohenstein, D.C. von 22-28, 138
Louis XIII 7
Louis XIV 7, 144, 146
Lucretia 27, 56, 58-60
Lucretius 9
Lupton, J.R. 5-6
Luther, M. 10
Lyons, J.D. 7, 147

Machiavelli, N. 10-11, 131-132

Macrobius 118
Mahon, D. 115
Maillard, J.-F. 145
Mairet, J. 26, 133
Mander, C. van 82
mannerism 5, 9
Maravall, J. 5
Margolis, J. 97, 114
Marin, L. 7, 16, 78-79, 146
Marlowe, C. 133, 135-136
Marx, K. 13
Marxism 18, 20-21
materialism 12, 18-21, 167-170; *see also* history; immanence; metaphysics; naturalism; ontology
Maximilian I of Bavaria 119-121
memento mori; *see* vanitas
Merleau-Ponty, M. 61, 98
Metaphysical poets (English) 5
metaphysics
    and allegory 25
    and the baroque 5
    Cartesian 16, 148-149, 151-152
    and history 21
    of immanence 15, 81-82, 103, 170
    and materialism 21
    and science 67
    and truth 1
    see also history; immanence; materialism; ontology; truth
Michelangelo Buonarotti 9, 78, 80-82, 92
Milton, J. 26-27, 137
mind, philosophy of 63-64, 97-99, 132-139, 144, 147-173
Minerva 123, 155
Mitchell, W.J.T. 79
modern subject 111-114, 132-139, 146
modernity 12, 14, 17-21, 44, 111-114, 132-139
Molina, L. de 86
Montaigne, M. de 9, 12, 14, 97, 113, 136, 162-163
Montchrestien, A. de 133
Moriarty, M. 149
Mulvey, L. 46
Murer, C. 119-120

Narcissus 91-92, 169
naturalism 9, 42, 82-84, 88-89, 103, 124; *see also* idealism; imitation; nature; painting; realism; representation
natural philosophy; *see* science
natural science; *see* science
nature 12, 14-15, 28-29, 43
    and gender 47-61, 111
    and idealism 80-84, 103
    imitation of 78-84
    and science 47-48, 151, 167
    and truth 48, 103, 111, 136
    see also idealism; imitation,; naturalism; realism; science
Newton, Sir I. 11, 169
New World; *see* America
nominalism 44
Norton, T. 133

Ockham, William of 44
ontology
    and modernity 10, 15, 65, 127, 137-138
    and painting 15, 64-65, 76, 102-103, 111, 127, 137-138, 144
    and science 48
    see also history; immanence; materialism; naturalism; truth
optics 6, 8, 45; *see also* science; vision
Oresme, N. 44
Orsini, F. 114, 124
Ovid 59, 91, 148, 163, 166

painting
    in Alberti 90-92
    in Caravaggio 88
    in Descartes 45-46, 150-151
    and gender 48-61
    and 'history' 80-81
    and idealism 80-84
    and imitation of nature 51, 78-81, 90-92, 103
    materiality of 75-76
    meaning in 114-115
    in Pascal 75-76
    and perspective 89-95
    and poetry 44, 78-82
    in Rembrandt 88
    and self-portraiture 92-95
    truth in 64-66, 68, 75-76, 79, 99-103
    see also imitation; representation

Pamphiles 80
Panofsky, E. 92, 118, 124, 131
Parker, P. 13
Parmigianino 82
Pascal, B. 9, 19, 43, 86, 97-98, 137
   apologetics 12-13, 156
   and Descartes 16, 148, 156-161,
      172-173
   dualism 157-161
   history 12-14, 24, 28, 173
   imagination 162-163, 170
   and Montaigne 12, 14
   painting 75-76
   Pensées 16, 30, 136, 145, 148, 156-161, 170
   scepticism 12
Paul of Tarsus, St 15-16, 81-82, 84-88, 96, 99-103, 144
Peirce, C.S. 98
perspective 8, 45, 64, 75-76, 89-95, 147
Peter, St 101-102
Pilate, P. 1-4
Piles, R. de 53, 80-84, 96, 102, 163
Plato 4, 137
Plautus 113
Pliny the Elder 78, 80
Plutarch 132
poetry 44, 78-82, 163; *see also* ut pictura poesis
Popkin, R. 113
portraiture 6, 8, 30, 42, 83, 92, 132; *see also* self-portraiture
Poulet, G. 154
Poussin, N. 114, 126
Pozzo, A. 76-77
Praz, M. 5
Prodikos of Chios 115, 117
Protagoras 114, 169, 171
Proust, M. 19
prudence 10, 129-132
Ptolemy 9
Pythagoras 115, 117, 119-120, 124, 152

qualities, doctrine of 48, 167
Quarles, F. 6

Racine, J. 78, 137, 139
Ranke, L. von 18
Raphael (Raffaelo Sanzio) 78, 80, 92-95, 118, 125
realism 9, 11, 86; *see also* naturalism
reason
   and appearances 29, 168-170
   dialectical 16
   and the Enlightenment 8
   and humanity 112, 132-133
   and imagination 14, 168-169
   moral 28
   and passion 8, 27
   and science 10, 47, 112
   and truth 144-145
reason of state 4, 10
Reformation, the 10
Reinhard, K. 5-6
relativism 1, 12; *see also* scepticism; truth
Rembrandt van Rijn 6, 9, 30, 163
   Bathsheba at Her Bath 127-128
   Belshazzar's Feast 62
   The Blinding of Samson 66
   and blindness 66
   and gender 53-56, 58-63, 66
   and iconoclasm 61-62, 75, 81-82
   Lucretia (1664) 56, 58-60
   Lucretia (1666) 56, 58-60
   The Night Watch 59
   and painting 75-76, 88
   and portraiture 83
   and representation 53-55, 59-63
   Self-Portrait as an Old Man Laughing 96-97, 99
   Self-Portrait as the Apostle Paul 16, 81-82, 88, 96, 99-103
   Self-Portrait with Saskia, as the Prodigal Son 96, 99
   and self-portraiture 88, 95-102
   Susanna and the Elders (1634) 15, 53-56, 60-63, 66, 90
   Susanna and the Elders (1645) 15, 53-56, 60-63, 66, 90
   and truth 99-103
   and vision 61, 98-99, 101
Renaissance, the 8-10, 44, 46, 64, 78, 89-90, 92, 95, 112, 136-139, 145
Reni, G. 126-127
representation 42-46
   and blindness 66
   and gender 46-61, 66-67, 111
   in Rembrandt 53-55, 59-63

representation (*cont.*)
   and science 44-45
   and truth 64-68, 76, 111
   see also imitation; painting
rhetoric 132-134
Richelieu, A. Du P., cardinal de 11
Ripa, C. 48
Rorty, R. 144
Rotrou, J. 133, 145
Rousset, J. 5, 7, 144
Rubens, P. P. 6, 9, 51-52, 55, 123-124

Sackville, T. 133
Sadeler, J. 119-121, 124
Saint-Amant, M.-A. de G., sieur de 7, 145
scepticism 1, 12, 14, 30, 131, 136, 150; *see also* relativism; truth
Schama, S. 6, 61
Schwartz, G. 6
science
   in Descartes 149-153, 156
   and gender 15, 46-48
   history of 9-11
   and iconoclasm 2, 61-63
   and imagination 164-168
   and modern subject 112
   and nature 29-30, 47-48, 151, 167
   and philosophy of mind 63-64
   and representation 44-45
   and truth 2, 15, 61-64, 66-68, 144
   see also cosmology; optics
Scipio Africanus 22, 26-27, 118
Scudéry, G. de 146-148
Scudéry, M. de 145
self-portraiture 15, 56-67, 111, 144
   in Caravaggio 87-88
   and naturalism 89
   and perspective 89-95
   in Rembrandt 88, 95-102
   see also portraiture
Shakespeare, W. 5-6, 78, 95, 97, 144
   Hamlet 21, 112-113, 133-134, 136-139
   The Merchant of Venice 63
   'The Rape of Lucrece' 59
   Richard II 133-134
   Twelfth Night 115
Sidney, Sir P. 78
Silverman, K. 46

Simon, R. 11-12
Simonides of Chios 44
Society of Jesus 24, 76, 86, 145, 152
Soggi, N. 120, 122-123
soliloquy 15-16, 111, 132-138, 144
Sorel, C. 7
specularity 8
Spenser, E. 55
Spinoza, B. 11-12, 14, 19, 21, 28-29, 98, 103
Steen, J. 55-56, 61, 90
Stein, M. von 118
stoicism 10, 15, 115, 118
Summers, D. 80-81, 92
Susanna 15, 53-56, 60-63, 66, 75, 90
Sustris, F. 119-121
Sypher, W. 5

Tacitus 9-10, 24, 132
Tapié, V.-L. 145
Tasso, T. 78
Thevet, A. 11
time 120, 123-139, 144, 173
Titian (Tiziano Vecelli) 78, 80
   Allegory of Prudence 129-132
   The Rape of Europa 51
   Venus of Urbino 49-51, 55
tragedy 6-7, 15-16, 21-28, 132-139
Trent, Council of 10
trompe-l'œil 2, 42, 76, 161; *see also* illusion
truth
   and art 4-5, 29-30, 76
   and belief 3-4
   definitions of 1-4
   in Descartes 149, 155-156
   and facts 3
   and falsehood 3, 8
   and the good 3
   and history 3-5, 98, 136-137, 144, 173
   and illusion 76
   and lies 2
   and metaphysics 1
   and nature 48, 103, 111, 136
   in painting 64-66, 68, 75-76, 79, 99-103
   in Rembrandt 99-103
   and representation 64-68, 76
   and speech acts 3-4

and 'true' 2-3
and 'the truth' 1-3
and truths 2
see also relativism; scepticism
Turing, A. 157
Tyndale, W. 99, 101

ut pictura poesis 44, 78-81, 103; *see also* aemulatio; imitation; poetry

vanitas 42-43
Vasari, G. 78
Vecelli, M. 131
Vecelli, O. 131
Velázquez, D. 9, 56-57
Vega, L. de 59, 138
Venus 48-51, 55-57, 80
Viau, T. de 145
Villiers, G., duke of Buckingham 1

Virgil 78
Virgin Mary 44, 82-83, 155
vision 8, 42-44, 55, 61, 65-66, 89, 91-92, 98-99, 101; *see also* optics; visual culture 42-44, 89; *see also* vision
Voiture, V. 7
Vuillemin, J.-C. 7

Webster, J. 6, 134
Wellek, R. 6
Weyden, R. van der 90
Winstanley, G. 11
Wittgenstein, L. 2, 4
Wölfflin, H. 5, 15, 125
Wroe, A. 3

Xenophon 115

Zeuxis 78, 80